# THE GOTHS IN ENGLAND

## A STUDY IN SEVENTEENTH AND EIGHTEENTH CENTURY THOUGHT

BY

## SAMUEL KLIGER

HARVARD UNIVERSITY PRESS

CAMBRIDGE, MASSACHUSETTS

1952

PRINTED BY E. J. BRILL, LEIDEN, THE NETHERLANDS

To the memory of
my mother

עליה השלום

## ACKNOWLEDGMENTS

I have already expressed my thanks to those who aided me in this study, but I owe the greatest debts to Professor Zechariah Chafee of the Harvard Law School and Professor Arthur O. Lovejoy, from whose advice I hope that I have profited; to the American Philosophical Society for a grant to study in England; to Deans T. Moody Campbell and Paul Gross for research grants. I am grateful to the editors of *Modern Philology* and the *New England Quarterly* for permission to use material which first appeared in their journals. Professors Moody E. Prior, Z. S. Fink, Howard Mumford Jones, and Warner G. Rice also gave me useful advice.

S. K.

New York, December 15, 1951

# CONTENTS

# A MOORING POST IN THE PAST

## MOTHER OF PARLIAMENTS

It is common knowledge that throughout the eighteenth-century discussion of aesthetic taste the term "Gothic" was in prevailing usage a *Modewort* of very wide currency and that as applied to literature and the fine arts the same term was used with both eulogistic and disparaging connotations. What is not common knowledge, however, is that the history of the "Gothic" begins not in the eighteenth but in the seventeenth century, not in aesthetic but in political discussion; stale platitudes drawn from the classic-romantic dichotomy made familiar by the simpler sort of literary textbooks simply do not suffice to explain the full phenomenon of the Gothic vogue in England.

The term "Gothic" came into extensive use in the seventeenth century as an epithet employed by the Parliamentary leaders to defend the prerogatives of Parliament against the pretensions of the King to absolute right to govern England. To this end the Parliamentarians searched the ancient records of English civilization for precedent and authority against the principle of monarchical absolutism. An antiquarian movement flowered, and in the ancient records the Parliamentarians discovered that the original forebears of the English were the Germanic invaders of Rome whom they called not Germans but Goths, substituting the name of only one of the Germanic tribes to denote all the barbarians collectively; the Goths, they thought, founded the institutions of public assemblies which, in its English parliamentary form, the Stuarts were seeking to destroy. The antiquarian researches, consequently, were directed to records more ancient than and anterior to specific accounts of early English institutions, to the histories composed by Tacitus, Saint Augustine, his disciple Salvian, Jordanes, and Paul the Deacon. The analysis of Gothic character found in these early texts described the Goths as a Teutonic folk to whom political liberty was dear. Furthermore, the early texts offered a quasi-scientific explanation of the Gothic propensity for liberty in a theory of climatic influence on character. According to this theory of environmental conditioning, the frigid temperature of the Gothic habitat in the northern regions was the physiological factor explaining Gothic vigor, hardiness, and zeal for liberty. (Conversely, the southern and Latin people were thought to be invertebrate and supine under the heels of despots as a result of the hot, enervating, southern climate.) The English, a branch of the Gothic-Teutonic folk, shared in these psychological characteristics. In the barbarian *adventus,* traditionally dated in Bede and the *Anglo-Saxon Chronicle* in 449, the barbarians implanted on English soil their tribal assembly, the seed of English parliaments. As the defenders of Parliament saw it, the Parliament had a continuous existence in England dating from the Saxon witenagemot despite the subsequent Danish and Norman conquests and the occasional efforts of power-hungry kings to uproot it, even William the Conqueror failing in this dastardly ambition. It was in this way that the Gothic *Völkerwanderungen* of antiquity supplied the basis of discussion out of which emerged the ideas which were destined to play a governing role in the seventeenth century in the bitter contest between the Stuart kings and Parliament.

## "EX SEPTENTRIONE LUX"

The arguments spread in abundance by the Parliamentary circle of writers, based on implications drawn from traditional political inheritances, were not the only factor aiding in the creation of the Gothic vogue in England. A powerful thought-current set in motion by the Reformation, known as the "translatio imperii ad Teutonicos," emphasizing this time traditional racial characteristics, brought about an association of the Goths with a tradition of enlightenment. The result was that the epithet "Gothic" became not only a polar term in political discussion, a trope for the "free," but also in religious discussion a trope for all those spiritual, moral, and cultural values contained for the eighteenth century in the single word "enlightenment". The picture drawn from Tacitus showed the triumph of Gothic humanity, honor, and simplicity over invertebrate Roman urbanism, effeminacy, and luxury. The Gothicists pictured, that is, a world rejuvenation or rebirth due to the triumph of Gothic energy and moral purity over Roman torpor and depravity.

The seventeenth and eighteenth-century understanding of the Goths has very little to do with the actual facts of Gothic history; but all that is necessary in the history of ideas is to determine the process of intellectual cross-fertilization which created the Gothic edifice into a living symbol of England's democratic past. Consequently, if the Gothic idea is to be understood it must be gathered up into its total: political, semantic, and aesthetic. Only less important than the "Gothic" inheritance itself was the fact that the Englishman's view of his Gothic past was affected by what he saw in his present.

## WHIG AESTHETICS

An anonymous essayist of 1739 not only admires the Gothic style of architecture but claims that a special taste, "A Constitutional sort of Reverence," is required to appreciate it. The Whigs of the period represented the party that made much of constitutions protecting popular liberties. Although it appears impossible now to identify the anonymous writer as either Tory or Whig, we do know, on the other hand, that William Whitehead, the Tory, unmistakably detects a parallel between the Whig clamor for increased popular representation and the debased Gothic taste.

It cannot be shown, as a matter of fact, that a fixed or general connection existed between Whiggism in politics and admiration of the Gothic style. Addison, a Whig, disapproved of Gothic architecture and spoke his disapproval of the strained metaphors of metaphysical poetry as an example of "Gothic" poetry. Walpole shifted from admiration to depreciation of the Gothic style yet he remained a Whig throughout. Instances can be multiplied. In fact, as Professor Lovejoy has pointed out, the use of the term "Gothic" as a word of abuse can be illustrated by the Whig practice of hurling the word at the Tories to designate the latter's hostility to Whig reforms. In addition, we must scrupulously avoid drawing the inference that the favorable connotation which the term "Gothic" had in Parliamentary circles either statistically outweighed the predominating use of the term unfavorably or that the favorable connotation was the main or even important cause of the actual building of Gothic structures. Nevertheless, even if actual party affiliation did not mean very much, the conception of Gothic freedom and energy depicted, so the century thought, in the inexhaustible imagination displayed in such "Gothic" poetry as Spenser's *Faerie Queene,* illustrates the way in which the Gothic tradition of the previous century brought about a cross-fertilization of aesthetic and politico-religious ideas. In other words, an association had been formed in some eighteenth-century minds between Whig principles of popular government and the freedom from neoclassical restraints displayed in the Gothic building; *per contra,* from the opposing Tory point of view, the symmetry and balance of the Grecian building apotheosized the Tory aim of maintaining national stability through a vested aristocratic interest and a strong monarchy.

On both sides, Tory and Whig, of the aesthetic debate, much if not all of the discussion was so much critical shadow-boxing in response to a need for overcoming what the Tories affected to think were Whig prejudices for excessive irregularity or, on the other hand, what the Whigs affected to think were Tory prejudices for excessive regularity. The disputants on both sides could have learned much from Batty Langley's *Gothic Architecture Improved* (1747). Langley admits the excessive ornamentation in the details of Gothic architecture but he insists that the Gothic edifice in its overall configuration does have regularity and balanced design; in other words, "art" in the sense of regularity and "nature" in the sense of overflowing, inexhaustible energy are reconciled to each other in the Gothic building.

The "Whiggish" aspect, therefore, of the Gothic revival is another manifestation of the complex history of the term "nature" in the eighteenth century. The eighteenth century sought to establish an equilibrium of opposites in which "reason" and "nature" were the opposed terms; "reason" stood for judgment, decorum, regularity, the rules, where "nature" stood for imagination, novelty, irregularity. The equilibrium of opposites was more or less stable, but its constant tendency was towards instability in the direction of undue emphasis on either "reason" or "nature," especially when such exterior forces as Tory politics with its intrenched beliefs in security and the *status quo,* or contrariwise, the force of Whig politics with its stress on progress and on an expanding future, tended to upset the equilibrium in either of the two directions. [1] The facts of Gothic freedom—the Whig protests against monarchical restraints—Gothic energy—the picture of a youthful, ardent people supplanting the decadent

[1] Deism in religion, as Professor Lovejoy has brilliantly shown, tended to shift the balance (and maintain it there) towards the neoclassical pole; see A. O. Lovejoy. "The Parallel of Deism and Classicism," *Modern Philology,* XXIX (1932), 281-299.

Romans and rejuvenating the world thereby—depicted an opposition between "nature" and "reason."

However, in the same way that the Gothic Parliamentary propaganda never quite resulted in demands for republican government, Batty Langley's effort to defend the Gothic style as composed both of regular and irregular elements remains the best indication of the way in which the Gothic taste figured as a Whig taste, always within the prevailing critical mode which sought a harmony in a judicious mixture of extremes. Under the exigent demands of partypolitics, the movement toward freedom from neoclassical restraints in literature and the fine arts found the same advocates and opponents as that towards freedom in political matters. But there was underlying a more persistent movement to establish in aesthetics what Edmond Burke called "Old Whiggism" in politics: a just mixture of popular sovereignty and a strong centralized monarchy. Thus, Humphrey Repton remarked of gardendesign, assimilating art to politics:

The neatness, simplicity, and elegance of English gardening, have acquired the approbation of the present century, as the happy medium betwixt the liberty of savages, and the restraint of art; in the same manner as the English constitution is the happy medium betwixt the wildness of nature and the stiffness of despotic government. [2]

[2] *Letter to Sir Uvedale Price* (1794); the letter is printed in *Sir Uvedale Price on the Picturesque* (Edinburgh, 1842), p. 413.

# CHAPTER ONE

# THE PROBLEM OF THE "GOTHS"

## GOTHIC LIBERTY

Writing in 1647, Nathaniel Bacon avers that English laws are largely Gothic in origin: "Nor can any nation upon Earth shew so much of the ancient Gothique law as this Isiand hath."[1]

In 1695, Sir William Temple calls the English a Gothic people: "The Saxons were one branch of those Gothick Nations, which swarming from the Northern Hive, had, under the conduct of Odin, possessed themselves anciently of all those mighty tracts of Land that surround the Baltick Sea."[2]

In the essay "Of Poetry," Temple refers to the "ancient Western Goths, our Ancestors."[3] Thomas Pope Blount (1694) also points to the "ancient Western Goths (our Ancestors)."[4] In 1694, Robert Molesworth argues that England's government in its origins was Gothic and Vandalic: "The Ancient Form of Government here was the same which the Goths and Vandals established in most if not all Parts of Europe whither they carried their conquests, and which in England is retained to this day for the most part."[5] According to Jonathan Swift, writing in 1719, parliaments are a peculiarly Gothic institu-

[1] *Historical and Political Discourse of the Laws and Government of England* (4th ed.; London, 1739), p. 40.

[2] *Introduction to the History of England,* in *Works* (London, 1731), II, 537.

[3] *Critical Essays of the Seventeenth Century,* edited by J. E. Spingarn (Oxford, 1909), III, 86. The essay "Of Poetry" first appeared in *Miscellanea, The Second Part* (1690).

[4] *De re poetica* (London, 1694), p. 3.

[5] *An Account of Denmark as it was in the Year 1692* (London, 1694), p. 42.

tion, implanted in England "by the Saxon princes, who first introduced them into this island, from the same original with the other Gothic forms of government in most parts of Europe." [6] Laurence Echard identifies the Saxon invaders of England as Goths: "And now a new Race of People began to inhabit this Island, call'd Saxons, a fierce and barbarous Nation, one branch of those Gothick Multitudes..." [7] John Oldmixon, writing in 1724, also assimilates Gothic to English history: "No nation has preserv'd their Gothic Constitution better than the English." [8] Lord Bolingbroke, similarly, sees Goths on the horizon of England's foundation: "Though the Saxons submitted to the yoke of Rome in the matters-of religion, they were far from giving up the freedom of their Gothic institution of government." [9] Molesworth not only domiciles the Goths in England, but appears to think of a Whig as a Goth *par excellence:* "My notion of a Whig, I mean of a real Whig (for the Nominal are worse than any sort of Men) is, that he is one who is exactly for keeping up to the Strictness of the old Gothick Constitution." [10] Batty Langley (1747) justifies the Goth-Saxon identification in reasonableness: "And 'tis very reasonable to believe, that as in all ages of the Saxon monarchy there was no distinction of Goths from Saxons, but in general all were called Saxons." [11] Henry Brooke's play, *Gustavas Vasa* (1739), based on the life of the

[6] "Abstract of the History of England," *Prose Works of Jonathan Swift,* edited by Temple Scott (Bohn ed.; London, 1897-1908), X, 225.

[7] *The History of England* (3d ed.; London, 1720), p. 17.

[8] *Critical History of England* (London, 1724), p. 25.

[9] "Remarks on the History of England," in *Works* (London, 1754), I, 315. The "Remarks" appeared originally in *The Craftsman* (1726- c. 1747).

[10] Quoted in John Ker, *The Memoirs* (London, 1726), II, 192; immediately following a translation by Ker of Paul de Rapin-Thoyras' *An Historical Dissertation upon Whig and Tory,* also translated by J. Ozell (London, 1717). Ker says "These just notions, entertained by M. Rapin, are fully confirmed by the Sentiments of the late Lord Molesworth.'

[11] *Gothic Architecture Improved* (London, 1747), p. 1.

celebrated Swedish monarch, ran afoul of Walpole's censorship. In the printed version of the play (subscribed to by over one thousand persons) Brooke's preface disclaims political satire and explains that his theme was taken from the principle of Gothic government, both Swedish and English: "I took my subject from the history of Sweden, one of those Gothic and glorious nations, from whom our form of government is derived." [12] The *World* (number 8, dated February 22, 1753) speaks of "the excellent Gothic constitutions, from whence we derive our own." [13] A dictionary, reprinted many times during the eighteenth century, explains under "Government" that "we in Great Britain have still happily preserved this noble and ancient Gothic constitution." [14] John Pinkerton (1787) venerates "the name of Goth" because it is "the sacred name of our fathers." [15] Sharon Turner (1828) roundly declares that "our language, our government, and our laws, display our Gothic ancestors in every part." [16] The most striking passage of all dates from 1656, when Sir James Harrington refers to those "inundations of Huns, Goths, Vandalls, Lombards, Saxons, which breaking the Roman Empire, deformed the whole world." [17] But, notwithstanding the subordination of the Goths in this passage, Harrington nevertheless in another context establishes the principle of "Gothic balance" as universally embodied in the land reforms effected as a result of *all* the migrations of the Germanic conquerors of Rome. [18]

[12] *Gustavas Vasa* (Bell ed.; London, 1779), p. 14.

[13] In Alexander Chalmers, *The British Essayists* (London, 1817), XXVI, 38.

[14] *A New and Complete Dictionary of Arts and Sciences..* by a Society of Gentlemen (London, 1763), *s.v.* "Government."

[15] *A Dissertation on the Origin and Progress of the Scythians or Goths* (London, 1787), p. viii.

[16] *History of the Anglo-Saxons* (London, 1828), I, 52.

[17] *The Commonwealth of Oceana* (Liljegren ed.; Heidelberg, 1924), p. 12.

[18] Liljegren makes no attempt to explain the "Gothic balance." On the Gothic balance, see *ibid.*, pp. 15, 54, 119, 124.

In view of this varied usage of the term "Gothic," the
primary problem in the investigation of the origins of the
Gothic vogue in England must be semantic. Historically, the
word "Gothic" describes only a single Germanic tribe out of
many who crossed the Danube in 376 A.D., and it is by no
means so clear as the writers quoted would have their readers
believe that the English are a Gothic folk and that "Gothic" as
a name is applicable universally to all the Germanic tribes.
The questions, then, are two: how did this extraordinary
expansion in the usage of the word take place? And, what hint
does its semantic history in the seventeenth century supply
toward establishing a relationship with the eighteenth-century
usage in aesthetic discussions which denoted, as is well known,
almost everything which was Germanic in origin and almost
everything which was medieval?

A widespread interest in what might be called "speculative
geography" was responsible for one use of the term "Gothic"
to denote all the Germanic tribesmen; political exigency, on
the other hand, determined the second use to denote the English people and English government in particular and hence
supplied the basis for such assertions as made by Bacon,
Temple, Molesworth, and the others.

The speculative geographers were interested in tracing the
origins of the people of the world to an ultimate beginning.
The Bible, in part, supplied answers to their inquiries; either
the Deluge and the subsequent spread of Noah's progeny or
the Babel episode offered a starting point. Trojan history and
the flight of the descendants of Aeneas subsequent to Troy's
fall appealed to other writers. But a growing awareness of the
large admixture of fable with fact in these stories turned
research into other channels. Earlier than the seventeenth
century—in fact, in the sixteenth century—an important group
of geographers in the Scandinavian countries, particularly a
circle of scholars centered at Uppsala University, led by a

nationalistic interest in the origin of their countries, evolved a theory of a *vagina gentium,* a "womb of nations," which, on the authority of Jordanes, sixth-century historian of the Goths, they placed in Scandinavia, or Scandza as Jordanes called it.

The history of the Goths, their conquests, their gradual spread over Europe, which to the unbiased student of history is—except perhaps for Theodoric—a sordid account of plunder and betrayal, was to Jordanes a magnificent record of Gothic greatness. [19] Jordanes' main purpose was to glorify the eastern Getes from whom he sprang so as to show them worthy of alliance with the Romans under the rule of Justinian. His first move, therefore, was to relate the Getes to the more splendid Gothic tribe by identifying the Getes as Goths. Following Orosius' statement, "Getae illi qui et nunc Gothae," Jordanes says that "the Getae we have proved in a previous passage to be Goths, on the testimony of Orosius Paulus." [20] This identification of the Getes with the Goths, as we shall presently see, was one of the determining factors in the process which, in the view of the seventeenth-century writers, domiciled the Goths in England.

The primary importance of Jordanes for the modern revival of interest in Gothic antiquity rests on the credence he gave to the theory that all the German tribesmen were generically "Goths," all stemming from the group which, migrating from Scandza in the north, peopled Europe. Jordanes says:

The same mighty sea has also its arctic region, that is, in the North, a great island named Scandza, from which my tale (by

[19] *De origine actibusque Getarum* (551 A.D.), text edited by Mommsen in the *Monumenta Germaniae historica,* Auctores antiquissimi, vol. V (Berlin, 1882). The English translation is by Charles C. Mierow, *The Gothic History of Jordanes* (Princeton, 1915). Following Mommsen's usage, the text is referred to briefly as the *Getica.*

[20] Bk. ix, ch. 58; in Mierow, p. 66, in Mommsen, p. 70. There is no previous passage, but in bk. v, ch. 40 (p. 61 in Mierow, p. 64 in Mommsen), Jordanes uses Goth interchangeably with Gete. For Orosius, see his *History Against the Pagans,* translated with notes by I. W. Raymond (New York, 1936), bk. i, ch. 16, p. 64.

God's grace) shall take its beginning. For the race whose origin you ask to know burst forth like a swarm of bees from the midst of this island into the land of Europe. But how or in what wise we shall explain hereafter, if it be the Lord's will. [21]

Returning later to the subject of Scandza, he explains, as he had promised, how "from this island of Scandza, as from a hive of races or a womb of nations, the Goths are said to have come forth long ago under their king, Berig by name." [22] The Goths, consequently, are, in Jordanes' theory, the aboriginal folk who spread over Europe and Asia and, dividing into two large branches—the Visigoths and the Ostrogoths—were also known in later history by their various separate names, Huns, Vandals, Lombards, and so on. Thus the application of the term "Gothic" to denote all Germanic peoples seemed entirely appropriate to the Renaissance geographers. In order to account for the implantation of Gothic institutions and government in the north, these scholars argued, on the basis of Jordanes' account, that the Goths returned in a second great wave of migration, repopulating Europe and the north. In a burst of nationalistic pride, Rudbeck, Joannes and Olaus Magnus, and others declared that Sweden was Jordanes' Scandza, or cradle of nations. [23]

In England, the starting-point of speculation about Jordanes' Scandza theory was inevitably the barbarian *adventus* in England, traditionally dated in Bede and the *Anglo-Saxon Chronicle* in 449 A.D. From Bede downward, the Angles, Saxons,

[21] Bk. i, ch. 9; p. 53 in Mierow's translation, p. 55 in Mommsen.

[22] Bk. iv, ch. 25; p. 37 in Mierow.

[23] The Uppsala circle of scholars is described by Thor J. Beck, *Northern Antiquities in French Learning and Literature (1755-1855): A Study in Preromantic Ideas* (New York, 1934). Miss Ethel Seaton has described the trade channels, diplomatic and scholarly correspondence which extended knowledge of the Uppsala discussions to England in *Litterary Relations of England and Scandinavia in the Seventeenth Century* (Oxford, 1935). F. E. Farley's *Scandinavian Influences in the English Romantic Movement* (Boston, 1903) is a valuab'e bibliographical guide.

and Jutes were recognized as a Germanic folk. Within Jordanes' agglutinative Gothic tradition it was possible to describe the barbarian invaders as "Goths" and their institutions as "Gothic". Thus there came about the predominance of the term "Gothic" to describe almost everything primitive which was Germanic, and also to indicate almost everything which was medieval (since Roman culture was first recovered in the Renaissance, everything preceding the recovery was non-Roman). Norse poetry, ballads, cathedrals, native common law, parliaments—known as the modern form of the ancient Germanic tribal assemblies described in Tacitus' *Germania*—all were Gothic in this sense. [24]

At the same time, a second set of circumstances was operating to bring the Goths into English history. The tradition formed in Bede and the *Anglo-Saxon* chronicle with respect to the Germanic conquest of England was the determining factor which reinforced and was mutually reinforced by the influence previously described.

Bede says distinctly (departing from his source, Gildas, to supply his own information) that England was colonized by three Germanic tribes—Angles, Saxons, Jutes: "Advenerant

[24] Admittedly, it is ludicrous to find Englishmen describing England's government as carried on under a "Gothic" constitution. Yet even modern linguistic science can accept the term, or, at least, it can comprehend, quite aside from Jordanes' spectacular theory, why the early English writers resorted to the term. A glance at the *Oxford English Dictionary* will reveal how late the adjective "Germanic" appears. The early period had the nouns "German" and "Germany," but lacking the adjective "Germanic" it is understandable why they seized on the adjective "Gothic" as a substitute for what we call "Germanic." "Germanic" is still unsatisfactory except as a convention; Gudmund Schütte (*Our Forefathers, the Gothonic Nations,* translated by J. Young, Cambridge, 1929) suggests "Gothonic" as a substitute to avoid the confusion with anything pertaining exclusively to territorial Germany. Even Grimm notably wrote a *Deutsche Grammatik* when obviously he did not mean the language of territorial Germany but the general adjective "Germanic." I am indebted to Professor F. E. Magoun, Jr., of Harvard for this explanation.

autem de tribus Germaniae populis fortioribus, id est, Saxoni-
bus, Anglis, Iutis. De Iutarum origine sunt Cantuari et Victuari,
hoc est, ea gens quae Vectam tenet insulam, et ea quae
usque hodie in provincia Occidentalium Saxonum Iutarum
natio nominatur, posita contra ipsam insulam Vectam." [25]
Bede remarks that the Germanic forces were captained by
Hengist and Horsa, and, without stating explicitly that Hengist
and Horsa were Jutes, he rather implies that they were. At any
rate, what is certain is that as the seventeenth century read
Bede the Jutes were given a preponderance in the invasion
and in the subsequent political history of England in such a
way as to establish the term "Gothic" to denote the origins
of the English people and their culture.

The "Alfredian" translation of Bede's Latin text supplies
the key to this most important development in the Gothic
cult in England. On strict linguistic grounds, the Latin of
Bede's *Iutis, Iutarum* when translated into any of the dialects
of Old English cannot possibly be identical with a Gēat-form:

| Northumbrian | Īote, Īotan |
| Mercian | Ēote, Eota |
| Early West Saxon | *Īete, *Ietan |
| Late West Saxon | Ȳte, Ȳtan |

Nevertheless, within two centuries after Bede, the "Alfredian" translation does supplant the normal Old English equivalent of Latin *Iuti* with a *Gēat*-form: "Comon hi of Þrim
folcum ðam strangestan Germanie Þæt [is] of Seaxum and
of Angle of Geatum. Of Geata fruman syndon Cantware and
Wehtsætan..." [26]

It is interesting that in a second passage the same "Alfre-

---

[25] "Historia ecclesiastica gentis Anglorum," *Opera historica*, bk. i,
ch. 15; (Loeb ed.; London and New York, 1930), I, 70. The Plummer
text of Bede (Oxford, 1896) agrees with the Loeb text.

[26] *The Old English Bede*, Early English Text Society, o.s., XCV
(London, 1890-1898), 52.

MS. SELD. SUPRA 63. FOL. 61v. (BODLEIAN LIBRARY)

An Old English vocabulary by Laurence Nowell, written about 1550, illustrating the Geat-Goth-Jute equation.

FOL. 19v.

FOL. 132

ADD. MS. 43703 (BRITISH MUSEUM)

A transcript made by Laurence Nowell in 1562 of the Alfredian translation of Bede's *Ecclesiastical History,* illustrating the variant tribal names: *geata, geatum, eota (lond).*

dian" translation inconsistently renders *Iutorum* as *Eota:* "in
Þa neahmægðe, seo is gecegd Eota lond in sume stowe seo is
nemned Aet Stane." [27] Is the scribe correcting his error of i,
15, or is he employing both forms as equivalents? Modern
scholarship can only conjecture, but what is certain is that
as the seventeenth century read Bede not only were "Jute,"
"Eota," and "Geata" taken as equivalents but "Goth" as well.

It was this identification (or confusion, as modern scholarship would call it) which established the term "Gothic" to
denote the origin of the English in the Jutes. A double-text
edition of Bede, in both Old English and Latin, was made
available to the seventeenth century by Abraham Whelock,
probably the greatest Old English scholar of his day. [28]
Whelock follows the inconsistency of the "Alfredian" scribe.
The seventeenth-century evidence is clear beyond cavil, but
the mutual support of Bede and Jordanes must be recognized.
The point to observe is that the Latin authorities also confused
Gete with Goth. Jordanes, himself a Gete, tells the history of
the Goths but calls his history *Getica*. Orosius remarks: "Getae illi, qui et nunc Gothi," and this passage is cited, as will
be shown, by Robert Sheringham, who identifies them further
by adding "Jute" to the equation Goth equals Gete.

The first Old English dictionary, compiled by William
Somner, states the identification in the plainest terms. Under
"Geatar" we find the simple definition: "Jutae, Getae, Gothes." [29] The identification is, apparently, well established;
but for a fuller account which brings out the role of the Jutes
in the conquest, we must go back to Kentish political history.

[27] Bede's original (iv, 16) reads: "In proximam Iutorum provinciam
translati... in locum qui vocatur Ad Lapidem."

[28] Cambridge, 1643. The monumental work of Whelock and his
associates has been reverently described by David C. Douglas, *English Scholars* (London, 1939).

[29] *Dictionarium Saxino-Latino-Anglicum* (Oxford, 1649), *s.v.* "Geatar." William Lambarde's *Archaionomiea* (London, 1568).

Written in 1570 but first published in 1576, William Lambarde's *Perambulation of Kent* states: "The Saxons, Iutes, and Angles, were the Germaines that came over (as we have said) in aide of the Britons, of which the first sort inhabited Saxonie: the second were of Gotland, and therefore called Gutes, or Gottes. The third were of Angria, or Anglia, a countrie adioning to Saxony." [30] William Camden treats the three terms as equivalents, but cautiously does not assume responsibility for the identification: "The Iutae, who had that name (as many think) from the Gutes, Getes, or Gothes (for in a manuscript booke, we read Geatun) did for certaine inhabite the upper part of Cimbica [sic] Chersonesus, which still the Danes call Iuitland." [31] John Speed's *History,* in discussing "The Saxons Original," identifies the Jutes as Goths: "These Iutes, Gutes, Getes, or Gothes, or (as Beda calls them Vites) gave names to those parts of Britaine which they inhabited." [32] Sir Henry Spelman's *Glossarium Archaiologicum* (1626) also makes the identification. Under "Guti," the *Glossary* identifies Jute, Gete, and Goth. The statement is headed by a distich:

Gothorum variam appelationem
Cantiaros et Vectuarios nostros ab iisdem emanesse.

The definition itself reads in part: "*Guti.* Idem sunt qui Gotti, Gothi, & Goti: quibusdem Jutae & Jutones: Romanis Getae Anglo-Saxonibus geatas." The definition cites the law of Edward the Confessor which recognized the Jutes as possessing denizen rights in England: "Inde illud in Ll. Edouardi Confess. cap. 35 de his qui cohabitare debent in Britannia. 'Guti vero similiter cum veniunt, suscipi debent & protegi in

---

[30] *A Perambulation of Kent* (London, 1826), p. xiii.

[31] *Britannia* (London, 1586); the text used is Philemon Holland's translation, *Britain* (London, 1610), p. 130. Camden's original reads: "Iutis, quos a Gutis, Getis, sive Gothis dictos multi arbitrantur," and so on (1607 ed., p. 93).

[32] *The History of Great Britaine under the Conquests...* (3d ed.; London, 1632), p. 199.

regno isto, sicut conjurati fratres, sicut propinqui, & proprii cives Regni hujus'." [33]

Robert Sheringham controverts Cluverius, German scholar-geographer, who participated in the Continental discussion of Jordanes by pointing to Jordanes' error in confusing Getes with Goths. Sheringham asserts that they are the same. Chapter nine of his book *De Anglorum gentis origine disceptatio* (1670) is entitled "Getas Gothosque unam fuisse gentem ostenditur." He cites Orosius as authority for the identification: "Getae illi, qui et nunc Gothi," and brings together all the variant names of Goths: "Populi isti in legibus Edwardi Confessoris Gutae, & Annalibus Petroburgensibus Geatuni, ab iliis Jotuni & Jetae, a Scriptoribus Danicis Jutae & Juitae nominantur; nam Getae & Giotae, & Jotae, & Gutae, & Geatuni, & Jotuni, & Jetae & Jutae & Juitae unum idemq; nomen est." [34] Aylett Sammes asserts positively the identity of Jutes,

---

[33] "Hence the statement in the Laws of Edward the Confessor Chap. 35 concerning those who intend to live in Britain: 'The Guti, however, as soon as they come ought to be received and protected in this realm as sworn brothers, as kinsmen, and proper citizens of this realm.'" Any moderately well-read classicist among Spelman's contemporaries would have recognized the source of the statement "Romanis Getae." If not, the prefatory chapter "Concerning the Getes and Gothes" to the translation of Saint Augustine's *City of God* by Ludovico Vives (London, 1620) would have made the point clear. It is characteristic of Spelman, the lawyer, to confirm his point by citing the law. Spelman undoubtedly used the manuscript sources which were passed around and discussed at the meetings of the famous Society of Antiquaries of which he was a member. Whelock's edition of Bede also reprinted Lambarde's *Archainomia,* a collection of the old laws. DuCange (*Glossarium mediae et infimae latinitatis* ... Niort, 1883-1887), s.v. "Guti," merely repeats Spelman, as does Giles Jacob's *New Law Dictionary* (4th ed.; In the Savoy, 1734). "*Guti and Gotti,* Eng. Goths, called sometimes Jutae, and by the Romans Getae ... Leg. Edw. Confess. c. 35."

[34] *De Anglorum* (Cambridge, 1670), p. 36: "Those people are called Gutae in the laws of Edward the Confessor, and Geatuni in the Annales Petroburgenses; by others they are called Jotuni and Jetae; by the Danish writers, Jutae and Juitae; for these are one and

Getes, and Goths: "Getae, Jetae, Jutae, Juitae, Gutae, Giotae, Jotae, Geotuni, Jotuni, are all the same names, differing only in termination and writ after various orthography." [35] Laurence Echard's *History of England* follows its predecessors in identifying the Jutes as Goths:

There came great Numbers of People (in response to Hengist's and Horsa's call for reinforcements) of three Nations of Germany, namely, Saxons, Jutes, and Angles, which with those who were here before made up a compleated Army. These two latter People are suppos'd to be Branches of the Saxons, both inhabiting the Cimbrian Chersonese, from whom we have still the names of Juteland and Anglen; the former being call'd Jutes from the word Goth, and the latter Angles from the word Angulus or Corner. [36]

Edward Lye's Old English dictionary merely states: "*Geatar*. Getae. Jutae. Bed. I. 15." [37] Rapin's *History* casually makes the identification: "Great numbers of Goths mixed likewise with them [the Angles and Saxons] to share in their conquests. These are called Wites by Bede, and commonly known by the name of Jutes, or (which is the same) Goths." [38] The specific equation Goth equals Gete is present in the writings of the Continental writers, Rudbeck, Verelius, the Magnus brothers, Wormius, Bartholin, and so on. Naturally, however, they do not add Jute to the equation, since as Swedish patriots they were interested in tracing Jordanes' Scandza to Scandinavia. Consequently, they attach merely a toponymic significance to the name Goth by identifying the

the same name: Getae and Giotae, and Gutae, and Geatuni, and Jotuni, and Jetae, and Jutae, and Juitae."

[35] *Britannia antiqua illustrata: Or the Antiquities of Ancient Britain, Derived from the Phoenicians* (London, 1676), p. 417.

[36] Page 17.

[37] *Dictionarium Saxonico et Gothico-Latinum* (London, 1722), *s.v.* "Geatar."

[38] Paul de Rapin-Thoyras, *History of England*, translated by N. Tindal (London, 1732-1747), I, 27. Batty Langley (*Gothic Architecture*, p. 1) repeats Rapin's remark.

tribe as residents originally of the island of Gotland. Olaus Magnus seems to picture the Gothic *Urheim* as a kind of paradise; for example, the land was "good": "The Eastern part of Gothland is called so, as you would say a Good Land, or Land of the Goths. For Goth in their Mother tongue signifies good, or God, and Landia signifies Land." [39] On the other hand, Georges Hickes, English author of the monumental *Thesaurus,* refrains from the specific equation Goth equals Jute; nevertheless, his classification of the English language within what he calls the "Moeso-Gothic" family implies a Gothic-English relationship. [40] Hugo Grotius is apparently the only Continental writer who brings the Jutes into the formula; the fact that his book was widely cited by the English Gothicists establishes its importance for our discussion. [41]

The quaint etymologizing of the seventeenth-century writers, however, hardly tells the whole story. The tendency clearly was to establish the term "Gothic" as descriptive of the Jutes, *one* of the three Germanic tribes which invaded England. But account must also be taken of a second tendency to connect Gothic history with a national apotheosis of democracy in England. In a word, the political institutions which were implanted in England by the "Gothic" invaders were thought to be "free" or "democratic"; furthermore, the Gothic "free" institutions were thought to have had a continuous development in England despite the successive Danish and Norman invasions. Bolingbroke, we recall, definitely characterizes the

[39] *A Compendious History,* translated by "J. S." (London, 1658), p. 29, "Of the famous Island of the Goths called Gothland."

[40] Part I of the *Thesaurus* is entitled: "Institutiones grammaticae anglo-saxonicae et moeso-gothicae." The full title of Hickes's work is *Linguarum Vett. Septentrionalium Thesaurus Grammatico-Criticus et Archaeologicus* (Oxoniae, 1703-1705).

[41] Hugo Grotius, "Prolegomena," to his edition of *Historia Gothorum, Vandalorum, Langobardum* (Amstelodami, 1650), p. 10; the histories that Grotius edits are by Procopius, Isidore of Seville, Jordanes, and Paul the Deacon.

Gothic government as free: "Though the Saxons submitted to the yoke of Rome, in matters of religion, they were far from giving up the freedom of their Gothic institutions of government." [42] In fact, it is precisely out of such a contrast between Gothic freedom and Roman tyranny that the eighteenth century derived the term "Gothic" to denote the "liberal," the "enlightened," and similar meanings; thus a preference for the Gothic style of architecture might be characterized as a Whiggish taste. As we shall presently see, William Whitehead, the Tory, attacked the taste for the new-fangled style in architecture and suggested a parallel between the moral turpitude underlying Whig principles of popular government and the debased Gothic taste in the fine arts. Unless the term "Gothic" had been established as a trope for the "free" (and recalling Molesworth's description of a Whig as a true Goth), Whitehead could not have been able to point out the parallel. Nathaniel Bacon, whom we have observed designating English law as "Gothic" in origin, calls the barbarian founding fathers a free people: "The people were a free people, governed by laws, and those made not after the manner of the Gauls (as Caesar noteth) by the great men, but by the people; and therefore called a free people, because they were a Law to themselves." [43]

Temple describes Gothic government as "invented by the sages of the Goths, as a government of freemen." [44] He continues, describing the English constitution as Gothic, pointing out that "I need say nothing of this our constitution, which is so well known in our island," but going on, nevertheless, for a full page in which he heaps praises on the constitution:

However it be, this constitution had been so celebrated, as framed with great wisdom and equity, and as the truest and justest temper that has ever been found out between dominion

---

[42] See Note 9, above.
[43] *Laws and Government*, p. 9.
[44] *History of England*, in *Works*, I, 219.

and liberty... This seems to have been intended by these Gothic institutions, and by the election and representation of all that possessed lands. [45]

James Beattie declares: "Another thing remarkable in the Gothick nations, was an invincible spirit of liberty... To them there is reason to believe that we are indebted for those two great establishments, which form the basis of British freedom." [46]

In view of these descriptions of Gothic free institutions, it will become clearer why the Jutes, or the Goths as the seventeenth century denominated them, had a greater effect on English political history than the mere account in Bede would bear out. The role of the Jutes in English history, as the seventeenth century read it, was to create a psychological predisposition in the men of Kent (the county where the Jutes planted their seat) ever since 449 to be fiercely liberty loving. Furthermore, so determined were the Kentishmen to preserve their legacy of liberty from their Jutish forefathers that no conqueror, not even the Norman, could destroy their legacy. In other words, Jutish free institutions (their favorite example was *gavelkynd*) had a continuous history despite the various conquests. A curve of history bound England's future, as Temple, Swift, Bolingbroke, Bacon, and the others saw it, to England's Gothic past.

The tradition of Kentish valor and love of freedom was so proverbial that it appeared as a commonplace, apparently, in the literature of the period:

Middleton, *Roaring Girl,* act II, scene i
  The purity of your wench I would fain try, she seems like Kent unconquered.
Peele, *Jests*
  The fruitful county of Kent...a climate as yet unconquered.

[45] *Ibid.,* I, 220.
[46] "On Fable and Romance," in *Dissertations Moral and Critical* (Dublin, 1783), II, 261-262.

Middleton, *Father Hubburd's Tales*
  My honest nest of ploughmen! the only Kings of Kent.
*Henry VI, Part III,* act I, scene ii
  In them [Kentishmen] I trust; for they are soldiers, Witty,
  courteous, liberal, full of spirit.
*Henry VI, Part II,* act IV, scene vii
  Kent, in the Commentaries Caesar writ,
  Is term'd the civil'st place of all this isle.
  Sweet is the country, because full of riches;
  The people liberal, valiant, active, wealthy. [47]

*The Paston Letters* view Kent as a hotbed of dissension,
apparently in recollection of Jack Cade: "The comons of Kent,
as thei werre wonte, er not all well disposid, for there is in
doyng amongs hem what evere it bee." [48]

Thomas Fuller's *Worthies* includes in its description of the
county of Kent an account of the Kentishman's proverbial love
of liberty:

*Kent. Proverbs of Kent:* "A man of Kent": This may relate
either to the liberty or to the courage of this county man; liberty, the tenure of villanage (so frequent elsewhere) being here
utterly unknown, and the bodies of all Kentish persons being of
free condition. Insomuch that it is holden sufficient for one to
avoid the objection of bondage, to say "that his father was born
in Kent!" Now seeing "servi non sunt viri, quia non sui juris"
(a bond-man is no man because not his own man); the Kentish
for their freedom have achieved to themselves the name of
men. [49]

Richard Kilburne (1659) states the reasons for the preëminence of Kentishmen:

Fourthly, For the ancient valour of the people of this County,
they claime, and are allowed the front in Battailes. And they
onely of all England obteyned and reteyne the name of UNCON-

---

[47] The references are from that mine of Elizabethan lore, Edward
H. Sugden, *Topographical Dictionary to the Works of Shakespeare
and His Fellow Dramatists* (Manchester, 1925), *s.v.* "Kent."
  [48] *Paston Letters,* edited by James Gairdner (Edinburgh, 1910), I,
392, dated 1456.
  [49] *The Worthies of England* (London, 1840), II, 122.

QUERED: For (as if all the antient English valour were remaining in them) they only resisted King William the Conqueror (when all other Counties submitted) and (capitulating with him) reserved to themselves and their posterity, their antient Customes and Liberties. [50]

Kent is geographically in the front of battles (as Kilburne says) whenever England is menaced by foreign invasion. Wordsworth's poem "To the Men of Kent," inspired by the threat of a Napoleonic invasion, may mean no more than this. But Wordsworth, significantly, also traces the Kentish tradition of liberty:

Vanguard of Liberty, ye men of Kent,
Ye children of a Soil that doth advance
Her haughty brow against the coast of France,
Now is the time to prove your hardiment!

To France be words of invitation sent!
They from their fields can see the countenance
Of your fierce war, may ken the glittering lance
And hear you shouting forth your brave intent.
Left single, in bold parley, ye, of yore,
Did from the Norman win a gallant wreath;
Confirmed the charters that were yours before;—
No parleying now! In Britain is one breath;
We all are with you now from shore to shore:—
Ye men of Kent, 'Tis victory or death'. [51]

The dramatic story of William's submission to the Kentish demands for liberty was repeated in many chronicles of the Norman Conquest and in the same context of discussion with a description of Kentish psychology or in a discussion of *gavelkynd,* a free institution as the seventeenth century saw it, planted by the Jutes on English soil in Kent and unbroken in its development. Richard Grafton in his *Chronicle at Large* (1568-1569), for example, tells the story well. Flushed with

[50] *A Topographie or Survey of the County of Kent* (London, 1659), p. 6.
[51] In *Complete Poetical Works,* introduction by John Morley (London, 1898), p. 201.

victory, William moved on toward Kent. Archbishop Stigand of Canterbury aroused the Kentishmen, "and the whole people rather desyring to ende their haplesse lyfe, then to beare the unaccustomed yoke of servitude, with a comon consent decreed to meete Duke William, & to fight with him for their aunicent lawes and libertyes." The Kentishmen ambushed William's forces at Swanscombe by the trick of moving boughs. William agreed to their demands, and the story concludes:

And so the auncient liberties of Englishmen, and their Countries lawes and customes, which before the comming of William Duke of Normandy, were equally held through the whole realm of England, now was onely in the Countie of Kent...and is unto this day inviolably observed and kept that tenure which at this day is called Gavell kynde. [52]

This concluding passage is curious because it implies that *gavelkynd* is not strictly Jutish; it is a native, non-Roman, that is, a free institution; but apparently it once extended over all England. The Jutish Kentishmen, then, were apparently the most determined and most successful of Englishmen in preserving their original liberties. Camden, who, as we have seen, identified the Jutes as Goths, also tells the Swanscombe story to the effect that Kent is unconquerable: "This Country was never conquered, as the residue of England was but by concluding of a peace subjected themselves to the dominion of the Conqueror, retaining to themselves all their liberties, immunities, and customs, which they had, and used before time." [53]

John Rastell's law dictionary (1567) describes *gavelkynd* as a Kentish institution but as ultimately Germanic, in itself a clear indication of the overlapping or shift between the terms "German" and "Gothic," the particular denoting the general: "Gavel-kinde est un Custome annexe & currant ove terres en Kent, appel Gavel kinde-terres. Et est pense per les erudites

[52] *Chronicle at large* (London, 1809), I, 154-156.
[53] Holland's translation, p. 325.

en Antiquities, destre Gavel-kinde de *Give all kine,* cest adire, a touts les kinne en un line, accordant come est use enter les Germans, de que nous Anglais, & especialement de Kent, venomns." [54] Rastell's last phrase, "especialement de Kent," reflects the importance given to the Jutes in the invasion.

Michael Drayton's *Polyolbion* indites a song to "noble Kent":

Who, when the Norman first with pride and horror sway'd,
Threw'st off the servile yoke upon the English lay'd;
And with a high resolve, most bravely didst restore
That libertie so long enjoy'd by thee before.
Not suffring forraine Lawes should thy free Customes bind,
Then only showd'st thyselfe of th'auncient Saxon kind.
Of all the English shires be thou surnam'd the Free. [55]

It should again be noted how the terms have shifted. Drayton describes Kentish freedom as of the "auncient Saxon kinde," despite the clear statement in Bede that the Saxon seat in England was elsewhere than in Kent. But the poem stresses the essential ideas of freedom, its source in valorous character, and the continuity in England (or at least in Kent) of free institutions despite despots. Thus the tradition of Kentish valor and love of freedom became synonymous with the Gothic tradition in England through the intermediary of the etymologizing which brought about the identification of Kentish Jutes and Goths; Nathaniel Bacon states the matter succinctly: "Another custom of descent remaineth, and that is to the children indifferently, and it is called Gavel-kind or Gave-all kind... It seemeth to be first the laws of the Goths or Jutes." [56] The terms "Germanic," "Jutish," and "Gothic" shift, but

---

[54] *Les Termes de la ley* (Printed in the Savoy, 1721), *s.v.* "Gavel-kinde."
[55] "The Eighteenth Song," *Poly-olbion,* edited by J. William Hebel (Oxford, 1933), in *The Works of Michael Drayton,* IV, 381.
[56] *Laws and Government,* p. 66.

the meaning of "Gothicism" remained fixed throughout the seventeenth and eighteenth centuries to describe primitive Germanic culture and the medieval, in the sense of the stream of history outside of the classic Roman stream. These two meanings were the reasons for the transfer to aesthetic discussion in the eighteenth century of the term "Gothic" to describe cathedrals, ballads, Norse poetry, and even Arthurian legend. In the latter case, even if a dim awareness existed that its materials were Celtic and not Germanic, the Arthurian tales lay within these two meanings—the primitive, and the medieval—in the sense that they were clearly segregated from the stream of classical civilization; as a result, Thomas Warton and Richard Hurd wrote critiques of Spenser's "Gothic" *Faerie Queene,* the Arthurian materials of which, according to modern knowledge, could not conceivably be Germanic. [57]

Jordanes' Scandza theory and the importance given to the Jutish colonization of Kent explain, consequently, the domiciliation of the "Goths" in England. The actual facts of the historical Gothic conquest of mighty Rome and the Gothic *Völkerwanderungen* are never so strange as the peregrination which in the minds of the seventeenth-century English writers brought the "Goths" to England's shores. Their veneration of the Goths of antiquity was profound precisely because they could appreciate Gothic history as a phase of England's cultural, political, and moral evolution.

The aura of Gothic "freedom" as enshrined in England's Gothic laws arises unmistakably from eighteenth-century aesthetic and political discussions of the Gothic. Neoclassic standards of Greco-Roman symmetry and purity of style notwithstanding, not only was it possible to admire the Gothic style, but a very special taste of the "constitutional sort" was required to appreciate it:

[57] Warton, *Observations on the "Faerie Queene"* (London, 1754, enlarged 1762); Hurd, *Letters on Chivalry and Romance* (London, 1762).

Methinks there was something respectable in those old hospi-
able Gothick halls, hung round with the Helmets, Breast-Plates,
and Swords of our Ancestors; I entered them with a Constitutional Sort of Reverence and look'd upon those arms with Grat-
itude, as the Terror of former Ministers and the Check of Kings.
Nay, I even imagin'd that I here saw some of those good Swords
that had procur'd Magna Charta, and humbled Spencers and
Gavestons. And when I see these thrown by to make Way for
tawdry Gilding and Carving, I can't help considering such an
Alteration as ominous even to our Constitution. Our old Gothick
Constitution had a noble strength and Simplicity in it, which was
well enough represented by the bold Arches and the solid Pillars
of the Edifices of those Days. And I have not observed that the
modern Refinements in either have in the least added to their
Strength and Solidity. [58]

This was the Whig taste in the fine arts; *per contra,* from
the Tory point of view, the Whig taste for the Gothic was as
abominable as the Whig clamor for popular government was
politically irresponsible. According to William Whitehead,
Tory spokesman:

From a thousand instances of our imitative inclinations I shall
select one or two, which have been, and still are, notorious and
general. A few years ago everything was Gothic; our houses, our
beds, our book-cases, and our couches, were all copied from
some parts or other of our old cathedrals. The Grecian architecture, where, as Dryden says

"Firm Doric pillars formed the lower base
The gay Corinthian holds the higher space,
And all below is strength, and all above is Grace,"

that Architecture, which was taught by nature and polished by
the graces, was totally neglected. Tricks and conceits got possession everywhere... This, however odd it might seem, and
however unworthy of the name of Taste, was cultivated, was
admired and still has its professors in different parts of England. There is something, they say, in it congenial to our old
Gothic constitution, which allows everyone the privilege of

[58] Anonymous, *Common Sense,* no. 150 (December 15, 1739); also
reprinted in *Gentlemen's Magazine,* IX (1739), 641.

playing the fool, and of making himself ridiculous in whatever way he pleases. [59]

Thus the term "Gothic" appears on both sides of an antithesis; that is to say, it is used in praise or in censure. Party politics was intervening to condition the critic's taste in the arts.

Gothic liberty provides one of the themes for Gilbert West's poem on the beauties of Stowe, Lord Cobham's country showplace. The poet makes a circuit of the gardens and pauses before a "Sylvan Temple" sheltering "Saxon Gods." A sylvan temple falls into the category of Gothic building, as a cursory glance at eighteenth-century architectural plates will show. The temple is a symbol of liberty:

> Forsaking now the Covert of the Maze,
> Along the broader walks more open Space,
> Pass we to where a Sylvan Temple spreads
> Around the Saxon Gods, its hallowed Shades.
>
> Hail! Gods of our renown'd Fore-fathers, hail:
> Ador'd Protectors once of England's weal.
> Gods of a Nation, valiant, wise, and free,
> Who conquered to establish Liberty!
> To whose auspicious care Britannia owes
> Those Laws, on which She stands, by which she rose.
> Still may your Sons that noble Plan pursue,
> Of equal Government prescrib'd by you.
> Nor e'er indignant may you blush to see,
> The Shame of your corrupted Progeny!
>
> First radiant Sunna shews his beamy head,
> Moved to him, and scepter'd Tiw succeed;
> Tiw, ancient Monarch of remotest Fame
> Who led from Babel's To'rs the German Name.
> And warlike Woden, fam'd for martial Deeds,
> From whom great Brunswick's noble line proceeds.
> Dread Thuner see! on his Imperial Seat,
> With awful Majesty, and Kingly State... [60]

[59] World, no. 12 (March 22, 1753), pp. 59-60.
[60] Stowe, the Gardens of the Right Honourable Richard Lord Viscount Cobham (London, 1732), pp. 17-18.

*The Gothic Temple.*

## The *Gothic* Temple,

is a large Building of red Stone 70 Feet high, upon
a rifing Ground, adorned in the *Gothic* Way with
carved Work and painted Glafs. The Difpofition
within is very beautiful. You enter a Dome; round
which, on the fecond Story, is a Gallery: The third
affords a very extenfive View round the Country.

The Hill round the Temple is adorned with very
good Statues of the feven *Saxon* Deities, who gave
Names to the Days of the Week.—The Manfion
Houfe, and *Greeian* Temple, have a beautiful Effect
from the Place.

(FROM STOWE: A DESCRIPTION ..., LONDON, 1766)

Tiw is Tuisto, the eponymous hero of the Teutons. The poem is notable also in that it shows a new shift in terms. Now it is Britannia which is free, despite the fact that actually the Saxons defeated the Britains. One recalls in this connection Thomson's "Rule, Britannia." West's idea that Tuisto led his people from Babel is founded on an Oriental version of the Jordanes myth, to be discussed later.

West's poem *The Institution of the Order of the Garter* places beyond dispute the fact of the close and necessary connection between the Gothic style of architecture and a national apotheosis of liberty. The poem traces the beginnings of the Garter in Edward's invitations to the reigning monarchs to state their claims to membership. The Genius of England presides over the council as each applicant appears and is rejected as unworthy of the honor. The bards, led by the Genius of England, burst into Pindaric odes in praise of Edward's elevated standards of morality. The Pindarics also commend

> That Law of Freedom, which to Britain's shore
> From Saxon Elva's many-headed Flood
> The valiant Sons of Odin with them bore,
> Their national, ador'd, inseparable good. [61]

The closing epode establishes the specific connection between liberty and the Gothic style of building:

> Hail happy Prince! on whom kind Fate bestows
> Sublimer joys and glory brighter far
>         . . . . .
> To make dependent millions blest,
> A dying nation to restore,
> And save fall'n Liberty with kingly power;
> To quench the torch of discord and debate
> Relume the languid spark of publick zeal,
> Repair the breaches of a shatter'd state,
> And gloriously complete the plan of England's weal,

[61] *The Institution of the Order of the Garter* (London, 1742), p. 62. Garrick staged the poem as a masque.

> Complete the noble Gothick pile
> That on the rock of Justice rear'd shall stand
> In symmetry, and strength, and fame... [62]

Edward Lovibond's poem, "On Rebuilding Combe Neville," also sees in the Gothic building a symbol of liberty. Stanza two addresses "thy Gothic tower," and the poem continues: "There patriot passions fir'd my breast With freedom's glowing themes." [63]

Samuel Boyse's poem, "The Triumphs of Nature" (1742), is also written on Lord Cobham's Stowe. The poem confirms our interpretation of West's "sylvan temple" as a Gothic edifice, symbolical of liberty:

> High on a summit all below commands,
> Fair liberty (4) thy destin'd temple stands.

Note 4, below, reads: "A Gothic temple 70 foot high on the brow of the hill, to the right, intended to be dedicated to Liberty." The poem continues:

> For lo conspicuous stands the awful grove
> Sacred to Woden, and the Saxon Jove:
> Around the central altar seem to stand,
> The gods ador'd by Hengist's valiant band;
> Life seems each breathing figure to inform
> A godlike freedom, and a noble scorn!
> O glorious race! O nation dear to Fame!
> From whom exalted Albion grateful draws
> Her long-establish'd rights—her sacred laws.
> Tho in the Gulph of wasting time were lost
> Each antient monument your name can boast,
> Yet in the hallowed shrine shall one remain,
> While Freedom lives to bless Britannia's plain! [64]

William Julius Mickle's *Almahida Hill* (1781) describes the

---

[62] *Ibid.,* p. 63.

[63] In Alexander Chalmers, *Works of the English Poets* (London, 1810), XVI, 289-290.

[64] In *Gentleman's Magazine,* XII (June, July, August, 1742), pp. 324, 380.

defeat of Rome and the spread of the "northern hordes" over Europe. The gift of Germanic democracy, however, was not universally distributed; only "Saxony" was its recipient:

> When Rome's wide empire, a luxurious prey,
> Debas'd in false refinement nerveless lay,
> The northern hordes on Europe's various climes
> Planted their ruling virtues and their crimes;
> Cloister'd by Tyber's stream the slothful staid,
> To Seine and Loire the gay and frivolous stray'd,
> A sordid group the Belgian marshes pleas'd,
> And Saxony's wild forests freedom seized,
> There held her juries pois'd the legal scales. 65

"Saxony" probably means Germany, but, in any event, England would ultimately receive the gift.

The outstanding poem in the period on Gothic freedom is James Thomson's *Liberty* (1735-36). That its ideas were not lightly considered may be gathered from the fact that Thomson thought the poem his greatest work. In it, the sight of Rome's ruins fills Thomson with a nostalgic longing for the grandeur of the past, and he invokes the spirit of Liberty to give him an account of the causes underlying Rome's decline. Liberty delivers a lengthy monologue, explaining that Rome's liberty departed when the empire suffered military reverses, but that fundamentally the true cause for its downfall was the spiritual corruption of the Romans which made them an easy prey to the invading barbarian armies. Liberty then traces her migrations, and in part four, the climax of the monologue, describes her happiest of all homes in England. It is understandable how Thomson could have persuaded himself that *Liberty* was his finest poem. His imagination was afire with the spectacle of the valorous, liberty loving men of the North, because he could appreciate their history as a phase of England's moral and political growth. The poem could be con-

---

65 In *The Poetical Works of W. J. Mickle,* edited by T. Park (London, 1808), p. 80.

sidered great because its theme—the increment of history turned back to enrich the lives of England's humblest citizens —was great.

The Goths, in Thomson's account, are the original democrats of the world. Rome once had liberty but lost it in spiritual decay. Happily, the Gothic invaders brought about a rebirth of liberty, for,

> Long in the barbarous heart the buried seeds
> Of freedom lay, for many a wintry age. [66]

Liberty fled to the North, as a stopover on its way to England:

> Thence, the loud Baltic passing, black with storm,
> To wintry Scandinavia's utmost bound—
> There I the manly race, the parent hive
> Of the mixed kingdoms, formed into a state
> More regularly free. [67]

The "yellow-haired, blue-eyed Saxon" (part IV, line 670) brought with him to England the gift of Gothic free institutions:

> Untamed
> To the refining subtleties of slaves,
> They brought a happy government along;
> Formed by that freedom which, with secret voice,
> Impartial nature teaches all her sons,
> And which of old through the whole Scythian mass
> I strong inspired. [68]

Another passage describes the Gothic gift of liberty to England:

[66] *Liberty,* edited by J. Logie Robertson (Oxford, 1908), part III, ll. 539-540, p. 355.

[67] *Ibid.,* part IV, ll. 370-374, p. 368. Jordanes' *officina gentium* is obviously the ultimate source of Thomson's reference to a "parent hive"; for Jordanes on the *officina gentium,* see note 21, above.

[68] *Ibid.,* part IV, ll. 689-695, p. 377. Scythian and Gothic are frequently interchangeable, as in Pinkerton's *Dissertation on the Scythians or Goths* as the title itself shows.

that general liberty...
I through the northern nations wide diffused.
Hence many a people, fierce with freedom, rushed
From the rude, iron regions of the north. [69]

Gothic antiquity had become for England a Golden Age, a symbol of a successful democracy. Nor was the tradition of Gothic democracy a mere pseudo-learned creation of Renaissance antiquarians and a mere novelty for eighteenth-century poets wearied of classical themes. The fact of the case is that Englishmen fought and died in a cause which they themselves called "Gothic"; it was the challenge flung down to the English nation by the ambitions of the Stuart monarchs to destroy Parliament which was, as this study will show, the "efficient cause" which brought the Gothic ideas to the surface of English life during the seventeenth century.

## GOTHIC ENLIGHTENMENT

The arguments spread in abundance by the English writers during the seventeenth and eighteenth centuries, based on implications drawn from traditional democratic political inheritances, were not the only factor aiding in the creation of the Gothic vogue in England. A powerful thought-current set in motion by the Reformation, known as the "translatio imperii ad Teutonicos," was a second factor, emphasizing not so much political inheritances as traditional racial characteristics, and shaping the modern understanding of the role of the Goths in history.

The *translatio* suggested forcefully an analogy between the breakup of the Roman empire by the Goths and the demands of the humanist-reformers of northern Europe for religious freedom, interpreted as liberation from Roman priestcraft. In other words, the *translatio* crystallized the idea that humanity was twice ransomed from Roman tyranny and depravity—in

[69] *Liberty* (Robertson ed.), part IV, ll. 798, 801-803, p. 379.

antiquity by the Goths, in modern times by their descendants, the German reformers. In their youth, vigor, and moral purity, the Goths destroyed the decadent Roman civilization and brought about a rejuvenation or rebirth of the world. In the same way, the Reformation was interpreted as a second world rejuvenation. The result was that the epithet "Gothic" became not only a polar term in political discussion, a trope for the "free," but also in religious discussion a trope for all those spiritual, moral, and cultural values contained for the eighteenth century in the single word "enlightenment."

The "translatio imperii ad Teutonicos" invoked for the Renaissance reader a complex of traditional ideas associated with the preëminence of Rome as the cultural center of the world, composed of the following strands: (1) the classical (pagan) conception of the *urbs aeterna* proclaiming the preminence of Rome; (2) the patristic (Christian) acceptance of the classical *urbs aeterna,* abetted by the irresistible authority of Scripture, especially the prophetic Book of Daniel; (3) the significance attached to the accession of Charlemagne to the imperial title of the Holy Roman Empire, a literal "translatio imperii ad Teutonicos," that is, a world empire given over to the Germanic peoples.

## THE "URBS AETERNA"

The classical conception of the *urbs aeterna,* voiced by a long line of Rome's poets and orators, proclaimed the august, enduring, and universal grandeur of Rome. Two forces, political and religious, shaped the literary tradition. The last century of the republic was marked by extreme disorder, prevented only by the prudence and sagacity of Augustus from becoming worse; as a consequence, the poetic celebrations of Rome's imperial grandeur were, in reality, elegies for a departed past. The Goths had appeared within the borders. A new religion had appeared to supplant the old gods. On the

other hand, however, the popular belief in the assurance stated
in three different passages of the Sibylline oracles that Augustus would succeed in establishing in his dynasty the perpetuity
of the empire, was a second source of inspiration rather more
forward-looking than retrospective, less elegiac and more
hopeful; certainly Virgil's great claim of Rome's eternity
enlarges on the latter inspiration.

It was primarily due to Virgil as the literary interpreter of
the Roman sentiment of the *urbs aeterna* that the conception
survived the downfall of the material empire. To Virgil, Rome
was the steward of civilization, the giver of world order, and
it was destined, therefore, to be the universal city of peace and
justice:

> Tu regere imperio populos, Romane, memento;
> hae tibi erunt artes; pacisque imponere morem,
> parcere subiectis, et debellare superbos. [70]

The underlying conception, indeed, of the entire sixth book
of the *Aeneid* is of Rome's world-dominion. As Anchises tells
the story of Rome's founding and bares the prophecy of its
glorious future, he stresses that he is not simply telling the
story of a few stragglers from Troy but that he is revealing
the purpose of divine creation itself in the founding of Rome.
The Eternal City was to have universal and eternal world-
dominion because it represented the consummation of the
divine ordering of the world and the long process of civilizing
barbarous humanity:

> En, huius, nate auspiciis illa incluta Roma
> imperium terris, animos aequabit Olympo,
> septemque una sibi muro circumdabit arces,
> felix prole virum. [71]

[70] *Aeneid,* bk. VI, ll. 851-853; Greenough and Kittredge edition
(Boston, 1895), p. 184. "Roman, be this thy care—these thine arts—
to bear dominion over the nations and to impose the law of peace,
to spare the humbled and to war down the proud," *Virgil,* translated
by J. Jackson (Oxford, 1921), p. 258.
[71] Book VI, ll. 781-784; Greenough and Kittredge, p. 181. "Look.

As Anchises speaks, Rome's empire, "imperium sine fine dedi," from its western to its eastern limits, comes under his view.

The powerful attraction exerted by the city of Rome is thus seen to be closely related to the imperial idea. It was even the conviction of Rome's panegyrists that if Rome fell, so would the entire world: "Quando cadet Roma, cadet et mundus." [72]

### THE "URBS SACRA"

Rome's superiority, as an ideal, was never canceled. Like Rome's pagan poets, the early Christian thinkers—St. Augustine, Lactantius, Tertullian, and Prudentius—were interested intentionally to obscure the fact that Rome's power was declining. Consequently, the Christians also sponsored the idea of the *urbs aeterna*, blending scriptural notions from the Book of Daniel with the Roman notions. The early Christian thinkers were conciliatory. Christianity took up the Roman strand and wove into it a new thread, spiritualizing it beyond even Virgil's noble vision: the Christians were the noblest Romans of all. Thus the continuity of the idea of the *urbs aeterna* was assured. It survived to enter into the thought-complex centering on the *translatio*.

The effort at Christian reconciliation may be described simply as an attempt to convert the *urbs aeterna* into an *urbs sacra*. The pagan belief in the city's providential creation by the gods aided in the process; it is, in fact, another manifestation of that ever attractive theme, the classical legacy to the modern, Christian world. For example, one of the more famous

---

my son, and know that under his [Romulus'] auspices shall glorious Rome bound her empire earth, her pride by Olympus, and one in self, circle with her battlements the seven hill, blest in a warrior race," Jackson translation, p. 256.

[72] [Pseudo-] Bede, *Exceptiones patrum, in Opera paraenetica,* Migne, *Patrologia Latina,* vol. XCIV, col. 453; see also Arturo Graf, *Roma nella memoria e nelle immaginazioni del Medio Evo* (Torino, 1882), vol. I, ch. i.

"stations-of-Rome" or pilgrim poems, "O Roma nobilis," expresses a veneration of Rome. But its mood of piety is different. The poem venerates Rome because it was the stage which witnessed the spectacle of the martyrs:

> O Roma nobilis, orbis et domina,
> cunctarum urbium excellentissima,
> roseo martyrum sanguine rubea,
> albis et virginum liliis candida
> salutem dicimus tibi per omnia,
> te benedicimus; salve per secula. [73]

The *Peristephanon* of Prudentius hails Rome as "parent of men," "ruler of the world,"

> Antiqua fanorum parens
> Jam Roma Christo dedita...

Like "O Roma nobilis," it connects the city with a martyr cult: once great as ruler of the world, Rome is now greater in the reflected glory of the martyrs. [74]

Another panegyric of Rome commences in the manner of the pagan encomia, stressing Rome's glory; but the city replies to Hildebert (the author of the poem) that under Peter, Rome will be more glorious than under Caesar:

> Quis gladio Caesar, quis sollicitudine consul,
> quis rhetor lingua, quae mea castra manu
> tanta dedere mihi? Studiis et legibus horum
> obtinui terras; crux dedit una polum. [75]

[73] Quoted in F. J. E. Raby, *History of Christian-Latin Poetry* (Oxford, 1927), pp. 233-234. "O noble Rome, and mistress of the world, most excellent of all cities, red with the blood of the martyrs, shining with the white lilies of the virgins, we greet thee, we bless thee throughout all ages, hail forever."

[74] "Hymnus II," *Peristephanon*, (Amstelodami, 1657), p. 58. "Rome, ancient mother of shrines, now given up to Christ..."

[75] Quoted in F. J. E. Raby, *Secular Latin Poetry* (Oxford, 1934), I, 324. "What Caesar with his sword, what consul with his vigilance, what orator with his tongue, what camp with my might gained for me such great achievements'. By the efforts and the laws of all these, I obtained the earth; but one cross gave heaven to me."

These poems were patently written under the influence of
the pagan city encomia, but insofar as their authors seek to
reconcile their Christianity with the pagan belief in Rome's
destiny, they solve their problem very superficially. We must
turn to other Christian panegyrists to see the complexity of
the problem faced by Christian thinkers in reconciling the
ecumenical character of Rome with its imperial character
which they were far from denying.

The specific statement "quando cadet Roma, cadet et mundus" is, as a matter of fact, of Christian composition. [76] The
reasons why the Church arose to propagate anew the faith
in the universal empire and intentionally to obscure the facts
of the imperial dissolution are not difficult to trace. The
Fathers recognized the positive services which Rome rendered
to the cause of humanity by providing the earthly order on
the basis of which it was the Church's mission to create a
spiritual order. The Church accepted Rome's earth-encircling
claim, denouncing, to be sure, the empire's moral decay and
oppression, but accepting, nevertheless, the principle of
authority on which the imperial order rested. The Christians
had no national traditions and had never known a national
existence, and for this reason they were as much, or perhaps
first, citizens of Rome before they were members of the Church.
The following passage, of anonymous authorship, reveals
how Christianity came into existence within the Roman empire

[76] *Vita S. Adelberti,* ch. xxi (Anno 996) quoted in A. J. Carlyle,
*Medieval Political Theory in the West* (Edinburgh, 1927-28), III, 171:
"Roma autem cum caput mundi et urbium domina sit et vocetur, sola
reges imperare facit," and so on. For additional passages, making the
same point of Rome, the capital of the world, see Lactantius, *Divina-
rum institutionum,* bk. VII, chs. 14, 25; in Migne, *Patrologia Latina,*
vol. VI, cols. 779-784, 811-813. Ambrosius, *Expositio in Lucam,* bk. IV,
ch. IV, and discussion by H. Fischer, "Belief in the Continuity of the
Roman Empire among the Franks of the Fifth and Sixth Centuries,"
*Catholic Historical Review,* n.s. IV (1925), 536-553. Also useful is the
synopsis of a dissertation by William Haller, *Latin and German Encomia of Cities* (Chicago, privately printed, 1937).

and formed a constituent element in a civilization which it gradually permeated:

Christians are not distinct from the rest of mankind in land or language or customs. For they nowhere inhabit cities of their own, nor do they use any different form of speech, nor do they practise any peculiar mode of living... They inhabit cities, Greek or Barbarian, wherever the lot of each has cast him, and they follow local custom in their clothes, food, and general way of living. [77]

As Domenico Comparetti has said:

The ideals of Christianity would have remained mere Utopian visions had they not found so many diverse peoples made homogeneous by the legions of Rome... As Christ stood at the fountain-head of the religious records of Christian history, so, its political records began with the first emperor, Augustus, in whose reign Christ was born. By a coincidence, on the miraculous nature of which the Christians were never tired of dilating, the beginning of Christianity had been contemporaneous with the beginning of the Empire, and Christ had been born at the moment when Rome was at the zenith of her power, when peace reigned throughout her vast dominions. [78]

In St. Augustine's view, the empire was even due to the will of God. Attacking the pagans' belief that their empire was divinely instituted, St. Augustine points out that even if true, the pagan gods were powerless since, obviously, they had left the Romans to their fate at the hands of the Gothic invaders. But, he continues, deliberately obscuring the fact that because of the barbarian eruption the empire was dissolving, the end is not fatal since the true God had providentially created the empire in preparation for the spiritual kingdom to follow: "Cause ergo magnitudinis imperii Roma nec fortuita est nec fatalis... Prorsus divina providentia regna

---

[77] *Epistola ad Diognetum,* cited and translated by W. R. Halliday, *The Pagan Background of Early Christianity* (London, 1925), p.l.

[78] *Vergil in the Middle Ages,* translated by E. F. M. Benecke (London, 1895), p. 175.

constituuntur humana." [79] Rome's greatness, according to
St. Augustine, was the reward of the pagan intellectual effort:
"Honorati sunt in omnibus fere gentibus, imperii sui leges
imposuerunt multis gentibus, hodieque litteris et historia
gloriosi sunt paene in omnibus gentibus." [80]

The implication of the metaphor which forms the very
substance of St. Augustine's book becomes comprehensible in
terms of his belief that Rome's imperial greatness, her universal and eternal empire, was the earthly order necessary to the
creation of the heavenly order, although ordinarily most commentaries stress that St. Augustine rejected the "earthly city."

Proinde per illud imperium tam latum tamque diuturnum
virorumque tantorum virtutibus praeclarum atque gloriosum et
illorum intentioni merces quam quarebant est reddita, et nobis
proposita necessariae commonitionis exempla, ut, si virtutes,
quarum ista utcumque sunt similes, quas isti pro civitatis terra-
nae gloria teruerunt, pro Dei gloriosissima civitate non tenueri-
mus, pudore pungamur. [81]

In the view of Lactantius, the earthly order provided by
Rome's universal empire is necessary since it preserves the
world, otherwise on the brink of destruction: "Cuius vastitatis
et confusionis haec erit causa, quod Romanum nomen, quo
nunc regitur orbis (horret animus dicere: sed dicam, quia
futurum est) tolletur de terra et imperium in Asiam revertetur,

---

[79] *Civitas Dei*, bk. v, ch. i. "Wherefore the cause of this was neither
fortune, nor fate... But the God of heaven, by his only providence,
disposes of the kingdoms of earth," John Healey's translation, edited
by R. V. G. Tasker (Everyman ed.; London, 1945), p. 153.

[80] Book v, ch. xv. "Honored they are almost all the world over: all
nations very near received their laws; honored were they then in all
men's mouths, and now in most men's writings through the world,"
Everyman ed., p. 163.

[81] Book v, ch. xviii. "Wherefore that empire, so spacious and so
continual and renowned by the virtues of these illustrious men, was
given both to stand as a reward for their merits, and to produce
examples for our uses, that if we observe not the laws of those virtues
for attaining the celestial kingdom, which they did for preserving one
but terrestrial, we might be ashamed," Everyman ed., p. 168.

ac rursus Oriens dominabitur, atque Occidens serviet." [82]

According to Tertullian, it was necessary for the Christians to pray for the emperor's life since a lease on life was given to the world by the duration of the empire. [83] Thus it is clear that the Church accepted—in its own way—the claim of Rome's universal and eternal empire. The Christian thinkers affirmed (in the words of Pope Leo the Great, 390?-461 A.D.: "Ut ennarabilis gratiae per totum mundum diffunderetur effectus, Romanum regnum divina praeparavit." [84]

## THE DANIELIC "TRANSLATIO"

Whether the Christian panegyrists were able without reservation to accept the Roman claim is exceedingly dubious. There were, as a matter of fact, three ideas, not merely the *urbs aeterna* and the *urbs sacra,* fertilizing the Christian thinking. Account must be taken of the third idea, the famed *translatio,* in order better to understand why the Christians appear to have accepted the Roman claim, although they must like St. Augustine ultimately reject the pagan *civitas Roma* in favor of the *civitas Dei.*

The *translatio* represents a reworking of the prophecies contained in chapters 2 and 7 of the Book of Daniel. To the Jews, Daniel was a prophecy of Jewish national resurgence, but to the Christians (primarily because of Jerome's commentary) it meant a consummation of the divine purpose in

---

[82] *Div. instit.,* bk. VII, ch. XV, in Migne, *Patrologia latina,* vol. VI, col. 787. "Of this desolation and confusion the cause will be this, that the Roman name by which the world now is ruled (my mind shudders to say it: but I shall say it because it is going to be so) will be removed from the earth and dominion will return to Asia, and again the East will be the lord and the West will be the slave."

[83] *Apologia,* ch. xxxii, edited by William Reeves (London, n.d.), pp. 95-96.

[84] "That the working of unspeakable grace might be spread abroad throughout the whole world, Divine Providence prepared the Roman Empire"; quoted and translated by Grant Showerman, *Eternal Rome* (New Haven, 1924), I, 185.

allowing Rome to prosper simultaneous, paradoxically, with release from the Roman empire. (Later, however, to the medieval German historians and to the German humanist-reformers, Daniel meant again a resurgent national ideal, but specifically a German national resurgence.)

The statue and the beasts, allegorized in Daniel 2 and 7, represent the four empires of antiquity and the transference (translatio) of power from each decaying empire to its successor, the process culminating in the rise of Rome:

| [Ch. 2 (statue)] | [Ch. 7 (beast)] | [Empire] |
|---|---|---|
| golden head | lion | Babylonian |
| silver breast | bear | Medo-Persian |
| brazen belly and thighs | leopard | Grecian |
| iron legs, iron and clay feet | the fourth beast | Roman [85] |

The point that we shall have occasion to observe is that Bishop Otto of Freising (a German historian), for example, regards the imperial idea from a double viewpoint, prefiguring the shift which was to become more and more predominant in Germany as the Reformation approached. Bishop Otto, like Virgil, is deeply imbued with the pacific dream of the empire. On the other hand, however, by directly linking Daniel with a German imperial concept, Bishop Otto appears to be espousing what might be called a "Fifth Monarchy," that is to say, a "translatio imperii ad Teutonicos," a conception of Rome's decaying power passed on to its successor, Germany.

The affinity between Daniel and the Virgilian vision was natural. Virgil was, for the Middle Ages, at once the prophet of Rome's imperial destiny and the supposed foreteller of the advent of Christ. It is not a priori impossible (Virgilian scholars continue to debate the point) that Virgil's fourth

[85] James Hastings and John A. Selbie, *Dictionary of the Bible* (Edinburgh, 1898), *s.v.* "Daniel." For Jerome's commentary on Daniel, see Migne, *Patrologia Latina,* vol. XXV, col. 504 and discussion by E. M. Sanford, *The Mediterranean World in Ancient Times* (New York, 1938), p. 557.

eclogue, prophesying the birth of Christ, was strongly tinctured with Judaized (Alexandrian) Sibylline prophecy; the vision of Aeneas of "better things to come" may have been similarly inspired. At any rate, whether the "Judaizing" interpretation is correct or not, it is a fact to be established here that the tradition formed among the German historians of a German *translatio* actually unites Daniel and the Virgilian imperial conception. Thus, as far as German historiography is concerned, the *translatio* flowed (ultimately, at any rate) from two heads: Scripture and the Virgilian-Christian dream of empire. [86]

## CHARLEMAGNE, THE LITERAL "TRANSLATIO"

Medieval political and religious history continued to gravitate toward the one great idea of the empire. The medieval theory of Charlemagne's accession to the Roman imperial title is the last restatement but one of the imperial idea. Under the impact of the Reformation, the ideal of Gothic enlightenment, based squarely on the concept of the German *translatio* and incomprehensible without it in fact, stands, as we shall see, at the apogee of the development of the imperial idea. Absolutely decisive for this subsequent political and religious history was Charlemagne's accession in 800 to the imperial crown. Because of the imperial diadem resting on Charlemagne's brow, the whole of history, as in Daniel, continued to be looked upon as a succession of great monarchies, successively entrusted by God with the sovereignty of nations. Now, sovereignty was entrusted to the Germanic peoples.

[86] R. S. Conway is sympathetic to the Judaizing interpretation of Virgil; see his essay in *Virgil's Messianic Eclogue, Three Studies* (London, 1907) by Joseph B. Mayor, W. Warde Fowler, R. S. Conway, H. J. Rose is sharply critical of the interpretation, *The Eclogues of Vergil* (University of California, 1942), ch. viii, "A Child is Born." See in Rose, especially pp. 180, 195, on eastern conceptions of "better things to come" possibly available to Virgil and certainly floating about at the time. Comparetti is, of course, classical on the medieval Virgil.

However illusory the Frankish emperor's real power, however shadowy his title as compared with the Papal claim of surpremacy, or even however unwilling Charlemagne was (as some records suggest) to accept the imperial diadem, the Roman imperial idea persisted as a result of Charlemagne's accession. [87] Charlemagne is referred to by later historians as "most serene Augustus." Like the first Augustus, his mission was conceived as an effort to spread peace and civilization over the world. One of Charlemagne's seals reads: "Renovati Romani imperii."

The early biographer of Charlemagne, known to us as the Monk of St. Gall, dips into Scripture and revives the Danielic prophecy, connecting it with the crowning of Charlemagne: "After the omnipotent ruler of the world, who orders alike the fate of kingdoms and the course of time, had broken the feet of iron and clay in one noble statue, to wit the Romans, he raised the hands of the illustrious Charles the golden head of another, not less admirable, among the Franks." [88]

In 871, Emperor Louis II wrote to Basil of Byzantium: "The race of the Germans has brought forth the most abundant fruits to the Lord... For as God was able to raise up children like Abraham, so from the barbarism of the Germans He had been able to raise up successors to the Roman emperors." [89]

[87] Herbert Fisher, *The Medieval Empire* (London, 1898), vol. I, ch. 1, "The Survival of the Imperial Idea"; consult James Bryce, *The Holy Roman Empire* (London, 1904), ch. ii *et passim;* also useful are: F. Schneider, *Rom und Romgedanke im Mittelalter* (Munich, 1926); P. E. Schramm, Kaiser, *Rom und Renovatio* (Leipzig, 1929); Walther Rehm, *Der Untergang Roms* (Leipzig, 1930); F. Gregorovius, *Geschichte der Stadt Rom im Mittelalter* (4th ed.; Stuttgart, 1886-1896), also available in translation by Annie Hamilton (London, 1894-1902), see especially volume one.

[88] A. J. Grant, translator *Early Lives of Charlemagne* (London, 1926), p. 59.

[89] Cited by James Westfall Thompson, *Feudal Germany* (Chicago, 1928), p. 367.

In 1239 Frederick II protested against the action of Gregory IX in stirring up enemies against him; he asks his enemies to remember the dignity of the German empire, holding the monarchy of the world: "Exurgat igitur invicta Germania, exurgite populi Germanorum. Nostrum nobis defendatis imperium, per quod invidiam omniun nationum, dignitatem omnium et mundi monarchiam obtinetis." [90]

The *Chronica* of Bishop Otto of Freising is a landmark of the interim development of the transformed imperial idea. The Danielic spirit dominates Bishop Otto's viewpoints towards history, as is made clear in his dedicatory letter:

Preterea, quo ordine currat haec historia, breviter exponam, ut hoc incognito qualitas operis facilius pateat legenti. Quatuor principalia regna, qua inter cetera eminerent, ab exordio munde fuisse, in finemque eius secundum legem totius successive permansura fore ex visione quoque Danielis percipe potest. Horum ergo principes, secundum cursum temporis enumeratos, primos Assirios, post, suppressis Chaldaeis, quos inter ceteros historiographi ponere dedignantur, Medos et Persas, ad ultimum Grecos et Romanos, posui, eorumque nomine usque ad presentem imperatorem subnotavi... [91]

Bishop Otto directly connects in turn the Danielic prophesy with the "translatio imperii ad Teutonicos": "Et de potentia

---

[90] Carlyle, *Medieval Political Theory,* V, 142.

[91] Ottonis Episcopi Frisingenses, *Chronica sive historia de Duabus civitatibus,* edited by Adolphus Hofmeister (Leipzig, 1912), p. 5. "Next I shall briefly explain the order in which this history proceeds, that, when this is known, the nature of the work may be the more readily apparent. That therefore from the beginning of the world four principal kingdoms which stood out above all the rest, and that they are to endure unto the world's end, succeeding one another in accordance with the law of the universe can be gathered in various ways, in particular from the vision of Daniel. I have therefore set down the rulers of these kingdoms, listed in chronological sequence, first the Assyrians, next (omitting the Chaldeans, whom the writers of history do not deign to include among the others) the Medes and the Persians, finally the Greeks and the Romans," translation by C. C. Mierow, under the title of *The Two Cities* (New York, 1928), p. 91.

quidem humana, qualiter a Babilonius ad Mesos et Persa ac inde Macedones et post ad Romanos rursumque sub Romano nomine ad Crecos derivatum sit, sat dictum arbiteror. Qualiter vero inde ad Francos, qui occidentem inhabitant, translatum fuerit, in hoc opere dicendum restat." [92]

Interpreting the significance of Charlemagne's crowning by the Pope, Bishop Otto concludes triumphantly: "As Rome fell, Francia arose to receive her crown." [93] Of royal lineage himself, Bishop Otto was at once (as Mierow points out) a prince of the realm and a servant of the Church. If there is not in Bishop Otto (as there is unquestionably among the German reformers later) a nationalistic bias, there is at least a dynastic bias which tends toward an aggrandizement of Germany at the expense of Rome's fame. Bishop Otto is of considerable importance, therefore, as a transitional figure.

The exact difference between Bishop Otto and the Reformation historians is indicated in his lack of assurance in his attempt to explain in final terms exactly why God transferred the gift of empire to the Germans: "Quare autem populi vel illi urbi hanc potius quam aliis gratiam contulerit, discutere non possumus...si quis vero contentiosus est, audiat in potestate figuli esse, aliud vas in honorem, aliud facere in contumeliam." [94]

Such lack of assurance is not to be found among the Pro-

---

[92] *Chronica,* prologus, lib. v; Hofmeister ed., p. 227. "Regarding human power—how it passed from the Babylonians to the Medes and the Persians and then again to the Greeks under the Roman name—I think enough has been said. How it was transferred from the Greeks to the Franks, who dwell in the West, remains to be told in the present book," Mierow's translation, p. 322.

[93] Mierow, p. 322; text in Hofmeister, p. 226: "Cum iam Roma cadente Francia ad accipiendam coronam surrexerit."

[94] Hofmeister, p. 134. "But why He bestowed this boon [eternity] upon that people or that city rather than on others we cannot even discuss...but if any man is contentious let him hear that it is in the power of the potter to make one vessel unto honor and another unto dishonor," Mierow, p. 221.

testant reformers discussing the same ideas; Luther, as we shall see, denounces the entire idea of Rome's empire although, interestingly, he employs the same arguments, based on certain racial inheritances, which the humanists developed in support of their theory of a German *translatio*. The Reformation, in other words, supplied the fulcrum for applying the *translatio* lever to the very foundation of the Roman claim of universal supremacy. In the hands of the German humanist-reformers, the *translatio* became a loud and insistent summons to Germans to a renewed faith in the religious meaning of what their ancestors had accomplished in the past and what they themselves might hope to accomplish in the future. The *translatio* summoned the Germans to a rebirth or rejuvenation of the world. As a direct parallel to the secular victory of their Gothic ancestors in freeing the world from Roman political tyranny, the Reformation was to ransom humanity again, this time from Roman religious tyranny. The reformers approached their task with an apocalyptic fervor. While denouncing Roman depravity, they were making it perfectly clear that the era of justice promised both in the Danielic and the Virgilian visions of "better things to come" would be created by the morally pure, humane Germanic peoples. Thus Virgil's centuries-old divine prophecy ironically gave birth with the passing of time and under religious exigency to a new prophecy of Gothic enlightenment. Even while representing Virgil's deeply felt conception of a palladium of mankind, the prophecy of Gothic enlightenment at the same time represented the culmination of Rome's might. Before, the propitious stars shone on Rome; now it was the German's day. God was with the Germans and they were lucky!

## THE REFORMATION IN GERMANY

"Omnia Romae est venalia"—the many satirical effusions denouncing the corrupt Roman clergy have been too well canvassed in standard literary histories to require additional mention. Our purpose will have been achieved if we bring to light the fact that the indignation of the reformers was based on arguments drawn from implications resting on a theory of traditional German racial characteristics. It was the *translatio* which was causing the ferment of racial ideas. On the basis of the *translatio,* the humanists were enabled to offer an antecedent explanation of the divine strategy in bringing about a transfer of world-dominion to the Germans in contrast to Bishop Otto who does not even feel that an explanation can be forthcoming. The humanists found—or pretended to have found—a sharp contrast between an over-ripe, decadent, immoral Latin culture and a youthful, vigorous, morally pure Germanic culture. [95] God had evidently willed that the decaying Roman empire give over world-dominion to the Germans, who in their vigor and purity qualified to usher in "better things to come," a glorious period of justice and faith. Hence the analogy between the Gothic victory in antiquity over the Romans, Daniel's prophecy, Charlemagne's crowning, and the reformers' own demands for freedom from Roman religious tyranny. Hence the humanists' creation and fulfillment of their own demand for a thorough historical research into Gothic and German antiquities in order to establish the antithesis of *Deutschtum* with *Romanitas.*

Luther's is an interesting case to begin with because he is so similar and dissimilar to his humanist allies. It is true that Luther argued not for a revolution in the Church but for a restoration or a continuation of the pure, primitive Christianity which existed before it was defiled by Rome. It is also true, however, that as compared with the humanists, Luther is

[95] The notion of a youthful, vigorous, Germanic culture was given a pseudo-scientific basis by a climate theory; see Appendix A: Climate and Liberty.

devoid of a historical sense. He disdainfully turns away in his *Address to the German Nobility* from the *translatio*. Yet in doing so, it is significant that he reflects the discussion of the *translatio* going on about him, and, more importantly, that he pictures at the same time, the same contrast between Latin depravity and German purity which the more historical minded humanists were never tired of stressing. Luther's first move in the *Address* is to point out that the Roman empire proper had long disappeared from the face of the earth: "There is no doubt that the true Roman empire of which the prophets spoke was long ago destroyed." [96]

Luther explains Pope Leo's crowning of Charlemagne as a typical act of Roman knavery. Unable to control the eastern line of rulers, the Pope cunningly devised the scheme of transferring the imperial diadem to the unspoiled Germans, hoping thereby to dominate the Germans:

Since the Pope could not force the Greeks and the emperor at Constantinople, which is the hereditary Roman emperor, to obey his will, he invented this device to rob him of his empire and title, and give it to the Germans, who were at that time strong and of good repute, in order that they might take the power of the Roman empire and hold it of the Pope.

It was only a trick, however, depending for success on the vulnerability of the Germans because of their simplicity. Here is the typical contrast between Latin depravity and German kindliness: "Therefore the Pope and his followers have no reason to boast that they did a great kindness to the German nation in giving them this Roman empire; firstly because they intended no good to us in this matter, but only abused our simplicity to strengthen their own power against the Roman emperor at Constantinople..." [97]

If the *translatio* theory had never existed, Luther would

[96] *Luther's Primary Works,* edited by Henry Wace and C. A. Buchbeim (London, 1896), p. 235.
[97] *Ibid.,* pp. 235, 237.

4

nevertheless have attacked Rome. Yet his view of Roman
cunning and Germanic simplicity sounds suspiciously like the
racial doctrines which the humanists were spreading in
response to the call of the most indefatigable protagonist of
German historical research, Matthias Flacius Illyricus: "Historia est fundamentum doctrinae." [98] Illyricus himself was to
show the way to solve contemporary problems by going back
to the past, not only in the *Magdeburg Centuries* but also in a
text entitled *De translatione imperii Romani ad Germanos.* [99]

Secular histories of the German past, but powerfully shot
through with the apocalyptic fervor imparted by the conception of a *translatio* brought about with the aid of God, blos-
somed in support of the German claim for religious freedom.
Ironically, it was an Italian and Papal legate (later a pope),
Aeneas Sylvius, who stimulated the study of the German past.
In 1454, in order to encourage the Germans to take a leading
role in the crusade against the Turks, he praised German
virtue by calling attention to what Tacitus had written in the
*Germania* of German moral purity, vigor, and invincibility. [100]
His publication in 1496 in Leipzig of his German history,
entitled *Descriptio de situ moribus et conditione,* stimulated
a whole series of German researches into their ancestors by
the German humanists Bebel, Aventinus, Celtis, Beatus Rhe-
nanus, Sebastian Münster, and others. [101]

[98] In a letter to Archbishop Parker in England, quoted by Eleanor
N. Adams, *Old English Scholarship in England from 1566-1800* (New
Haven, 1917), p. 14.

[99] Basilae, 1566; for Daniel, see p. 3; for Charlemagne, see ch. iii,
"De translatione imperii occidentalis in Carolum magnum." Cardinal
Bellarmine refuted Illyricus and similar theorists in *De translatione
imperii Romani ... adversus Illyricum* (Ingolstadt, 1589). See E. A.
Ryan, *Historical Scholarship of St. Bellarmine* (Louvain, 1936), pp.
69-70, 158-163.

[100] See Wilhelm Pauck, "Nationalism and Christianity," pp. 286-
303 in *Environmental Factors in Christian History,* edited by J. T.
McNeill, M. Spinka, H. R. Willoughby (Chicago, 1939), p. 293.

[101] For a good working bibliography of the German humanists, see

P. S. Allen, with his matchless knowledge of the Reformation, comments on the Germanic-Latin contrast; it will not pass unnoticed that he also points to the *translatio:* "Italy might vaunt the glories of ancient Rome; but Germany also had deeds to be proud of. Rome might have founded the World-Empire; but Charlemagne had conquered the dominions of the Caesars and made the Empire Germanic." It was vitally necessary and even a duty, therefore, for the German humanists to study German antiquities, especially as recorded in Tacitus' *Germania.* Professor Allen says further:

Classic antiquity, too, could not be denied to the land and people whom Tacitus had described; and Germans were not slow to claim the virtues found among them by the Roman historian... German faith and honour, German simplicity, German sincerity and candour—these are insisted upon by the Transalpine humanists with a vehemence which suggests that while priding themselves on the possession of such qualities they marked the lack of them in others. 102

Preserved Smith, also a competent historian of the Reformation, stresses the Germans' self-awareness of their distinct entity, particularly as it contrasted at all points with the Latin entity. The Reformation, as the Germans conceived it in the light of the Gothic conquest of Rome in antiquity, was to free the world from tyranny a second time:

In two aspects, the Reformation was the religious expression of the current political and economic change. In the first place, it reflected and reacted upon the growing national self-consciousness, particularly of the Germanic peoples. The revolt from Rome was in the interests of the state-church and also of German culture. The break-up of the Roman church at the hands of the Northern peoples is strikingly like the break-up of the Roman Empire under pressure from their ancestors. 103

James Westfall Thompson, *The History of Historical Writing* (New York, 1942), vol. I, ch. xxx, "The Historiography of the German Reformation."

102 *The Age of Erasmus* (Oxford, 1914), pp. 266, 274.

103 *The Age of the Reformation* (New York, 1920), p. 747.

Italian arrogance, in particular, was galling to the Germans, for did not the historical facts make clear that the mantle of world-dominion had fallen not on Italian but German shoulders? Who then were the barbarians, Italians or Germans? Martyn Mayr, chancellor to the Elector of Mainz, asks these questions in a letter to Aeneas Sylvius (1457) and summons the Germans to regain their old liberties:

A thousand cunning devices are being resorted to ingeniously for the purpose of extorting money from us barbarians. Therefore our nation, once of great fame, who acquired with her courage and blood the Roman empire and was the mistress and queen of the world, has become poor and a tribute-paying maid; in this misfortune she has now for many years been complaining of this miserable lot. Now, however, our heads have awakened as it were from their slumber and are beginning to consider measures with which to check this evil. They have determined to throw off the yoke and to regain their old liberties [104]

The letter is striking evidence of the Germans' pride in their acquisition of Rome's empire.

A deep evangelical fervour throbs in Heinrich Bebel's "De laude," in which he explains the reasons why God chose the Germans as the only people qualified to inherit the empire: "Nostri vero virtute ac laboribus pro deo susceptis, digni visi sunt vel universo ecclesiae Romanae senatui qui imperium orbis agerent quique quod virtute acquisiverunt te rege te auspice in aeternum servabunt." [105]

German *tugend, tüchtigkeit, treu, standhaft* are the reasons for the superiority of the German peoples; above all, for their true faith, the Germans are set apart to propagate true religion:

[104] Quoted by Hans Kohn, *The Idea of Nationalism* (New York, 1944), p. 389.

[105] *Opera* (Basel, 1504), fol. Cl: "Our people, furthermore, by their valor and by undertaking labors for God, have seemed worthy of the universal senate [?] of the Roman church to exercise control over the world, and they who have gained this [right] by their valor will keep it forever under you as their king, under you as their leader."

Quae est enim gens alia servantior aequi omnisque iustitiae, quae constantior quae tante tamque syncerae fidei quo autem nostri amore et veneratione divinum cultum christianamque religionem prosecuti sint testantur non solum templa Christi sumptuosissima, Coenobia utriusque sexus castissima arae innumerabiles, verumetiam illustria facta maiorum nostrorum et bella domi forisque pro Christiani nominis conservatione et incremento suscepta. [106]

Johann Nauclerus addresses his countrymen as "nobilissimi Germani," and shows why Germans are the most fortunate of peoples: "Nobis dedit Deus imperium, dedit gloriam et nomen excellentissimum." [107]

The world empire was placed in the hands of Charlemagne: "Nam imperium fuit translatum a Graecis, non in Italos neque in Gallos. i. occidentales Francem, sed in Germanos s. in persona Caroli magni." [108]

Germany alone of all the nations deserved the gift of empire: "Quod plane intelliges, si cogitabis imperium ob sola in ecclesiam Ro. merita, in Germanam fuisse translatum, quod ad singulare eius nationis decus et ornamentum accedit." [109]

---

[106] Ibid., fol. C8: "For what other nation is more careful to observe right and all justice, what other is more constant, what other shows such great and sincere faith? Moreover, the love and veneration with which our people have practiced divine worship and the Christian religion are evidenced not only by the most sumptuous temples of Christ, the purest convents of both sexes, and innumerable altars, but also by the illustrious deeds of our ancestors and wars both domestic and foreign undertaken for the preservation and increase of the Christian name."

[107] *Chronica* (Coloniae, 1563), fol. 630: "God has given us empire; He has given us glory and a most excellent name."

[108] *Ibid.*, fol. 658: "For empire was transferred from the Greeks not to the Italians, nor to the Gauls, i.e., the Western Franks, but to the Germans, viz. in the person of Charlemagne."

[109] *Ibid.*, fol. 629: "As you will understand clearly, if you consider that the dominion, [once given] to the Roman church on account of merit alone, was transferred to the German church because the matchless of this nation added honor and glory [to the church]."

Under the rubric *Laus Germaniae,* Nauclerus proclaims the incomparable virtues of the German People:

Quae êm est natio alia sub caleo, ubi tanta & tam syncera nobilitas, ubi tot generosi proceres, ubi tot fortissimi milites, quibus ex innata animi fortitudine cõtra hostes videt quiddã inesse quasi vitae cõtemptus dũ malle inueniuntur exuere hořem & mortalitatẽ, q̃ salutẽ fuga quaerere? Quam longa vero & lata fit Germania, q̃ religosa q̃ veri tenax, q̃ iusta, q̃ populosa, quãtus splẽdor urbũ, q̃ colli facies, q̃ terrae ubertas, magis admirari q̃ recensere volebimus. [110]

Hans Sachs traces the imperial idea and recounts how the Roman empire fell into the hands of the "löblich teutsche nation":

> Ein tags ich ehrenholt fragt
> . . . . .
> Wie das [Romc] euch entlich kommen wer
> Auff löblich teutsche nation. [111]

In the polemic of Ulrich von Hutten one finds the main ideas in the Reformation-created tradition of German enlightenment and Roman obscurantism. Hajo Holborn, Hutten's biographer, suggests that lectures on Tacitus' *Germania,* given by Aesticampianus and attended by Hutten, aroused in him the conception of a distinctive German national history. [112] In a work by Hutten, Dame Italy addresses the German

[110] *Ibid.,* fol. 620: "For what other nation is there under heaven in which there is such great and genuine nobility, in which there are so many worthy noblemen, or so many valorous soldiers who seem to have, from an inborn fortitude of mind in the face of their enemies, almost a contempt for life, so that they are found to prefer to lay down honor [only] along with mortality, rather than to seek safety in flight? And in addition, how long and wide Germany is, how religious, how tenacious of truth, how just, how populous, how splendid in her cities, how beautiful in her hills, how fruitful in her land—all these things we shall be better able to wonder at than to recount."

[111] *Histori: Das Romich Reich, in Litterarischen Vereins in Stuttgart,* CLXXIX (1886), 192, edited by A. von Keller and E. Goetz·.

[112] *Ulrich von Hutten* (New Haven, 1937), pp. 43-44.

emperor and says: "Thy people is now the greatest. Formerly it was Rome." [113] Here, Hutten's viewpoint is balanced: the emperor is to consider himself the heir of the Roman empire but also the proud recipient of a distinctively German legacy. As his animosity toward Rome became aroused, however, Hutten expresses himself in terms of a biting contrast between German manliness and Roman effeminacy, and also in unrestrained praise of Maximilian as heir to the Roman title: "Exaudi nos Caesar, exaudi, innocentum patrone, conservatore iustitiae, libertatis vindex, cultor pietatis; exaudi nos, successor Augusti, aemule Traiani, dominator orbis, rector humani generis." [114]

The Romans are "weibisch":

> Ein weibisch volck, ein weyche schar,
> On hertz, on mut, on tugent gar,
> Der keiner hatt gestritten nye,
> Von kryegen weissz nit was, noch wie,
> Da sind wir uberstritten von,
> Im hertzen thut mir wie der hon. [115]

In Hutten's *Inspicientes,* a Lucianic dialogue between Sol and Phaeton, the Germans are "starck":

*Phaeton:* Wei sind sye [the Germans] von leib?
*Sol:* So gesund, starck, wolgeschicht und vermüglich als keine anderen. [116]

---

[113] "Epistola ad Maxilianum Caesarem Italia ficticia," *Opera Ulrichi Hutteni,* edited by Eduard Bocking, (Leipzig, 1859-1870), I, 106; see Holborn, p. 75.

[114] *Opera,* V, 82, *In Ulrichum Wirtembergensis, Oratio Quarta:* "Hear us, Caesar, hear, patron of the innocent, preserver of justice, protector of liberty, lover of piety; hear us, successor of Augustus, emulator of Trajan, conqueror of the world, ruler of the human race."

[115] *Ibid.,* III, 513: "An effeminate people, a soft nation, without heart, without courage, even without virtue, none of whom have battled, know nothing of war; that we should have been conquered by them is a deep shame to rue."

[116] *Phaeton:* How are the Germans in body?
*Sol:* So healthy, strong, skilled and capable as no others.

The Germans are also invincible: "Seind die Sachsen un-
überwindliche kryegs leut." In a discussion of the topic, "Gut
vertrawen der Teutsche" (the trustworthiness of the Germans) and "Der Italianer untreu" (the unfaithful Italian),
even the complexions of the two peoples contrast, and for
good reason says Hutten: the Italian is pale, "bleych von ange-
sicht," whereas the German is "rotfarbig" (ruddy), a sign that
"sye leben in freuden, un gutem vertrawen" (they live in joy, in
good trust). [117] In another tract the Germans are again hailed
as a free and invincible folk: "Semper enim liberi fuerunt
Saxones, semper invicti." [118] The title of another essay assures his German readers "Quod Germania nec virtutibus nec
ducibus ab primoribus degeneraverit." [119] The *Germania* of
Tacitus is patently the source of Hutten's conception of the
manly, kindly, morally pure German of antiquity. In connection with Tacitus, Hutten's wit leaps to the occasion in the
dialogue, *Vadiscus.* The Pope had given Beroaldus, Italian
scholar of Bologna, a ten-year stay on any other printing of
Tacitus as a reward for printing the 1515 edition. Hutten
knows the facts but pretends ignorance and professes to be
mystified why the one historian who has spread the fame of
the old German people should not be printed further: "Auch
mich ärgert diess vor allem Andern...Warum also, versetzte
ich, scheuest du dich, Tacitus den Deutschen vor Augen zu
bringen, einem Schriftsteller, der mehr als irgend ein andrer um
den alten Ruhm unsres Volkes sich verdient gemacht hat?" [120]

Based on Tacitus' praise of German valor, Hutten founded
an Arminius cult. Hutten created in Arminius a symbol of
German national character. Reading the history of Arminius'

[117] *Opera*, IV, 287, *Inspicientes.*
[118] *Opera*, I, 389, *Ad Fridericho Saxonum.*
[119] *Opera*, III, 331ff.
[120] Quoted from the German translation of the Latin original by
David Friedrich Strauss, *Gespräche von Ulrich von Hutten* (Leipzig,
1860), p. 102.

smashing defeat of the Roman armies under Varus, Hutten made Arminius the German liberator par excellence: "Arminius Cheruscum liberrimum, invictissimum et Germanissimum." [121]

John Carion's *Chronica* (1532; translated 1550) brings together the arguments drawn from Daniel, the *translatio,* and the literal *translatio* of the imperial power to Charlemagne. In his preface on the "use of readynge histories," Carion proclaims not only the transfer of power but God's providence in selecting the Germans for a special role in history:

> The fyrst was of the Assirians, ye second of the Persians, after them the Grekes, the last ye Romans. And to the honor of such an empire or superiorite, hath God exalted ye Germanes before other nations in these latter times... The Germane princes, and chefely the electors ought to estime greatly this their honour, that they have such high authoritye comitted of God, to preserve religion, justice and commune peace. [122]

Carion's chapter "Of the Germanes" begins: "Carolus Magnus was crownde Emperor of Leo III, the very Christmasse, thys was the begynnynge of translatynge the empyre to the Germanes." [123]

John Sleidan's famous *Commentarii* (1555; translated 1560) also fits German history into the *translatio* framework:

> And of those four greate Monarchyes of the Worlde, theyr greate alternation and succession, be taught us by the Prophette Daniell... The Romain Empire whyche should both be the last,

---

[121] *Opera,* IV, 46, *Arminius.* See also Paul Joachimsen, *Geschichtsauffassung und Geschichtsschreibung in Deutschland unter dem Einflus des Humanismus* (Leipzig, 1910), p. 106. Also useful on the subject of German nationalism are: Paul Ulrich, *Studien zur Geschichte des Deutschen Nationalbewusstseins im Zeitalter des Humanismus und der Reformation* (Berlin, 1936); Hans Tiedemann, *Tacitus und das Nationalbewusstsein der Deutschen Humanisten am Ende des 15. und am Anfang des 16. Jahrhunderts* (Berlin, 1913).

[122] *Chronica,* translated by Walter Lynne under the title *The Thre Bokes of Cronicles* (London, 1550), fol. b4, verso.

[123] *Ibid.,* bk. III, fol. cxxvii.

and also much greater than the rest, the prophet said should be devided, and brought from that huge and unmeasurable great quantity, to a right small thing, as it is now manifest, whiche consisted within the limites of Germany. [124]

Sleidan's *De quator summis imperiis* (1561; translated 1695) is devoted exclusively to the *translatio:*

Thus the Empire of the West was translated to the Germans: For there is no doubt but Pepin and Charles were Germans... Thus the Western part of the Roman Empire, torn to pieces, as evidently appears from what I have already said, after the Seat of Empire was translated from Rome to Constantinople, was restored by the Emperor Charles, and as it were, received a new Face, so many, and so great Provinces being restored to one Body, by his Valour and Success. [125]

Sleidan calls upon the authority of Daniel to explain what might be called the German "fifth monarchy": "Last of all, I'le explain how Daniel foretold this vicissitude of these Empires, and the fall of that of Rome." [126] He concludes: "From what I have said, we may see how that Great and August Empire of Rome, whose Power never was, nor never will be equalled, sunk from all its Grandure, and was wholly torn to pieces and dissipated." [127]

The *translatio,* as we have already seen, goes hand in hand with antiquarian research either into the Carolingian imperial title or, in remoter history, in an attempt to find in the Gothic victory in antiquity over the Romans the psychological or racial reasons for the success of the Germans. Maximilian and Charles V both had realized the value of employing the humanists to shore up their imperial pretensions. The corona-

[124] *A Famouse Cronicle of Oure Time, Called Sleidanes Commentaries,* translated by John Daw (London, 1560), fol. Aiiii, recto.

[125] *De quator summis imperiis. An Historical Account of the Four Chief Monarchies or Empires of the World*...now newly Englished (London, 1695), pp. 131, 140.

[126] *Ibid.,* p. 143.

[127] *Ibid.,* p. 199.

tion of Hutten, Bebel, and Celtis as laureates was the device for rewarding the historical researches of the humanists. The arguments of Celtis rest not so much on the *translatio* as on a racial theory, apotheosizing German manliness, piety, courage, and so on. Celtis, in his *Germania generalis,* goes back to the past in order to the past in order to establish the distinctive qualities of the German folk. The German is manly: "Vox quae nil muliebre sonat, set tota virilis"—a voice which has no feminine sound, but is altogether masculine; he is pious: "Religionis amans superumque et cultor honesti" — a lover of religion and the gods and devoted to honor; he has courage: "Nec signis timidusque mori roseumque cruorem pro patria et caris certans effundere amicis atque avidus caedis, si qua illam iniuria laesit." [128] They are called Germans because they live together in amity like brothers: "Germanos vocitant Latii, Graii sed adelphos. Quod fratrum soleant inter se vivere more..." [129]

In his "Public Oration Delivered in the University of Ingolstadt" Celtis exhorted his audience: "Assume, O men of Germany, that ancient spirit of yours, with which you so often confounded and terrified the Romans ... O free and powerful people, O noble and valiant race, plainly worthy of the Roman empire." [130]

Johannes Stumpf also perceives in the tribal name the German capacity for living in brotherly love: "Germanos das ist

[128] "In battle not afraid to die, but striving to shed his red blood for his fatherland and his dear friends, and eager for slaughter if his country has suffered any injury."

[129] Quoted from *Deutsche Literatur, Reihe Humanismus und Renaissance,* edited by H. Rupprich (Leipzig, 1935), II, 286-288. See L. Sponagel, *Konrad Celtis und das Deutsche Nationalbewusstsein* (Baden, 1939), pp. 20-34.

[130] The text of the "Oration" is edited and translated by Leonard Forster, *Selections from Conrad Celtis* (Cambridge, 1948), pp. 46-47; for his valuable commentary on German historiography, see pp. 106-109.

Bruder genenne worden/werden das/sy in Frieden einander
also bruderlichen un treülich beystandind." [131]

Sebastian Brant discusses the meaning of the *translatio*
for German history in his work entitled, *De iuribus et translatione imperii.* [132] His *Carmina* (1498) also reflect the idea:

> urbemque sacratam
> continuo in nostro reximus imperio... [133]

The *Carmina* also record Brant's conception of the high
destiny of the German emperor. In June 1495 Brant had seen
a number of falcons flying southward; he sees in the falcons
a symbol of Maximilian on his southern expedition. The poem
ends:

> Theutones o fortes: nomen retinete vetustũ:
> sitis Alemanni: fortiter ire decet.
> est aliquid totiens monitos: totiensque vocatos
> a superis; satis credere; & illa sequi.
> victoris deus ipse facit: qui causa triumphi:
> et dator est: ab eo gloria cũcta venit. [134]

*Deutsche treue,* a conception of German national and racial
character became, during the period of the Reformation, a
proverbial expression. [135] The Nordic--Latin contrast gave

[131] Johannes Stumpf (and Joachimes Vadianus, part collaborator),
*Gemeiner loblicher Eydgnoschoft Stetten ... Chronica Germanie ...* (Zu-
rich, 1586), pp. 18-19: "A German is called brother for the reason
that they live together in brotherly and faithful compassion." See also
ch. vi; "Von Stercke and Mannheit Teutschen."

[132] Argentoraci emisit, 1508. Also printed in Charles Schmidt, *Histoire Litteraire De L'Alsace* (Paris, 1879), I, 280f.

[133] *Varia carmina* (Basel, 1498), fol. a⁷, verso: "and we have ruled
the consecrated city within our continuous dominion."

[134] *Ibid.,* 5, recto: "O brave Teutons: retain your ancient name: be
Alemanni: it becomes you to go forth bravely. It is something that
you have been so often admonished, so often called by the gods
above; that you have faith enough, and pursue your ancient course.
God himself makes you victorious: He is the cause and giver of your
triumph: from Him all glory comes."

[135] Archer Taylor, *Problems in German Literary History of the
Fifteenth and Sixteenth Centuries* (New York, 1939), pp. 19f.

the expression a sharp edge. Johann Agricola's *Drei Hundert Gemeyner Sprichwörter* (1529) includes the proverb:

"Sinte mal gemeynelich mit der sprache auch die sittē/ist zubesorgē der Deutschē treu v̄n glauben bestand/warheit/welche tugent der Deutschē auch die Walen als Cornelius Tacitus zugeschribe v̄n geruhmet/werdē auch fallen. [136]

Johann Fischart's *Eikones* (1573) also contains the idea.

Standthafft und Treu, vnd treu vnd Standschafft,
Die machen eyn Recht Teutsch verwandtschafft. [137]

Sebastian Münster teaches a *deutsche wesen* by suggesting an etymon for the national name "German" as descriptive in itself of German vigor, manliness, and so on. In his *Cosmographia Universalis* (1544), book 3, chapter vi, entitled "Wie das Teutschland vor Alten Zeiten her Genennt ist Worden," Münster explains the names "German" and "Aleman": "Die vierden nennen Alemannia sen ein Teutsch Wort un so viel alss Aleman und senen die Teutschen ihrer grossen stercke und starckes Gemutshalb Alemann genennet worden... Etliche andere nennen Germania sen ein Teutsch Wort gleich wie Almand un sen so viel also Garmann oder Ganzman." [138]

The pugnacity of the German, Münster goes on to explain, is an attribute of his manliness. The German is invincible in battle:

[136] Quoted in Taylor, p. 21, n62. Tacitus, *Annals* ch. xiii, l. 14 is referred to in the mention of "Cornelius Tacitus." "Whereas, generally, the language and also the customs, agree on German fidelity, which virtue the Welshmen like Cornelius Tacitus [a *Welscher* in German means a foreigner] ascribe to the Germans and made famous, German truth will also be made famous."

[137] Quoted in Taylor, p. 22. "Steadfast and faithful, faithful and steadfast—these are the bases of a real German family."

[138] *Cosmographia* (Basel, 1628), a German translation from the Latin original, p. 604: "The fourth say that Alemannia is a German word and is the same as Aleman and the Germans have been called Aleman for their great strength and strong temperament...Some others say that Germania is a German word meaning the same as

Wie mit grosser muhe und arbeit ja kosten und verlust die
Romer vorzeiten gestritten haben wider das Teutschlandt ist
niemandt unwissend welche gelesen haben die alten Historien.
Es ist ihnen gering gewesen under ihren Gewalt zu bringen
Hispaniam, Galliam, Brittaniam, Greciam, Asiam, Egypten,
Macedoniam, und andere viel Lander: aber Teutschlandt wolt
sich nicht so liederlich ergeben besonder das Teutschlandt das
der Rhein von Occident und die Thonaw gegen Mittag als
starcke Rinckmawren beschleusst. Es hat mach tausent Man
daruber mussen zugrund gehen zu beuden senten wie du horen
wirst Dan die Teutschen theten solchen gewaltigen Wider-
standt den Romern und allen ihren Feinden das under ihren
Nachbawren ein solch Sprichwort ausgieng: Will einer ubel
Stritten so reib ey sich an die Teutschen. Und will einer Streich
losen so fahe er ein Zanck an mit den Teutschen. [139]

Peter Schott in his *Lucubratiunculae* (1498) states the
whole matter much more succinctly:

> Quod cum Romulides totum sibi vicerit orbem:
> germanos numquam subdidit ipse sibi. [140]

The *Sachssiche Chronica* by Cyriacus Spangenberg also
traces the *gar*-man etymology: "Das ist/gar solche Manner/

Almand and is the same as Garmann or Ganzman" (Ganz: completely
or entirely, a man).

[139] *Ibid.*, p. 611: "How with great effort, work, cost, and losses the
Romans have in the old days fought against Germany is known to
everybody who has read in the old histories. It was a little thing for
them to conquer Spain, Saul, Britain, Greece, Asia, Egypt, Macedonia,
and many other countries. But Germany would not surrender so
easily, especially as Germany, which is enclosed like a strong wall
within the Rhine from the West and the Danube from the South.
Thousands of men had to die because of that fact on both sides as
you will hear. For the Germans put up such powerful resistance to
the Romans and all their enemies that the proverb sprang up among
their neighbors: if anyone wants a bad fight, he should rub against
the Germans; if he wants to lose a fight, he should arouse a conflict
with the Germans."

[140] Quoted by Tiedemann, p. 130: "But although the heir of Romulus
won all the world for himself, he never reduced the Germans to submission to him."

oder alle solcher Helden..." [141] The *gar*-man etymology passed into the dictionaries of the time as standard information. Ambrosii Calepini, under "Germanis," says: "Eruditi tamen inter Germanos huius vocis etymolgicam ex sua lingua petunt. Illi enim *Gar* sive *Ger* totum dicunt & *Man* virum, quasi plane virum." [142]

Jean Bodin, the French jurist, was not as easily swayed by the winds of Protestantism. His remark is interesting because it reveals how widespread was the doctrine of the German *translatio:*

A long established, but mistaken, idea about four empires, made famous by the prestige of great men, has sent its roots down so far that it seems difficult to eradicate. It has won over countless interpreters of the Bible; it includes among modern writers Martin Luther, Melancthon, Sleidan, Lucidus, Funck, and Panvinio—men well read in ancient history and things divine. [143]

No better summary within a single text of the range of the ideas we have been surveying can be found than in an essay by Drouet de Maupertuy (prefatory to his translation of Jordanes). First he discusses the *urbs aeterna,* and he almost pities the Romans for having permitted themselves to hold faith in that myth:

Mais enfin qu'arrive-t-il, quand Rome est élevée a cet exces de grandeur? L'esprit de l'homme qui auparavant regardoit un Empire universel comme impossible & chimérique, s'imagine maintenant que Rome une fois établie est eternelle, & on ne

---

[141] *Sachssiche Chronica* (Frankfort, 1585), p. 12.

[142] *Dictionarium* (Lugduni, 1634): "Learned men of Germany seek the etymology of this word in their own language. For they say *Gar* or *Ger,* 'all' and *Man* 'mon'—together meaning 'completely man.'" See also Charles Estienne, *Dictionarium historicum...*(Oxonii, 1671), *s.v.* "Germania"; also Bochart's *Geographiae Sacrae* (1712), bk. 1, ch. lxii, col. 667.

[143] *Method for the Easy Comprehension of History,* translated by B. Reynolds (New York, 1945), p. 291. As a patriotic Frenchman, Bodin insists (p. 294) that Charlemagne was a Frank, not a German.

conçoit plus par ou son pouvoir peut s'abolir. Cette idée favorise
sur tout les Poëtes, auxquels elle fournit des expressions mer-
veilleuses, & un stile de Prophetie qui est incomparable pour les
vers. Elle se glisse insensiblement dans l'eloquence dont elle
releve le sublime, & par malheur elle passe enfin chez les His-
toriens, & les Philosophes, qui ne distinguant pas assez le beau
& le grand, avec le vrai & le certain, se laissant emporter comme
les autres à cette opinion magnifique, mais trompeuse, de l'im-
mortalité de Rome.

The real fact is, he goes on to say, that the Goths "ont
renouvellé le face du monde":

Choisir pour abattre, & pour détruire l'Empire Romain, ils
concurent des sentimens conformes a cette haute destinée, & l'on
vit en la personne des Alarics & des Théodorics, des Héros
dignes de l'éducation Romaine... Voilà les Nations qui dans le
quatre, le cinq, & le sixième siècle ont renouvelé la face du
monde, & dont pour en parler sincèrement nous sommes tous
descendus...

Maupertuy admits that there were also Attila and Genseric
who came only to destroy; but all things considered, is not
the modern world universally in debt to the Goths?

Il me semble que nous devions laisser aux Romains à déplorer
leur propre sort, puisqu' enfin nous ne sçaurions prendre leur
parti, & reprocher aux Goths l'invasion qu'ils ont faite de l'Empire, sans leur reprocher en quelque sorte la naissance qu'ils
nous ont donnée, ou du moins l'inhabitation qu'ils nous ont
acquise par leurs armes. 144

144 "Discours," *Histoire générale des Goths, Traduite du Latin de
Jordanes* (Paris MDCIII [really 1703]), pp. vii, xviii ff: "But finally,
what happened when Rome was elevated to this excess of grandeur?
The spirit of man which previously regarded the idea of a universal
empire as impossible and like a dream now imagined that Rome, once
established, is eternal and one finds it impossible to conceive any
longer how its power can be destroyed. This idea gains the attention
of all the poets, to whom it supplied marvellous expressions and a
prophet-like style, incomparable for verse. It insinuates itself insen-
sibly into eloquence which it carries to the sublime; unfortunately, it
finally passes over to historians and philosophers who do not distinguish sufficiently the beautiful and great from the true and certain.

So low, then, had sunk the proud Augustan *Romanus sum*. It is important to note that Maupertuy places the whole world, or, as it appears, all non-Roman peoples, in debt to the Gothic liberators. It was out of precisely such discussions, with their roots in the German Reformation, that the term "Gothic" emerged not as a synonym for barbarism but as enshrining the highest moral and spiritual values.

In their polemic against Rome the German reformers had endeavored to show first of all the "translatio imperii ad Teutonicos," a world-empire given over to the German people; to them, Charlemagne, a German, had conquered the lands lost by the Romans. They argued also for the essential moral purity of the Germans as attested by Tacitus; Roman priest-craft had corrupted this moral purity. They emphasized the distinctive entity of the German people, a folk united in spirit and temperament; hence, Roman Catholicism was Latin and alien. They pictured the mass migration of the German peoples as the means for bringing about a world renewal; restlessness (as in Celtis), constancy of purpose, and industry were the traits of Germanic character impelling the Germanic people onwards. They stressed strongly the analogy between the German demand for freedom from Roman ecclesiasticism and the break up of the Roman empire by the Goths; the Arminius cult, generated by Hutten, was representative of the alliance in the

---

They allow themselves to be carried away as the others to the magnificent but erroneous opinion of the immortality of Rome...chosen to attack and to destroy the Roman empire, they concurred in the sentiments appropriate to this high destiny and one could see it in the persons of the Alarics and the Theodorics, heroes dignified by a Roman education... Here then are the nations which in the fourth, fifth and sixth centuries renewed the face of the world and from whom, to speak sincerely, we have all descended... It seems to me that we should leave it to the Romans to deplore their own fate since finally we come to their defense and reproach the Goths for the invasion of the empire, without reproaching them in any way for the birth which they have given to us, or, at least, for the inhabitation which we have acquired by their arms."

5

period between historical research and reform; the researches of the humanists demonstrated what their forefathers had accomplished in the past against Rome and hence demonstrated at the same time what the Germans might accomplish in the present and the future. Daniel and Virgil together made a potent brew whose heady effects on the German reformers were noticeable in the apocalyptic fervour with which they awaited the "better things to come" once the "translatio imperii ad Teutonicos" had effected the entrance to the better destiny.

## ITALY AND THE RENAISSANCE

The importance of the Italian Renaissance for the complex semantic history of the term "Gothic" arises from the fact that the pejorative use of the epithet "Gothic" to denote the barbarous first leaped into prominence among the Italian humanists. The motivations were as deep as those which brought the term to the surface of German life to denote the opposite pole of Gothic enlightenment. It is not difficult to see that the retrospective view of the Italian humanists, while gazing on the sacred stones commemorating the glory of the old empire, would be bounded by Rome in a way impossible for the Germans or, certainly, different from the Germans. In fact, but for the intervention of the Carolingian and Hohenstaufen dynasties in Italian political life, the glorification of the imperial ideal is imaginable only in Italy. Venerating, therefore, the sacred soil because it had supported the old empire in the days before the Gothic onslaught, the Italian humanists would perforce look upon the Goths as barbarians and uncouth destroyers.

This is not to say that the political unification of Italy which would correspond to the imperial ideal was more of a fact in Italy than in Germany—it occurred in neither land. The imperial power, as a political reality, lay prostrate in both countries, steadily weakened by feudal decentralization and localization of power. In Germany the imperial ideal fructified, at least, in religious unification. The peculiar difficulty in Italy, hampering even the spread of the ideal as an ideal, arose from the fact that the King of the Germans was the feudal head of the invaders of Italy, whereas the Emperor of Rome represented all the native aspirations toward the Virgilian ideal of Roman civilization. The difficulty was that because of the Papal coronation of Charlemagne, the King of the Germans and the Emperor of Rome were the same person, representing conflicting tendencies.

Symptomatic of the Italian ambivalent attitude are Dante's contradictory views of the role of the Goths in Italian history. The *Convivio* is neutral with respect to the Goths; it is Virgilian in its conception of the sacred Roman empire: "Divine reason was the beginning of the Roman Empire." [145] *De Monarchia* repeats the Virgilian theme, but the viewpoint is now Ghibelline: since the Emperor receives his title not from the Pope but from God, the Emperor is above the Pope. In the *Divine Comedy*, we find the final expression of Dante's position. He hails the German monarch, and it would appear that his Ghibelline viewpoint persists: "O German Albert... Come and see thy Rome that weepeth widowed and alone, and day and night doth cry: 'Caesar mine, wherefore dost thou not companion me?' " [146]

But the point of view shifts once again. In the "Argument," preceding canto vi of the *Paradiso*, Justinian rebukes both

[145] *Convivio*, bk. IV: ch. iv: "Ma ragione, e ancora divina, e stata principio del Romano Imperio."

[146] *Purgatorio*, bk. VI, ll. 112-114, the Carlyle-Wicksteed translation (Modern Library Illustrated ed.; New York, 1944), p. 226. The original reads: "O Alberto Tedesco...Vieni a veder la tua Roma che piange vedova sola, e dì e notte chiama: Cesare mio, perchè non m'accompagne?" Albert I, Emperor from 1298-1308, like his father Rudolph, neglected Italy. He was succeeded by Henry of Luxembourg, on whom Dante rested all his hopes.

Guelph and Ghibelline factions. He recites the history of Rome, and while describing the triumphant flight of the Roman eagle over the conquered lands, pauses to extol his general, Belisarius. Belisarius is famous because having defeated the Goths and Vandals in battle he upheld the Roman glory against the marauding barbarians. Such passages support the possibility of the use of the term "Gothic," on one side of an antithesis, with unfavorable connotations. On the other hand, however, Justinian's recital also includes mention of Charlemagne, who is extolled as a champion of Christendom who succored the Papacy against the assaults of the Lombards. Such passages stand close to Dante's plea to "German Albert"; in fact, they stand close to precisely those claims of the German historians whose discussion of Charlemagne created the possibility of the use of the term "Gothic" with eulogistic connotations.

Dante is idealizing, of course; it is the source of his greatness and of his unique combination of history and Christian philosophy. As Comparetti astutely points out, [147] there appear in the *Paradiso* the ideal emperors Aeneas, Caesar, Augustus, Trajan, and Justinian, but not the bloody Nero. Dante can accept Charlemagne, Albert, or Henry of Luxembourg only by idealizing them, by endowing them, that is, with the spiritual capacity to seize the high Virgilian ideal which dominates Dante's vision.

The same ambivalent situation existed in Germany, even if that land failed to produce a singer of empire as sublime as Dante. Bishop Otto, we recall, balances his dynastic pride in the German ruling house against his admiration of the classical past. Hutten, at the beginning of his writing career, before his animosity against Rome was aroused and before he came into contact with the humanist circle which was discussing the relevance of Tacitus' *Germania* to contemporary

[147] *Vergil in the Middle Ages,* p. 220.

German life, also had a balanced viewpoint toward Rome on the one hand, and the specific German destiny on the other. An end to the ambivalence would have to be determined, in Italy and Germany both, by external causes.

In Germany, the accumulation of Papal abuses leading to the Reformation upset the equilibrium, and, as a result, the Goths and Romans emerged in a new equilibrium symbolic of a deep and abiding conflict between Gothic moral purity and Latin decadence. In Italy, the external cause upsetting the equilibrium was the rise of the free communes. The new city-culture brought to the surface that conception of a *rinascita* which created the parallel Gothic-Roman antithesis but in reverse: the Romans symbolized the classic ideal of culture, the Germans stood for barbarism and ignorance. The great difference between the two manifestations was that in Germany the historical writing continued within the framework of supernatural teleology; the German historians are never far from Daniel or its kind of religious historiography. In Italy, on the other hand, pride in the ancient imperial ideal became secularized almost entirely, either in republican pride in the local liberties of the free communes, as in the history of Leonardo Bruni (*Historiarum Florentini populi libri xii,* 1610), or in a chronology derived from a fantastic astrological scheme, as in Giovanni Villani (*Chronice,* 1539). The ideal of ancient Rome was still the predominant fact on the historical horizon of the Italian humanists, but in the foreground there were the thriving communes whose newness alone suggested the idea of a *rinascita,* in a new and modern form, of the grandeur that was old Rome. Thus it is that Italian secular pride in the communes compelled the civic humanists (they were writing to please local patrons) to conceive a "dark period" or "middle ages," in order to give expression to their self-awareness of the modernity of the communes. Add to this new periodization of history embracing the conception of a "dark period" the notion of a decline supposed to have set in with the Gothic invasions, and the conception of the "barbarian Goths" becomes fixed. Thus it was that the Italian humanists began the modern vogue of disparaging the Goths as barbarians. Medieval histories refer again and again to the barbarian Goths, but as "barbarians" probably on linguistic grounds alone; that is to say, they did not speak Latin. Even the medieval references to the *furor Teutonicos* are probably as much commendatory as not— praise of German military valor and manliness were intended. Not until the abusive term is linked by the Italian Renaissance humanists to the view of history contained in the word "middle ages" or "dark period" do we find that conception of a *rinascita* involving a decline supposed to have set in after Rome's fall which fixed the term "Gothic" as a trope for everything barbarous and ignorant. [148] Even the title of Trissino's epic is revealing: he calls his poem *L'Italia liberata dai Goti* (1547). Belisarius, in Trissino's account, expelled the Goths from Italy and safeguarded, as a result, the survival of classical traditions in Italy.

Mutual recriminations by Italian and German humanists only aided in disemminating further the Gothic-Roman antithesis. Rudolphus Agricola, for example, is resentful of Italian arrogance:

I predict that we shall one day succeed in wresting from proud Italy that ancient renown for eloquence of which she has hitherto retained almost undisputed possession, and shall wipe away that approach of barbarian slothness, ignorance, poverty of expression and whatever marks an unlettered race,

[148] See Nathan Edelman, "The Early uses of *Medium Aevum, Moyen Age, Middle Ages,*" *Romanic Review,* XXIX (1938), 3-25; also XXX (1930), 327-330. Valuable is a study (containing a full bibliography) by Wallace K. Ferguson, "Humanist Views of the Renaissance," *American Historical Review,* XLV (1939), 1-28. Ferguson quotes fully from Bruni's republicanism, Villani's astrology, and so on, and stresses the importance of the secular civic humanism.

which she unceasingly assails us, and Germany shall be seen to be in learning and culture not less Latin than Latium herself. [149]

Erasmus' wit reveals the squabbles agitating the Italian and German humanists: "The Italians affirm they are the only Masters of good Letters and Eloquence, and flatter themselves on this account, that of all others they only are not barbarous. In which kind of happiness those of Rome claim the first place, still dreaming of somewhat, I know not what, of old Rome." [150] P. S. Allen supplies a revealing anecdote about this conflict. Willibald Pirckheimer, German humanist, commenting on a manuscript of Irenicus' *Germaniae exegensis* (1518), in a letter to the author suggested that "more stress might be laid on the connexion of the Germans with the Goths, which the dregs of the Goths and Lombards—by which I mean the Italians—try to snatch from us." [151]

One additional point, perhaps an obvious one, needs to be reëmphasized. The Italian humanists could not agree on dating the beginning of the "modern" period, but all point to the new and original creations of the Italian cities in the arts. Thus, Cimabue and Giotto were held to have created the "modern" style of painting. Brunelleschi in architecture was held to have created a style to replace the debased *maniera Tedesca* ("the German style") brought in, it was thought, by the Goths. Recurrences of the phrase "the barbarous Gothic style" are too many to be numbered; it is a cliché of Renaissance discussion of architecture.

---

[149] Cited and translated by James B. Mullinger, *The University of Cambridge* (Cambridge, 1873), p. 409, from a letter to Rudolf von Lange.

[150] *The Praise of Folly,* translated by John Wilson (1688) and edited by Mrs. P. S. Allen (Oxford, 1913), p. 89.

[151] *Age of Erasmus,* p. 274.

### THE "GOTHS" IN ENGLAND

The *gar*-man etymology, indicative of German manliness, is encountered in England with sufficient frequency to establish its importance as one element in the English tradition of Gothic enlightenment. [152] As a matter of fact, there is a direct literary connection between England and Germany, since Münster's *Cosmographia* is explicitly mentioned as a source in Richard Verstegen's *Restitution of Decayed Intelligence in Antiquity* (1605), where the author points out the *gar*-man etymology:

As touching there names, of Germans and Almans sundry supposals have bin made; & of some peradvẽture that wel understood now how both thease names are but one, & have but one signification: for as in the later silable man they agree both in sound and in sense, so do they also agree in the former silables Ger and Al to wit in lyke sense, though not in sound, for the Ger or Gar (for both are indifferently used) is asmuch in the Tuitsch or Teutonic toung as all and wee englishmẽ have a phrase to say drink Gar aus and some not knowing what they say, in steed of Gar aus which is to say All out do say Car aus and thus Gar and all being shewed to bee the equivalent both German and Alman is the asmuch to say as All or wholy a man. And this name the Germans may wel at some tyme and upon some occasion have atributed or assumed to themselves, in regard of their manlynesse and valor. [153]

Münster is also a direct source for Thomas Coryat's similar etymologizing. In *Coryat's Crudities* (1611) we find:

The best and most elegant etymologie of all is to derive it [Alemannia] (as some learned doe) from two German wordes

[152] It may be worth-while to remember that the English pronunciation of the word "German" would facilitate the acceptance of the *gar*-man etymology. "German" would be pronounced "Garman," as "clerk" is pronounced "clark." (A climate theory gave the notion of German virility a pseudo-scientific basis; see Appendix A: Climate and Liberty.).

[153] *Restitution* (printed at Antwerp but sold in London, 1605), pp. 12-13; for Münster, see p. 9.

which doe altogether agree with our English even for All man, as the people called Marcomanni (which are now of Moravia) had their name from Marck, which signifieth the bound of a country, and the word Man. So that they which deduce the name of Alemannia from All man (as Munster doth) give the reason for it, because the ancient Alemannes were very courageous and valiant men, yea, they were All men: as when we in our English idiome doe commend a man for his valour, we sometimes say such a man is all courage, all spirit: so the Aleman quasi All man, he is all valour, every part of him is viril, manly, and courageous, no jot effeminate, which indeede was verified by their fortitude and manly cariage in their warres against the Romans. [154]

Pierre d'Avity, in his *Estates, Empires, and Principallities of the World* (1614; translated 1615), also finds the name "Alemann" indicative of German character:

The Alleman, called sometimes Germann, by reason of their force according to some, for that in this word Germaine signifieth all masculine and strong; and according unto Strabo, for that they did imitate them in behaviour, and were as it were like unto them in disposition, and in the greatnesse of their bodies and their complexions... The Alleman I say have alwaies beene very valiant and courageous. [155]

Similarly, Peter Heylyn remarks:

Others will have the name to be meerly Dutch, deriving it from Ger, which signifieth all, and the word man, signifying it in that language as in ours; whence they derive the name of Almans; by which they would imply that the Almans or Germans are a very warlike nation, a people that have in them *nihil nisi virile,* nothing not worthy of a man. [156]

Adam Littleton's *Latine Dictionary* (1678) defines "Germania" thus: "Rect. ab ipso Germ. ger i gar prorsus & man vir, ob fortitudinus laudem, sicut Alemanus, qu. alle man, i totus vir." [157]

[154] *Crudities* (Glasgow, 1905), II, 179.
[155] Translated by E. Grimstone (London, 1615), p. 558.
[156] *Cosmographie* (London, 1652), p. 36.
[157] *Latine Dictionary* (London, 1678), *s.v.* "Germania": "Properly

In emphasizing the warlike propensities of the Germans, the etymon, at times, is blended with another which explains *ger* as derived from *guerre*, hence *guerre*-man or warrior. A margin note by John Milton, inscribed in a copy of Irenicus' German history, expresses the idea: "Germani quasi Gere man vir exercitus. Ph. Melancthon: in suo Chronico lib. 2 rubri N. 174. Ger mans, as if men of the army." [158] Sheringham establishes *German* in this sense of *homo bellicosus*, but his explanation is based on his derivation of the name German from the tribe of Kimbri, the latter suggesting *Kampfer*, or fighter: "Cimbris hoc nomen ex fortitudine et bellica virtute partum est: Cimbri enim Germanice significat, robusti milites, pugiles et palaestrici viri. Hinc etiam, ni fallor, Germanus suum nomē. Germanus enim idem valet quod Kimber, id est, homo bellicosus, a Guerre, quod bellum, et Man, quod hominem significat." [159]

The difference between *ger*-man and *guerre*-man may be of some importance. *Homo bellicosus* resembles the medieval *furor teutonicos* in that it may indicate censure (in the sense of a belligerent man) or praise (in the sense of a courageous man). Praise at times is clearly intended (contributory to the tradition of Gothic enlightenment) since both etyma tend to fuse, as in William Slatyer:

For Germany and Germans are thought by some to be names imposed by others, not themselves; others thinke of themselves

derived from German language itself ger or gar 'completely' and 'man,' in praise of bravery; cf. Alemanus, which is able man or 'all man.' "

[158] "Marginalia," The Columbia edition of *The Works of John Milton* (New York, 1932), XVIII, 345.

[159] *De Anglorum*, p. 56: "The Cimbri gained their name from their fortitude and prowess in war; for in German Cimbri signifies robust soldiers, fighters and athletic men. From this source also, if I am not mistaken, the German takes his name. For Germanus has the same meaning as Kimber, that is, a warlike man, from Guerre, which means war and Man, which means man."

imposed for terror to the Romans, and other Invaders, German
& Alman signifying a stout warrior, Gar being the same with
all, as Gar aus (whence our Carouse) all is out or off: so Garman or German, and Alman, wholly a Man or a stout man! The
like name took the Sycambrers or Sigh-Campers, of Sigh-Vic-
torie or Victorious and Campers, Fighters, or Combatters in the
old Teutonic tongue. 160

William Camden praises the Germanic martial spirit, but says
that it goes hand in hand with moral excellence: "The Germans, the most glorious of all now extant in Europe for their
morall and martiall vertues." 161

In John Dryden's *King Arthur* (performed 1691) the King's
gentlemen discuss the valiant character of Oswald, their
Saxon enemy:

*Conon:*      I know him well; he's free and open Hearted.
*Aurelius:*   His Countries Character: That Speaks a German.
*Conon:*      Revengeful, rugged, violently brave; and once re-
              solv'd, is never to be mov'd.
*Albanact:*   Yes, he's a valiant Dog. Pox on him. 162

James Beattie's *Minstrel* is another indication that praise is
intended in the description of the German warlike spirit, since
faith is its accompaniment or its source:

> There lived in Gothic days, as legends tell,
> A Shepherd swain ...
> Zealous, yet modest, innocent though free,
> Patient of toil, serene amidst alarms;
> Inflexible in faith, invincible in arms. 163

In Gilbert West's *Stowe* the Goths are not only valiant but

160 *The History of Great Britainie* (London, 1621), p. 43.

161 *Remaines* (6th ed.; London, 1657), p. 20.

162 Act I, sc. i; in *Dramatic Works* (Scott-Saintsbury ed., Edinburgh, 1884), VIII, 142.

163 In *The Poetical Works of Beattie, Blair, and Falconer,* edited
by Rev. G. Gilfillan (Edinburgh, 1854), p. 5. "Gothic" days may
simply mean medieval days, but the qualities of the shepherd-swain
are clearly Gothic.

wise: "A Nation, valiant, wise and free." [164] Henry Brooke's
*Gustavas Vasa,* which presents Gustavas as a doughty Gothic
monarch, also presents his valor as the fruit of his virtue;
the King says:

> A cause like ours is its own sacrament;
> Truth, justice, reason, love and liberty.
> The eternal links that clasp the world, are in it. [165]

Thomas Warton's "Ode on His Majesty's Birthday" (1788)
tells of the liberty which "soon to Britains's shore / The sons
of Saxon Elva bore." Though warlike, the sons of Saxon Elva
also had gifts for wise and humane government:

> They felt the fires of social zeal,
> The peaceful wisdom of the public weal;
> Though nurs'd in arms and hardy strife,
> They knew to frame the plans of temper'd life;
> The king's, the people's, balanc'd claims to found
> On one eternal base, indissolubly bound. [166]

Celtis' exaltation of Germanic kindliness was made known
to English readers through the incorporation of his poem in
Johann Boemus' *Manners, Lawes, and Customes of All Nations* (1556; translated 1611). Neither Boemus' Latin original
nor the translation acknowledge the source in Celtis:

> The reason why this country assumeth the name of Germany,
> is, for that there is such a sympathy and concordance amongst
> all the people, both in the disposition of their bodies, their man-
> ners and courses of life, as all of them agree and live together
> like brothers an equalls.
> These did the Greeks Adelphi name, whom Latines Germans call,
> Because in unity and love, they live like brethren all:
>           . . . . .
> Nor can the fear of grisley death their valiant mindes appall,
> If wrongs be done, they seek revenge: but for their countries
>                                                   good,

[164] Page 17.
[165] Page 16.
[166] Warton, *Poems on Various Subjects* (London, 1791), p. 250.

Or kin or friends, they will not stick to spend their deerest bloud.
They constant be in Christ his faith, and him do duly serve:
Nor from sincere religion, due seld or never swerve,
. . . . .
Their dealings honest, true, and iust, all lying they detest,
And evermore their toung declares whats hidden in their brest. [167]

As members of the Germanic family, Englishmen could and
did appropriate to themselves the qualities of faith, courage,
justice, constancy of purpose, and so on, attributed to the
Germans. That small portion of Boemus' work, translated
into English under the title of *Fardle of Facions* (1555) also
contained a passage praising the Germanic innate love of
justice: "Thei observed iustice, without constraint of lawe." [168]

If travel broadens the mind, according to Coryat, one should
visit Germany first because one encounters there the purest
national life:

To what end dost thou travell with the swallow leaving thy
nest? doth not Germany in respect of the plenty and commodity
of those things, by many degrees excell all other nations? who
as the Queene of all other Provinces, the Eagle of all kingdoms,
the Mother of all nations, doth shee not most plentifully impart
unto thee all those things which may tend as well to the happy
institution of a common-weale, as to integrity of manners, purity
of religion, and piety of life, the ornament of wit, and the elegancy of speech? for if thou desirest to know the formes of common-
weales, and the governement of a Monarchie, if thou wouldest
understand the manner of an aristocraticall rule, and of the
popular state, where shalt thou better and more exactly learne
these thinges then in Germany, which is as it were an abridge-
ment of the world? [169]

The *Crudities* is preceded (volume I, pages 122-148) by a

[167] Bk. III, ch. xii, translated by E. Aston (London, 1611) pp. 245-
247.
[168] Reprinted in the *Bookworm's Garner* (Edinburgh, 1888), III,
19. Boemus is quoting Tacitus, *Germania,* ch. xix: "Plus...boni mores
valent quam alibi bonae leges."
[169] *Crudities,* II, 74-75.

translation by Coryat of an "Oration in Praise of Travel" by one Hermann Kirschner, whom Coryat identified as a poet and professor of eloquence at Marburg. In the above passage, Coryat is quoting from the "Oration," and it may be that he has in mind moral qualities which pertain only to residents of Germany proper and not to all Germanic peoples. On the other hand, the specific phrases "Eagle of all kingdoms" and "Mother of all nations" appear to reflect the propaganda of the humanist-reformers, especially in the inferences they drew from Jordanes' conception of the *vagina gentium*. The conception of a world renewal flows from ideas of this sort. Milton's eagle passage in the *Areopagitica* may have been written with Coryat in mind.

The contrast of Roman depravity and Germanic honor was paramount in the mind of John Hare in 1647. He pictures also a world rejuvenation:

We are a member of the Teutonick nation, and descended out of Germany, a descent so honourable and happy, if duly considered, as that the like could not have been fetched from any other part of Europe, nor scarce of the universe... Scarcely was there any worth or manhood left in the occidental nations, after their so long servitude under the Roman yoke, until these new supplies of free-born men re-infused the same, and reinforced the then servile body of the west, with a spirit of honour and magnanimity. [170]

The question why it was that England and not Germany, on the basis of the same arguments drawn from traditional racial inheritances, forged ahead and succeeded in the name of their Gothic forefathers in creating a democratic government poses for formal historians an interesting problem which, in our primary concern with the "Gothic legend," need not concern us. At any rate, where Germany succeeded in bringing about in the Protestant Reformation only a Gothic religious

[170] *St. Edward's Ghost* (1647), in *Harleian Miscellany* (London, 1810), VI, 92, 95 of the 12 volume edition (London, 1808-11).

revolution, in England, where the Gothic propaganda domina-
ted the consciousness of the period as strongly as in Germany,
Gothicism was knit into a close moral-religious *and* political
unity. For this reason it will not come as a surprise that the
arguments for Gothic moral purity appear in the same context
as the discussion of Gothic political liberty. Sir William Penn's
impassioned plea for religious toleration rests, as we shall
presently see, on the basis of Gothic political sentiments. In
addition, the same phenomenon also explains why a tradition
in England, dating from Bede's day, contrasting native moral
purity with Romish corruption, meeting the stream of ideas
derived from the Gothic secular political propaganda, ramified
into a doctrine of Gothic moral enlightenment. England pro-
gressed confidently toward the double ideal of Anglo-Saxon
democracy and Protestantism. This is the "pure" doctrine, so
to speak, of Gothicism. The anti-democratic glorification of
the State, as in Heinrich von Treitschke's polemic and the
lurid National Socialist experiment, do not encourage one to
seek for "pure" Gothicism in Germany in its later development
during and after the "Sturm und Drang" period. [171]

The account in the second book of Bede's *Ecclesiastical
History* of Augustine's mission to England in 597 supplied the
starting-point of a discussion, which by a process of exaggeration could be made (and was made) into an evil picture of
Augustine and Latin depravity by the seventeenth-century

[171] Even Tacitus justifies the idea of "pure" Gothicism, since the
*Germania* praises both Germanic democracy and virtue. Religious
Gothicism was contaminated later in Germany. Treitschke, at least,
kept Luther's Christianity pure; but Erich Ludendorf's emphasis on
an autocthonous druidical religion antedating the Papacy ended in
a pagan blood-ritual. Dr. Stukeley's eighteenth-century druidism ended,
as we shall see, in Christianity—pure and Nordic—Dr. Stukeley
thought, in harmony with the general Gothic program of restoring
English institutions to their primitive, native purity. (For Ludendorf's
*Teutschtumelei*, from which the gentle Dr. Stukeley would have
recoiled in horror, see his *Die Judenmacht* (Munich, 1939) and other
of his fanatical writings.)

English reformers. In Bede, the English reformers found
memories of a native, undefiled Christianity contending with
Roman corruption. As the story of Augustine's mission is told
and retold countless times throughout the seventeenth century,
the Nordic-Latin contrast becomes explicit, and in Thomas
Salmon, for example, we find an echo of Luther's idea in the
*Address to the German Nobility*: because of their very simplicity, the native English clerics were an easy prey to the
wily schemes of the worldly Papal delegate sent to England
to crowd the English churches into the greedy Roman maw.
English seventeenth-century narratives, based on Bede, stress
Augustine's overbearing manner, his haughtiness, his recourse
to mystery mongering, and, finally, paint him as a blood
thirsty murderer. The humility and simple piety of the native
monks contrast at all points. [172]

The religious tracts of Sir William Penn, the great Quaker,
mark the stage of development in the Gothic propaganda in
England when the Nordic-Latin contrast latent in the picture
of Augustine broadens into that view of English traditional
political inheritances and racial characteristics, that complex
of religious and political ideas, which is the aftermath in England of the intellectual currents set in motion by the Reformation in Germany. We find in Penn a direct cross-fertilization
of Gothic political and religious ideas.

The cause to which Penn devoted his life was the winning
of toleration of the dissenting religious sects, including his
own. He recognized early, on abstract grounds of conscience,
that civil liberty was incomplete without religious liberty.
Since the various test acts disqualifying the dissenters were
justified on the ground that dissent was dangerous to the state,

[172] An almost endless lists of tracts could be made setting forth
these arguments. I mention three: Francis Godwin, *Catalogue of the
Bishops of England* (London, 1615), p. 43; Richard Bernard, *Look
Beyond Luther* (London, 1624), p. 31; Daniel Featley, *Roma Ruens*
(London, 1644), p. 42.

Penn's two main arguments were devoted to showing that it was possible for a dissenter to be a good citizen without being a member of the Anglican church and that, historically, the oldest English church of the Saxons was completely independent of the state, and that tradition and custom were against the test acts. But, in addition, Penn was concerned to show that racial or psychological predilection was also against the test acts. In the last connection, Penn argues (borrowing his ideas from Continental sources) from the viewpoint of the Nordic-Latin contrast: the English, a branch of the Nordic stock, display the qualities of manliness which spell defeat for any plan, political or religious, seeking to keep them in subjection. Penn's tract, entitled *England's Present Interest Discovered* (1675), exhibits the extent to which the Gothic propaganda has molded his thinking.

Penn's theory of the rights of Englishmen is based on an interpretation of Old England as the Golden Age of Saxon freedom; he calls attention to

those rights and privileges which I call English, and which are the proper birth-right of Englishmen, and may be reduced to three:

I.   An ownership, and undisturbed posession: that what they have is rightly theirs, and no body's else.

II.  A voting of every law that is made, whereby that ownership or propriety may be maintained.

III. An influence upon, and a real share in, that judicatory power that must apply every such law; which is the ancient, necessary and laudable use of juries: if not found among the Britons, to be sure practised by the Saxons, and continued through the Normans to this very day. [173]

Penn's affiliation with the Continental movement of reform is revealed in the fact that, like the German reformers, he goes back to Tacitus—in other words, to a historical record antedating his own nation's records—to find evidence of a

[173] *England's Present Interest Discovered,* in *Select Works* (3d ed.; London, 1782), III, 203-204.

general Teutonic predilection for liberty. In the proof of his first principle of the right to an "ownership, and undisturbed possession," Penn locates the evidence in Tacitus:

It is true that the footsteps of the British government are very much over grown by time... However, Caesar, Tacitus, and especially Dion, say enough to prove their nature and their government to be as far from slavish, as their breeding and manners were remote from the education and greater skill of the Romans. Beda and M. Westminster say as much... The Saxons brought us no alteration to these fundamentals of our English government; for they were a free people, governed by laws of which they were themselves the makers; that is, there was no law made without the consent of the people; de majoribus omnes, as Tacitus observeth of the Germans in general. [174]

This passage is noteworthy because it combines condemnation of German uncouthness with praise of their distinctive predilection for liberty. Later (eighteenth-century) Gothicists either suppress all references to German illiteracy or, admitting it, make capital of it: the Goths were illiterate in the sense of being "undeveloped"—eager to learn from the Romans, they recoiled from Roman decadence; but in their youthful ardour and vigor they soon matured and brought about a rejuvenation of the world.

In concluding his arguments for toleration, Penn returns to his principle of German liberty and cautions that any program of repression must fail: "Doth kindness or cruelty, most take with men that are themselves? H. Grotius with Campanella, well observed, 'That a fierce and rugged hand was very improper for northern countries.' English men are gained with mildness, but inflamed with severity." [175]

Penn's sources in Grotius and Campanella are worth noting as evidence of the success of the German historians in disseminating the idea of Germanic vigor. The passage in Cam-

[174] *Ibid.*, p. 205.
[175] *Ibid.*, p. 249.

panella is found in his *Aforismi politici,* beginning: "Alli sen-
tentrionalli per Natura feroci non conviene imperio stretto."
The ideas of Grotius on German liberty are recorded in his
history of Holland and in his great juridical work, *De jure
belli ac pacis.* [176]

In his proof of the second English birthright, "A voting of
every law that is made," Penn repeats the argument of
Germanic liberty: "[The Saxons] brought this liberty along
with them, and it was not likely they should lose it, by trans-
planting themselves into a country where they also found
it. Tacitus reports it to have generally been the German
liberty." [177]

With so much of an introduction, drawn from general
principles of Nordic psychological predilection, Penn proceeds
to the heart of his argument and makes his plea for toleration
and repeal of the Test Act. "Religion," he declares, "is no
part of the Old English government... Nigh three hundred
years before Austin set his foot on English ground, had the
inhabitants of this island a free government." [178]

Penn's ingenuity lies in his adaptation of ideas which were
first put into service in the cause of Protestantism against
Rome, for the purpose of winning toleration for dissenters
within the Protestant body itself. The battle for a national
English church having been won, Penn is not concerned with
attacking the Papacy. His arguments reflect, however, the
more extensive propaganda of the German reformers who, on
the basis of the *translatio,* established the concept of the
distinctive psychological quality of the German folk. On the

---

[176] *Aforismi politici,* no. 45, in *Opere,* edited by A. D'Ancona (Torino, 1854), II, 18. Penn had a reading knowledge of Italian, gained
from a stay in Italy. Hugo Grotius, *De antiquitate reipublicae Bata-
viae* (1630), translated in 1649 as *A Treatise of the Antiquity of
Commonwealths,* p. 25; *De jure belli ac pacis* (1625), translated by
Francis W. Kelsey (Oxford, 1925), II, 126.

[177] *Select Works,* III, 209-210.

[178] *Ibid.,* pp. 231-232.

other hand, the cross-fertilization of religious and political ideas is the uniquely English manifestation of the idea of Gothic enlightenment.

Interesting, because it recalls Luther's interpretation of the way in which the cunning Pope inveigled the simple Germans, is Thomas Salmon's description of the Augustinian mission to England. Salmon argues that Augustine deliberately raised the trivial issue of the type of tonsure which the native priests should wear, "not that these things were of any great importance in themselves, but because of their Consequence. If they could but get them to alter any thing for the sake of Rome, and bring so much as their Hair to be of the new Cut, the Way would be made easier for receiving of the Papal authority." [179]

The Romans were worldly; the native priests, in contrast, were meek and devout:

Such was their Pageantry when they landed in Kent, that they were taken for Conjurers, rather than Preachers of the Gospel; and if we compare their proceedings with the Acts of Christ's apostles, recorded in Holy Scripture, those Suspicions would certainly have entred into the Hearts of all those that had been Christians already. The old Britains, when they met with them went upon more undoubted Grounds. They were sure that our Saviour was Meek and Lowly and that he required his Disciples to be so... [180]

In English druidic lore, especially where the eighteenth century is concerned, we find another channel directing the flow of ideas derived from the *translatio* thought-complex toward the doctrine of Gothic enlightenment. The fact that the Celts and Celtic druidism are not (according to modern understanding) Germanic hardly disturbed the eighteenth century. The term "Gothic" was serviceable to include all

[179] *Historical Collections Relating the Originals, Conversions, and Revolutions of the Inhabitants of Great Britain to the Norman Conquest* (London, 1706), p. 269.
[180] *Ibid.*, p. 442.

non-Roman people. Pope, for example, confuses in his mind
Goths, Scythians, the Norse god Odin, and druids:

> Of Gothic structure was the Northern side
> O'er wrought with ornaments of barbarous pride:
> There huge Colosses rose, with trophies crowned,
> And Runic characters were graved round.
> There sat Zamolxis with erected eyes,
> And Odin here in mimic trance dies.
> There on rude iron columns, smeared with blood,
> The horrid forms of Scythian heroes stood,
> Druids and bards.... [181]

As the English writers stress the moral enlightenment of the
druids, their superiority even to the Greeks in learning, their
piety, and their love of liberty, the idea emerges of Gothic
enlightenment. Fletcher's *Bonduca* is an early idealization of
native liberty and moral purity, especially as the latter is seen
in contrast to Roman decadence. "Liberty we hold dear as
life," the Queen declares. Queen Bonduca flings down the
challenge to the "vitious" Romans:

> If Rome be earthly, why should any knee
> With bending adoration worship her?
> She's vitious; and your partial selves confess,
> Aspires the height of all impiety:
> Therefore 'tis fitter I should reverence
> The thatched houses where the Britains dwell
> In careless mirth, where the blest household gods
> See nought but chast and simple purity. [182]

William Cowper's poem, *Boadicea,* proclaims the *translatio;*
a druid in the play prophesies to the Queen:

[181] *Temple of Fame* in *The Works of Alexander Pope* (Elwin
Courthope ed.; London, 1871), I, 209-210. Pope's own note on Odin
is that he was "the great legislator of the Goths." Percy and Gray
were exceptional in the period in avoiding the Celtic-Germanic confusion; see E. D. Snyder, *The Celtic Revival in English Literature*
(Cambridge, 1923), pp. 9f.

[182] *Works of Beaumont and Fletcher,* edited by A. R. Waller (Cambridge, 1905-1912), VI, 158.

> Regions Caesar never knew
> Thy posterity shall sway,
> Where his eagles never flew
> None invincible as they.
>
> Ruffians, pitiless as proud [the Romans]
> Heaven awards the vengeance due;
> Empire is on us bestowed,
> Shame and ruin wait for you. [183]

William Mason's druidical play, *Caractacus,* echoes the theme of freedom:

> His very thought big with his country's freedom
> To fight the cause of liberty and Britain. [184]

Toward the close of the century, the French Revolution affected the interpretation of druidic liberty. In the preface to his translations from the Welsh poet, Llywarc Hen, William Owen Pughe points not only to druidic liberty but to druidic social equality. Edward Davies attacked Pughe's theory of druidic equalitarianism and demanded better proof: "It therefore rests with the advocates of this chair, to inform us, whether it [equality] was introduced into their code by the levellers of the seventeenth century or fabricated during the late anarchy in France, as a new engine, fit for immediate execution." [185]

The druidic effusions of the period not only awakened the consciousness of the period to the tradition of native liberty, but the equivalence and even the superiority of native learning to classical learning. It was not so much a question, it was pointed out, of the druids learning from Pythagoras as of Pythagoras learning from the druids. Abbé Pezron, a French antiquarian considerably popular in the eighteenth century,

---

[183] In *Works,* edited by W. Benham (London, 1893), pp. 175-176.
[184] In *Poems* (London, 1764), p. 121.
[185] *The Mythology and Rites of the British Druids* (London, 1809), p. 59, in reply to Pughe's *The Heroic Elegies of Llywarc Hen* (London, 1809), p. iiv.

spread the idea that the druids had civilized the Greeks. [186]

Dr. William Stukeley's *Stonehenge* (1740) and *Abury* (1743) reveal best the manner in which sentiments of a pure, native Christianity, as practiced by druids before the land fell under corrupt Roman domination, were leading to the notion of Gothic enlightenment. Dr. Stukeley's point is that druidism was an autochthonous religion antedating the Papacy. In the preface to *Stonehenge,* he says:

My intent is (besides preserving the memory of these extraordinary monuments, so much to the honour of our country, now in great danger of ruin) to promote, as much as I am able, the knowledge and practise of ancient and true religion; to revive in the minds of the learned the spirit of Christianity, nearly as old as the Creation, which is now languishing among us...to warm our hearts into that true sense of Religion, which keeps the medium between slovenly fanaticism and popish pageantry... And seeing a spirit of Scepticism has of late become so fashionable and audacious to strike at the fundamentals of all revelation, I have endeavoured to trace it back to the fountain of divinity, whence it flows: and show that Religion is one system as old as the world, and that is the Christian religion ...I shall shew likewise, that our predecessors, the Druids of Britain, tho' left in the extremest west to the improvement of their own thoughts, yet advanc'd their inquiries, under all disadvantages, to such heights, as should make our moderns asham'd to wink in the sunshine of learning and religion. [187]

In his preface to the companion-work, *Abury,* Stukeley again attacks the Papacy while asserting druidism to be the purest Christianity:

We may make the general reflexion from the present work, that the true religion has chiefly since the repeopling mankind after the flood, subsisted in our island: and here we made the

---

[186] *Antiquité de la nation et de la langage des Celts* (1703; translated 1706). Blake made a notable effort to weave the idea into his visionary system; see Denis Saurat, "Blake et les Celtomanes," *Modern Philology,* XXIII (1925), 175-188.

[187] *Stonehenge* (London, 1740).

best reformation from the universal pollution of Christianity, popery. Here God's ancient people the Jews are in the easiest situation, anywhere upon earth. [188]

William Owen Pughe likewise stresses the Nordic-Latin contrast: "It is one of the most remarkable circumstances in the history of the Welsh that, through the long and dark ages of Popish superstition, the Bards retained the Christian religion in its purity and simplicity." [189]

In John Ogilvie's *Brittania* (1801), a druid "with meek-eyed peace and simple innocence" prophesies a new order of life to arise with the success of Northern arms. This Celtic prophecy is indistinguishable from a Gothic prophecy, particularly since that phrasing definitely recalls Jordanes' conception of a northern *vagina gentium:*

> I see the North
> Pour forth like insects, her innumerous sons,
> To heave th' unwieldy fabric from its base,
> Of Roman greatness, rais'd through many an age! [190]

The evidence gathered from the druidic lore in England is clear beyond dispute. The idealization among the English writers of druidic liberty, philosophic capacity, and religious purity is the parallel in England to the ideas engendered in Germany by the conception of the *translatio;* the discussions

---

[188] *Abury* (London, 1743). The reference to the Jews is incomprehensible, unless one notes his description of Adam, Noah, and Abraham as druids. Blake's cryptic symbolism in *Jerusalem* is derived from the same theory of druidic origins: "Jerusalem the emanation of the Giant Albion... Your ancestors derived their origin from Abraham Heber, Shem and Noah, who were Druids," *Poetry and Prose of William Blake,* edited by G. Keynes (New York, 1936), I, 597. Edward Williams also traces druidism back to the Jews and emphasizes the contrast of pure druidic religion with corrupt Romanism: "Ancient British Christianity was strongly tinctured with Druidism. The old Welsh Bards kept up a perpetual war with the Church of Rome," *Poems,* "Preface" (London, 1748).

[189] *Llywarc Hen,* p. xxxii.

[190] *Brittania, A National Epic Poem* (London, 1801), xvi, p. 492.

both in Germany and England aroused memories of the wholesomeness of old Germanic institutions. The idealization of primitive Germanic purity fell in with a great vogue in the eighteenth century of primitivistic speculation (as it may have, indeed, to a considerable extent aroused this kind of speculation). Even in the primitivistic frame of reference, Rome's colonization of England enters the picture as a symbol of an alien, corrupting influence. William Shenstone's "Elegy XV" is inspired by current notions of "hard" primitivism and anti-luxury, but the poem would nevertheless supplement and be fed by the propaganda of Gothic enlightenment. Shenstone writes:

> 'Twas on those downs, by Roman hosts annoy'd
> Fought our bold fathers, rustic, unrefin'd.
> Freedom's plain sons, in martial cares employ'd!
> They tinged their bodies, but unmask'd their mind.

> 'Twas there in happier times, the virtuous race,
> Of milder merit, fix'd their calm retreat;
> War's deadly crimson had forsook the place,
> And freedom fondly lov'd the chosen seat.

> No wild ambition fir'd their tranquil breast,
> To swell with empty sounds a spotless name;
> If fost'ring skies, the sun, the shower, were blest,
> Their bounty spread; their field's extent the same.

> Those fields, profuse of raiment, food and fire,
> They scorn'd to lessen, careless to extend;
> Bade luxury to lavish courts aspire,
> And avarice to city breasts descend. [191]

Samuel Daniel's *Defence of Rhyme,* written early in the seventeenth century, is an even more interesting example of

[191] In *Works in Verse and Prose* (London, 1764), I, 52-53. Shenstone's reference to the tinged bodies of the natives is intended to describe the Picts, so-called in current theory because they painted their bodies. This demonstrates again the agglutinative quality of the Gothic tradition in the manner in which any of the non-Roman people are assimilated to the Gothic tradition.

"adventitious" Gothicism. A literary controversy over rhyming in verse, not politics or reform, supplied the *point d'appui* for his statements, which raise Gothic culture to equivalence with the culture of Greece.

Daniel argued that the fact that classical poetry did not employ rhyme was no argument against rhyme. The Greeks wrote to suit their own taste; English taste was different. Furthermore, genius is distributed universally, and it was sheer presumption on the part of the Greeks to condemn their non-Greek neighbors as barbarians. The fact of the case was that the non-Greeks were far from ignorant; the German tribesmen, for example, even created the prototype of all modern governments:

The Goths, Vandales, and Lombardes, whose coming downe like an inundation overwhelmed, as they say, al the glory of learning in Europe, have yet left us still their lawes and cus-tomes, as the originalls of most of the provinciall constitutions of christendome; which well considered with their other courses of government, may serve to cleare them from this imputation of ignorance. [192]

In his *History of England,* Daniel specifically idealizes the natives of old England, contrasting them favorably with the tyrannical Romans:

And such was then the state of Brittaine, Gaule, Spaine, Germany, all the west parts of Europe, before the Romans...did by strength, and cunning, unlocke those liberties of theirs... And though the Brittaines were then simple, and had not that firebrand of letters, yet seemed they more just, and honest, and brought forth on the stage of action men as magnanimous (and toucht with as true a sence of honour, and worthinesse) as themselves. [193]

Once the identification had been made of the Englishmen

[192] I.1 J. H. Smith and E. W. Parkes, *The Great Critics* (New York, 1932), p. 198.
[193] *Collection of the History of England,* edited by A. Grosart (Spenser Society, 1896), IV, 87-88.

as Goths, it is understandable why, on the basis of the etymologizing tendency (descriptive of Germanic innate manliness), the picture of pre-Augustinian church purity, the idealization of the druids, and other contributing sources (as in Daniel) of the idea of Nordic moral advancement, Englishmen thrilled to the new consciousness of the people of England as bearers of a divine mission, builders of a democratic and Protestant destiny at a new turning-point in history from which an era of enlightenment was to start. In this mood of Gothic veneration, Bolingbroke writes: "How barbarous were those nations, who broke the Roman empire, represented to be, the Goths, for example, or the Lombards? And yet when they came to settle in Italy, and to be better known, how much less barbarous did they appear, even than the Greeks and the Romans? What prudence in their government? What wisdom in their laws?" [194]

Sir William Temple's high regard for the Goths is reflected in the fact that he endows them with the rare and precious quality of "heroic virtue." His essay "Of Heroick Virtue" begins: "Among all the Endowments of Nature, or improvements of Art...there are two only that have had the honor of being called Divine...which are Heroick Virtue and Poetry." [195] Those who have founded kingdoms and established stable governments are, in Temple's estimation, especially rich in heroic virtue. He would save, therefore, the Goths from opprobrium and establish their right to fame:

The Writers of those times content themselves to lay the Disgraces and Ruins of their countries, upon the Numbers and Fierceness of these Savage Nations that invaded them, or upon their own Disunions and Disorders, that made Way for so easy Conquests; but I cannot believe that the strange Successes and victorious Progresses of these Northern Conquerors should have been the Effect only of Tumultuary Arms and Numbers, or that

[194] "Fragments or Minutes of Essays," in *Works*, V, 111.
[195] In *Works*, I, 191.

the Governments erected by them and which have lasted so long in Europe should have been framed by unreasonable or unthinking Men. 'Tis more likely, that there was among them some Force of Order, some reach of Conduct, as well as some Principle of Courage above the Common Strain; that so strange Adventures could not be atchieved, but by some enchanted Knights. [196]

The Goths, says Temple, had great creative energy:

From this name of Getae came that of Gothae; and this part of Scythia, in its whole northern extent, I take to have been the vast hive out of which issued so many mighty swarms of barbarous nations, who...broke in at several times and places upon the several provinces of the Roman empire, like so many Tempests, tore in Pieces the whole Fabrick of that Government, framed many new ones in its room, changed the Inhabitants, Language, Customs, Laws, the usual Names of Places and of Men, and even the very face of Nature where they came, and planted new Nations and Dominions in their Room. [197]

Recalling Temple's identification of the English as Goths, Temple's praise of their virtue is of the highest significance:

For, of all the Northern nations, the Goths were esteemed the most civil, orderly, and virtuous; and are for such commended by Saint Austin and Salvian, who make their conquests to have been given them by the justice of God, as a reward of their virtue, and a punishment upon the Roman provinces for the viciousness and corruption of their lives and governments. [198]

Not even the German reformers surpass Temple in his Gothic evangelicalism.

David Hume's view encompasses a vision of a world renewal through the mass migration of the Germanic tribesmen. His account of "Anglo-Saxon Government and Manners" begins: "The government of the Germans, and that of all the northern nations, who established themselves on the ruins of

[196] *Ibid.*, I, 213.
[197] *Ibid.*, I, 212.
[198] *Ibid.*, I, 218-219, the references are to *De civitate Dei* and *De gubernatione Dei.*

Rome, was always extremely free." [199] He continues, picturing the rebirth:

Europe, as from a new epoch, rekindled her ancient spirit, and shook off the base servitude to arbitrary will and authority, under which she had so long laboured. The free constitutions then established, however impaired by the encroachments of succeeding princes, still preserve an air of independence and legal administration, which distinguish the European nations, and if that part of the globe maintain sentiments of liberty, honour, equity and valour, superior to the rest of mankind, it owes these advantages chiefly to the seeds implanted by those generous barbarians.

Thomson's *Seasons* discusses the Gothic renewal through mass migration:

Wide o'er the spacious regions of the north,
That see Boötes urge his tardy wain,
A boisterous race, by frosty Caurus pierced,
Who little pleasure know and fear no pain,
Prolific swarm. They once relumed the flame
Of lost mankind in polished slavery sunk;
Drove martial horde on horde, with dreadful sweep
Resistless rushing o'er the enfeebled south,
And gave the vanquished world another form. [200]

The discussion of Montesquieu's *Esprit des lois* belongs properly to French history, but the popularity of his book in England requires mention of his special version of the Nordic-Latin contrast. He sees in the formula a natural affinity of the transalpine people for Protestantism, and for southern people a natural affinity for Catholicism:

When the Christian religion, two centuries ago, became unhappily divided into Catholic and Protestant, the people of the north embraced the Protestant; and those of the south adhered still to the Catholic.

[199] "Appendix 1," *History of England,* (London, 1754-1762), I, 144f.
[200] "Winter," in *Seasons* (Oxford ed.; London, 1908), p. 216, ll. 835-842.

The reason is plain: the people of the north have, and will for ever have, a spirit of liberty and independence, which the people of the south have not; and therefore a religion, which has no visible head, is more agreeable to the independency of the climate than that which has one. [201]

The civilized Romans and the barbarian Goths completely reverse positions in a *Dialogue on Taste* (1762):

I see you smile at the mention of my friends the Goths; but allow me to tell your Lordship the Goths were not so Gothic as they are generally imagined. The arts, indeed, of poetry and painting seem to have been unknown or neglected among them; but in that they could be little worse, and in some respects they were much their [Romans] superiors. Civil discord, and all the evils that attend anarchy when joined to a most contemptible superstition, had produced in the Roman empire a poverty of every kind, and an almost total obliteration of those arts and sciences for which the same nations had been, but a few centuries before, so justly celebrated. Among the Gothic nations, the art of war was well understood as appears by their constant superiority, whenever they appeared in the field; and all the states of Europe, who at this day enjoy any of the blessings of good government, are ready to own that from this Gothic source those blessings were derived. But they were not like the Romans, a gang of meer plunderers, sprung from those who had been, but a little while before their conquest of Greece, naked thieves and runaway slaves. [202]

The preface to John Pinkerton's *Dissertation on the Origin and Progress of the Scythians or Goths* reveals how securely the doctrine of Gothic enlightenment had been established by 1787:

[201] *Spirit of the Laws,* translated by Thomas Nugent (London, 1750), XXIV, v; see also his *Lettres persanes* (Cologne, 1720), letter cxxxvi. Thor J. Beck (in *Northern Antiquities*) oversimplifies the sources of Montesquieu's ideas, as he fails to benefit by the monograph of Jacques Barzun (*The French Race,* New York, 1932) which traces a French democratic tradition dating from the Renaissance. It is also entirely probable that Montesquieu was in touch with the whole Gothic literature of England.

[202] Anonymous, *Dialogue on Taste* (2d ed.; London, 1762), pp. 39-40.

Yet such is our ignorance, who are but slowly eloping from barbarism, that the name of Goth, the sacred name of our fathers, is an object of detestation... Instead of turning our admiration to that great people, who could annihilate so potent an empire, instead of blessing the period that delivered all kingdoms from the dominion of one, we execrate our progenitors, to whom we are indebted for all our present happiness!

"Rome, Rome," Pinkerton continues, "what were thy laurels to these? Great and divine people!" [203]

Fundamental to Gilbert Stuart's survey of the progress of societies is the contrast of Germanic energy and fidelity with Roman torpor and depravity: "The Romans corrupted and servile in every quarter of the empire, were unable to oppose the valour and the activity of the Germanic tribes. And, the manners of the conquerors and the conquered being essentially different, and even contradictory, the revolution produced in the condition of Europe was total and decisive." [204]

In Gibbon's monumental *Decline and Fall of the Roman Empire,* a revenge-motivation enters into the Nordic-Latin contrast. Gibbon tells the story of Odin, the hero of the northern people, fleeing from Asia to the North before the pursuing army of Pompey, the Roman general. With this Odin legend, concocted by monkish chroniclers of the Middle Ages, Gibbon connects a prophecy that Odin and his followers will emerge from the North to chastise the Romans as enemies of mankind.

That Odin, yielding with indignant fury to a power which he was unable to resist, conducted his tribe from the frontiers of the Asiatic Sarmatia into Sweden, with the great design of forming, in that inaccessible retreat of freedom, a religion and a people, which, in some remote age, might be subservient to his immortal revenge; when his invincible Goths, armed with martial fanaticism, should issue in numerous swarms from the

[203] Page viii f.
[204] *A View of Society in Europe* (Edinburgh, 1778), p. 17.

neighborhood of the Polar circle, to chastise the oppressors of mankind. [205]

Gibbon's return-and-conquer theme thus enhanced the idea of Rome as a blight and pictured the northerners as a rescue party. It is significant that Gibbon is going beyond his sources. Chapter Five of Snorri's *Heimskringla,* for example, merely says that Odin's Ases fled from Asia in fear of the conquering Romans. In stressing or introducing a revenge-motif, Gibbon is being affected by the *translatio* thought-complex [206].

The revenge-motif reappears in Paul Henri Mallet's *Northern Antiquities* (1770) which, in Bishop Percy's translation, became a popular book on the North. According to Mallet,

Several learned men have supposed that a desire of being revenged on the Romans was the ruling principle of his [Odin's] conduct. Driven from his country by those enemies of universal liberty, his resentment, they say, was so much the more violent as the Teutonic tribes esteemed it a sacred duty to revenge all injuries, especially all those offered to their relations and country. [207]

Mallet is somewhat skeptical about the legend, but the reason why he accepts it reveals how compelling the concept of Gothic enlightenment had become: "I cannot prevail on myself to raise objections against so ingenious a supposition. It gives so much importance to the history of the north, it renders that of all Europe so interesting, and, if I may use the expression, so poetical, that I cannot but admit these advantages as so many proofs in its favour." [208]

[205] *Decline and Fall,* Bk I, ch. X (London, 1846), I, 254-255.

[206] Gibbon may have had access to certain eighteenth-century Italian histories which definitely execrate Rome as a curse and praise the Goths as liberators; for Carlo Denina and Vincenzo Cuoco and their break with the Italian humanist tradition, see F. Masciolo, "Anti-Roman and Pro-Italic Sentiment in Italian Historiography," *Romanic Review,* XXXIII (1942), 366-384.

[207] Bishop Percy's translation, revised by I. A. Blackwell (London, 1847), p. 82.          [208] *Ibid.,* p. 83.

Mallet is moved also by the idea of a world-renewal; he employs, however, another figure of speech:

We see the same people [the Goths] like a tree full of vigour, extending long branches over all Europe; we see them also carrying with them, wherever they came, from the borders of the Black Sea to the extremities of Spain, Sicily, and of Greece, a religion simple as martial as themselves, a form of government dictated by good sense and liberty, a restless unconquered spirit...

He repeats the horticultural figure and adds the revenge-motif:

By these means was liberty preserved among the inhabitants of Germany and the North, as it were in the bud, ready to blossom and expand through all Europe, there to flourish in their several colonies... Its [Rome's] celebrated name, that name which had been so long its support, was only a signal of vengeance, which served at it were to rally and assemble at the same instant all the northern nations. [209]

The revenge-motif found its poet in Sir William Drummond, author of *Odin* (1817). In the poem, the Genius of the river Goths prophesies that

> From my name
> The lords of Europe shall their name derive.
> The Goths victorious shall subdue the land. [210]

The Genius continues, addressing Pharnaces (an alias for Odin):

> Thou soul, O mortal, soars above thy state!
> Then give it wing, and let it win the skies.
> Thou woud'st eclipse the Roman in his pride,
> And overthrow his empire. Bold emprise,
> Yet vast and noble; worth Ambition's aim!

Book I ends with Pharnaces' acceptance of his destiny:

[209] *Ibid.*, pp. 56, 126.
[210] *Odin, A Poem* (London, 1817), p. 32.

> My sons shall raise new temples to new Gods;
> And wrest the sceptre of the world from Rome. [211]

The revenge theme also motivates Wilkie Collins' nineteenth-century novel, *Antonius, or, the Fall of Rome.* Alaric addresses his army of Goths on the march toward the conquest of Rome: "The curse of Odin, when in the infancy or our nation he retired before the myriads of the Empire, it is now our privilege to fulfill!... Our prey awaits us! Our triumph is near! Our vengeance is at hand!" [212]

A glorious destiny awaits the Gothic people when Odin's revenge will be completed. Alaric reads "runic" characters on a shield and finds concealed in the "runes" the message beckoning the Goths to their destiny:

> Behold the characters engraven here! They trace the curse denounced by Odin against the great oppressor, Rome! Once the words made part of the worship of our fathers; the worship has long since vanished, but the words remain; they seal the eternal hatred of the people of the north to the people of the south; they contain the spirit of the great destiny that has brought me to the walls of Rome. Citizens of a fallen empire, the measure of your crimes is full. The voice of a new nation, calls through me for the freedom of the earth, which was made for man, not for Romans. [213]

Hutten's Arminius cult had an auspicious revival in England. William Paterson's *Arminius, a Tragedy* (1740), has as its themes Germanic piety, faith, humanity, and invincibility, in fact, all of the virtues celebrated by Hutten, Bebel, and Celtis. In Paterson's play, Segestes is jealous because Arminius' fame has become greater than his. In the absence of Arminius, Segestes signs a dishonorable peace with the Romans and promises Varus, the Roman general, the hand

---

[211] *Ibid.,* pp. 42, 52.
[212] *Antonius* (New York, 1874), p. 25.
[213] *Ibid.,* p. 248.

of his daughter who is already promised to Arminius. Egbert reminds Segestes that he has broken his word:

> think how thus your Name
> Must suffer in th' opinion of the Germans,
> Whose pride of Soul is to maintain their Faith. [214]

When Arminius arrives, Segestes defends his acts on the ground that an alliance with Rome will teach the Germans "elegance of life" and will correct their manners. Arminius replies that the Germans are already rich in the virtues of kindness, and so on:

> What is her [Roman] wisdom? poor Deceit and Cunning.
> Her Elegance of Life? luxurious poison?
> And what her Virtues all but splendid Crimes?
> Give me, ye Gods! the plain unconquer'd German,
> Rich in hard toil, and opulent in Freedom;
> Unpolish'd into Vice, and void of Guile,
> Of rough, but kind and hospitable Heart. [215]

Arminius barely escapes from a Roman ambush, and he ascribes his good fortune to divine intervention:

> Yes, even for this, the Gods have set me free;
> To teach th'unconquer'd Nations of the North
> To crush the Tyrant. [216]

The prologue, in fact, announces the theme of Germanic "better things to come" at the very outset of the play:

> When Fate had fix'd th' irrevocable Doom,
> And Liberty forsook degenerate Rome,
> Strait to the Regions of the Rugged North,
> She took her Flight in Search of Manly worth. [217]

Arthur Murphy's play, *Arminius* (1798), is affected by the revolution in France. In Murphy's play, Arminius foretells in

---

[214] *Arminius* (London, 1740), p. 3.
[215] *Ibid.*, pp. 18-19.
[216] *Ibid.*, p. 36.
[217] *Ibid.*, p. v.

advance of the event the coming of the Saxons, and leaping
ahead centuries foretells the advent of a line of German kings
to England's throne. What is remarkable in the play is the
spirit of liberty and faith which breathes through it. As Arminius is dying he sends a prophetic message to the Saxon
confederates in his army:

> Bear to my Saxon friends my last advice.
> Let them embark for Britain; there they'll find
> A brave, hardly race... [218]

In Britain, the Saxons and Britons together will found a free
government:

> when landed on that happy shore
> Let my friends join in union with the natives.
> Britons and Saxons there may form one people;
> And from the woods of Germany import
> A form of government, a plan of laws
> Wise, just, and equitable.

Arminius then prophesies the House of Hanover:

> A time may come, when Germany shall send
> A royal race, allied to Britain's kings,
> To reign in glory o'er a willing people.
> I see the radiant dawn; I see
> The great event, when in a distant age
> A monarch sprung from that illustrious line
> Shall guide the state, give energy to laws,
> And guard the rights of man; his throne encircl'd,
> Adorn'd, illumin'd by a train of virtues,
> That win all hearts, and arm each honest hand
> In the great cause of freedom, and the laws,
> For which their ancestors in ev'ry age
> Toil'd, fought, and bravely conquered; then bequeath'd

[218] *Arminius* (London, 1798), p. 87. Arminius has been betrayed
by the Gauls in his army—Murphy's way of attacking the French
revolutionaries. He later (p. 88) warns against treacherous France:
"Let Britons guard against the Gauls." As a translator of Tacitus,
Murphy was in direct touch with the original story of Arminius in the
*Annals*.

> Seal'd with their blood a glorious legacy,
> A sacred trust to all succeeding times. [219]

Virtue and freedom, then, were the glorious Gothic-Germanic legacy to the world: "Ex septentrione lux." [220]

The history of the idea of Gothic enlightenment during the Victorian period was affected by new influences. The triumph of liberalism in the Reform Bill of 1832 and England's rapid industrial expansion induced the Victorians to see their period as a fulfillment or maturation of the Reformation ideal. Liberalism, Protestantism, and Progress resulting from industrial enterprise suggested a contrast with the monarchy ridden, Catholic, agrarian states of the Continent. Thus the idea of Gothic enlightenment took on a new life. The Gothic trait, in particular, of restlessness was particularly dwelt upon by the Victorians, but it was steadied by another Gothic trait, constancy of purpose. A "Danish Ode," by Michael Bruce (1770), strikes the tone:

> On wings of wind we pass the seas,
> To conquer realms, if Odin please:
> With Odin's spirit in our soul,
> We'll gain the globe from pole to pole. [221]

The ode may have been "Danish," but no Englishmen, par-

---

[219] *Ibid.*, pp. 88-89.

[220] Murphy may have had knowledge of the Arminius revival in Germany. Kleist for example, wrote a play, *Die Hermannsschlacht*. Klopstock wrote *Bardiete, Die Hermannsschlacht,* and other pieces celebrating Arminius. Justus Moser wrote an Arminius play. Uz extolled in *An die Deutschen* the bravery of Arminius. Gottingen students formed a Hainbund, meeting in a grove of oaks to revere the memory of Arminius. It was the menace of Napoleon which inspired the Arminius revival: as Arminius had rallied the German tribesmen against the hated Roman foe, so the German romantic writers hoped to unite Germany against Napoleon. See R. R. Ergang, *Herder and the Foundations of German Nationalism* (New York, 1931), pp. 229-230; John C. Blankenagel, *The Dramas of Heinrich von Kleist* (Chapel Hill, 1931) pp. 174-200.

[221] In *Works,* edited by A. B. Grosart (Edinburgh, 1865), p. 209.

ticularly an Englishman bearing the "white man's burden," would find difficulty adapting the idea to England.

Bruce is writing in an earlier day than the Victorians, but he is indicative of the new wind which was blowing. Walter C. Parry, writing in 1857, sees the Germanic folk as "the people of the future":

If the Greeks and Romans are rightly called the people of the past, the Germans, in the wider sense of the appellation, have an undoubted claim to be considered the people of the present and the future. To whatever part we turn our eyes of the course which this favored race has run, whether under the name of Teuton, German, Frank, Saxon, Dane, Norman, Englishman, or North American, we find it full of interest and glory. Majestic in nature, high in spirit, with fearless hearts, on which no shackle had been laid, they came forth from their primeval forests to wrestle with the masters of the world. [222]

Macaulay's writings are attuned to the triple ideal of Liberalism, Protestantism, and Progress. The *History* is practically a hymn indited to William of Orange, the champion of the cause of Protestant Europe against Catholic France. But it is Macaulay's essay on Von Ranke, the historian, which reveals most of the Victorian phase of the movement of Gothic ideas: "Our firm belief is that the North owes its great civilization and prosperity chiefly to the moral effect of the Protestant Reformation, and that the decay of the Southern countries of Europe is to be mainly ascribed to the great Catholic revival." [223]

It is obvious that Macaulay has in mind a conception of traditional Germanic racial inheritances: "In the northern part of Europe, the victory of Protestantism was rapid and decisive. The dominion of the Papacy was felt by the nations of Teutonic blood as the dominion of Italians, of foreigners,

---

[222] *The Franks* (London, 1857), opening paragraph.
[223] "Von Ranke," in *Essays* (Oxford ed.; London, 1913), p. 506.

of men who were aliens in language, manners, and intellectual constitution." [224]

The Teutonic principle is basic to the entire historical outlook of Edward A. Freeman, one of the period's great historians. Freeman identifies Teutonism with moral heriosm; prosperity, liberty, and reformed religion are its fruits. In his essay on "National Prosperity and the Reformation," he asserts: "There can be no doubt that the Protestant theology suits a free people better than the Catholic theology does." [225] The Teutonophilia of Freeman's major opus, *The Growth of the English Constitution,* is too obvious to mention, but the point made of the quality of Teutonic restlessness is also evident and needs emphasizing:

> The wisdom of our forefathers was ever shown, not in a dull and senseless clinging to things as they were at any given moment, but in that spirit, the spirit alike of the true reformer and true conservative, which keeps the whole fabric standing, by repairing and improving from time to time whatever parts of it stand in need or repair or improvement. [He means, of course, the Teutonic forefathers.] [226]

Sharon Turner works out his conception of the Teutonic striving for progress in terms of a distinction between nomadic and civilized peoples. The nomadic people have the store of energy and moral heroism; the civilized people are soft and morally invertebrate. "The Saxons, Franks, Burgundians, Goths, and Northmen have been distinguished by these [nomadic] characteristics." [227] This is Turner's version of the theory of world renewal through migration. Turner was also (surprisingly) a poet, and he describes the transfer of Rome's decaying empire to the Goths:

[224] *Ibid.,* p. 486.
[225] *Historical Essays,* Fourth Series (London, 1892), p. 289.
[226] *Growth of the English Constitution* (London, 1887), p. 20.
[227] *Anglo-Saxons,* I, 19.

> While Rome's superior virtues spread their beam,
> Its empire floated in majestic stream.
> Corrupting in its day of glory, down
> It sank, despis'd, before the Gothic crown.
> Germania's skin-cloth'd salvages [*sic*] assume
> The virtues it forsook, and hurl'd its doom. [228]

Notes preserved of a lecture given by Coleridge reveal his acceptance of the doctrine of Gothic enlightenment: "The hardy habits, the steady perseverance, the better faith of the enduring Goth, rendered him too formidable an enemy for the corrupt Roman, who was more inclined to purchase the subjection of his enemy, than to go through the suffering necessary to secure it." [229]

Carlyle, Kingsley, J. R. Green, Creighton, Froude, Kemble, Bulwer-Lytton, Meredith, Matthew Arnold—the list of those who start from racial assumptions could be made to include nearly every writer of the period; in every case, the German is the protagonist of valor, piety, constancy of purpose, restlessness, and so on. There can be no question, as Sharon Turner says, that there was perpetual discourse in England of Gothic enlightenment: "Our language, our government, and our laws, display our Gothic ancestors in every part: they live not merely in our annals and traditions, but in our civil institutions and perpetual discourse." [230]

The positive genius of the Gothic writers was that they created an image, so easily understood, of the noble, humane, morally pure, brave, and free Goth. A tradition as old as Daniel and Virgil introduced into England, through the mediation of the German reformers, the conception of a Gothic rescue-party which had twice ransomed humanity: once in antiquity, the second time in the Reformation.

[228] *Prolusions* (London, 1819), p. 151.
[229] *Coleridge's Miscellaneous Criticism,* edited by T. M. Raysor (Cambridge, Mass., 1936), p. 11; see also Coleridge's *Watchman* (10 nos.; Bristol, 1796) essay, no. 3.
[230] *Anglo-Saxons,* I, 52.

The disenchantment with Rome was not so complete that the tradition formed by the Italian humanists about the Gothic barbarians did not persevere at times. The point hardly needs illustrating; it is too obvious. For all that the *translatio* was made an article of English faith, the eighteenth-century society still prized a gentleman's ability to exchange a Latin quotation, and the staple of education remained the classical texts wherein young Englishmen were trained to discover ideals of urbanity and grace. These could no more be obliterated than thinking can. Actually, there was no conflict between the classical ideal of serenity and grace and Gothic muscularity and irrespressible energy. The eighteenth century rationalistic temper always found excellence in a just mixture of opposing qualities; faults were always identified with excesses in any one extreme. The Englishman saw himself as imperturbable but morally earnest, quietly active; the antitheses could be extended. Possible he was worshipping, Narcissus-like, an ephemeral self, but the picture of that self was first drawn in discussions in England of Gothic and Roman antiquities. Furthermore, a curious feature of the ideas we have been surveying is the occasional inconsistency of a writer in both praising and condemning the Goths. Although Thomson, for example, is ardent for Gothic liberty, turning to Greece he says: "In architecture too thy rank supreme!" Gothic architecture violates the rules:

> Such thy sure rules that Goths of every age,
> Who scorned their aid, have only loaded earth
> With laboured heavy monuments of shame. [231]

Inconsistency both in ideas and in the usage of terms is no rare phenomenon in intellectual history; it is true even of philosophers and, still more, of popular writers. The inconsistent use of the term "Gothic" simultaneously in both eulogistic

[231] *Seasons,* II, ll. 373, 377-379, "Liberty."

and dyslogistic senses is only one small part of the larger
history of the Gothic movement of ideas, ramifying in the
strife of Parliament with the King during during the seventeenth century, and the Protestant Reformation, first in
Germany and then in England.

## NOTE ON THE GOTHS IN AMERICA

In America there was also a consciousness of Gothic enlightenment. Because, however, of the American Revolution, the
Gothic-Roman antithesis appears in a new perspective, revealing that England had succeeded in establishing only a defective version of Gothic life.

In a treatise published in America in 1843, the Goths
reappear on the stage of history as passengers aboard the
*Mayflower* and as the patriots who fought and died at Bunker
Hill! The treatise, entitled *The Goths in New England,* had
considerable authority by virtue of its being written by George
Perkins Marsh (1801-1882), who had already won fame as
a scholar and philologist. [232]

Marsh was not, of course, the first American to give expression to nationalistic sentiment. The key, however, to Marsh's
interpretation of American national development lies in the
dual facts that he takes pride in America's Gothic legacy from
the mother country at the same time that he deplores the
lingering Roman element in England which tended at times to
come to the surface of English political life. In other words, it
is Marsh's idea that in order to realize their Gothic destiny
unhampered, a band of hardy Anglo-Saxons migrated to
America. The *Mayflower* passengers were in this sense

[232] *Dictionary of American Biography, s.v.* "George Perkins Marsh."
Marsh's scholarship later received wider recognition in the form of
invitations to lecture on Anglo-Saxon philology at Columbia University and the Lowell Institute. In public life, Marsh served ably as
America's first ambassador to Turkey.

"Goths" escaping a "Roman" tyranny in England; Bunker Hill, in the next century, witnessed another struggle between "Goths" and their "Roman" oppressors. The "Gothic" pattern of life which England succeeded in establishing only in part would thus be completely realized in America. It was in these terms that Marsh visualized a "Gothic" future on the horizon of American life. His enormous erudition, to which the catalogue of his library of over twelve thousand volume testifies, put him in touch with every important scholar and linguist in England and on the Continent. The library bequeathed by Marsh to the University of Vermont is highly specialized and, for its day, appears to have been exhaustive in the field of German philology and ethnology. [233] Out of this storehouse of antiquarian researches into the past of the Germanic peoples Marsh derived the idea of Gothic democracy and Protestant enlightenment. The seachange preserved intact the English tradition of Gothic enlightenment except where the facts of George III's intransigent policy toward the colonies influence Marsh's reinterpretation.

"My country is my subject," Marsh declared in his *Goths in New England*. [234] His tract was deeply imbued with Gothicism, expressed simultaneously in a veneration of the morally pure, free Goth, and a plea to keep the strain free from European contamination. To be mindful of our Gothic past is the highest duty of the American citizen, he wrote. "The intellectual character of our Puritan forefathers is that derived from inheritance from our remote Gothic ancestry, restored by its own inherent elasticity to the primitive proportions, upon the removal of the shackles and burdens, which for centuries

---

[233] University of Vermont, *Catalogue of the Library of George Perkins Marsh* (Burlington, 1892).

[234] *The Goths in New England. A Discourse Delivered at the Anniversary of the Philomathesian Society of Middlebury College, August 15, 1843* (Middlebury, 1843), p. 6.

the spiritual and intellectual tyranny of Rome had imposed upon it." [235]

Cromwell and Milton are, for Marsh, examples of great moral leaders in the fight for political and religious freedom. It follows that the Restoration represented a reversion to Roman tyranny and a loss of Gothic freedom. In distinguishing, therefore, between English and American character, we must account, as he continued, for "discordant elements of the English character." [236] American character is Gothic pure and unalloyed:

That the mind of New England is plainly distinguished from that of the mother country, is due partly to the circumstances under which the colonies were planted...but chiefly to the fact that our fore-fathers belonged to that grand era in British history, when the English mind, under the impulse of the Reformation, was striving to recover its Gothic tendencies, by the elimination of the Roman element... The period to which I refer embraces the century extending from the accession of Elizabeth to the restoration of despotism, and the overthrow of British freedom, under the reign of Charles II. [237]

Marsh's rhetoric mounts to the highest praise of the Goths in the passage describing the *Mayflower* passengers and the Bunker Hill patriots as Goths: "The Goths, the common ancestors of North Western Europe, are the noblest branch of the Caucasian race. We are their children. It was the spirit of the Goth that guided the *Mayflower* across the trackless ocean; the blood of the Goth that flowed at Bunker Hill." [238]

Marsh constantly emphasized the Gothic-Roman discord in English character, implying where he does not explicitly state it the purity of American Gothic character: "England is Gothic by birth, Roman by adoption. Whatever she has of

[235] *Ibid.,* p. 10.
[236] *Ibid.,* p. 13.
[237] *Ibid.,* p. 11.
[238] *Ibid.,* pp. 13-14.

true moral grandeur, of higher intellectual power, she owes to the Gothic mother; while her grasping ambition, her material energies, her spirit of exclusive selfishness, are due to the Roman nurse." [239]

America's war of independence was interpreted as war for freedom from Roman tyranny:

The Goth holds that government springs from the people, is instituted for their behoof, and is limited to the particular objects for which it was originally established, that the legislature is but an organ for the solemn expression of the deliberate will of the nation, that the coercive power of the executive extends only to the enforcement of the will, and that penal sanctions are incurred only by resistance to it as expressed by the proper organ. The Roman views the government as an institution imposed from without, and independent of the people, that it is its vocation not to express but to control the will. [240]

In 1845, in a Thanksgiving Day address, Marsh again brought his vast scholarship to bear on the Gothic doctrine of democracy and moral purity:

But I may well invite to accompany us, on this Thanksgiving visit, not the descendants of the Pilgrims alone, but all who share their principles, and especially those brothers of the same blood, twin scions of the ancient Gothic stock, with whom you are now domiciliated, and whose ancestors, after having themselves nobly fought and triumphed in the same glorious struggle against the crown and mitre... [241]

Marsh fell back on the theory of climate to explain why Catholicism is as appropriate to the decadent peoples of the South as Protestantism is appropriate to the virile peoples of the North. He questioned why "those monastic institutions, which strike at the very root of the social fabric, and are eminently hostile to the practice of the noblest and loveliest

[239] *Ibid.,* p. 14.
[240] *Ibid..* pp. 16-17.
[241] *Address, Delivered before the New England Society of the City of New York* (New York, 1845), pp. 8-9.

public and private virtues, have met with less success, and numbered fewer votaries in Northern than in Southern Christendom." [242] Marsh concluded: "Under such impulses [climate and the Reformation] as I have described, the Gothic mind attained to its most perfect development, in the character of the great sect to which the Pilgrims belonged." [243] It is interesting that at least one writer took sarcastic exception to Marsh's Gothic propaganda: "About the only part of the human race worth mentioning is the Gothic race. About the only part of the Gothic race worth mentioning are the Puritans who emigrated to New England and their present descendants." [244]

Thomas Jefferson had also drunk deeply from the Gothic fount. Like Marsh, he was a student of Anglo-Saxon philology, and in his commonplace book, we can trace the record of Jefferson's reading in the antiquarian literature published in England and on the Continent. Since, however, Marsh could not have had access to Jefferson's manuscript commonplace book, there is no question of a source of influence. [245] In any

[242] *Ibid.*, p. 20.

[243] *Ibid.*, p. 34.

[244] Anonymous, *Remarks on an Address Delivered before the New England Society of New York* (Boston, 1845), p. 9; the next page refers to Marsh by name; the authorship of the pamphlet may be conjectured from the fact that the copy in the New York Public Library is inscribed: "Mr. Everet A. Duyckinck with the regards of Rich. H. Dana."

[245] *The Commonplace Book of Thomas Jefferson: A Repertory of his Ideas on Government*, edited by Gilbert Chinard, Johns Hopkins Studies in Romance Literatures and Languages, Extra Vol. II (Baltimore, 1926). Chinard properly emphasizes in his introductory essay the large part played by Germanic antiquities in shaping Jefferson's ideas on government: "He had painstakingly collected every scrap of evidence to reconstruct the history of his 'Saxon ancestors,' and he remained firmly convinced that his conception of liberty and natural rights had been put into effect by the 'semi-barbarous' tribes whose wanderings he had traced through Pelloutier, Molesworth, Vertot, Sullivan, Kames and Blackstone during the studious years of his

event, even a cursory check of the authors listed in Jefferson's notebooks with the titles listed in Marsh's catalogue will indicate that both Jefferson and Marsh were drawing upon common sources of ideas known to America at their respective times.

---

youth" (pp. 64-65). Chinard, however, overlooks the significance, semantically and ideologically, of the specific equation, Jute equals Goth equals German, in Jefferson's thinking.

# CHAPTER TWO

## GOTHIC PARLIAMENTS

Without Jordanes' Scandza theory and the specific equation Jute equals Goth, there would have been a Germanic, not a Gothic, cult in England. Within the agglutinative tradition, however, it was possible to describe parliaments and the primitive folkmoot out of which they grew as Gothic. This explains why Tacitus' *Germania,* because it embodied the fullest description of what the seventeenth century called not Germanic but Gothic institutions, relegated Jordanes' *Getica* to the background and emerged itself as the most important text in the Gothic tradition in England.

Tacitus wrote an epitaph to Roman *virtus,* not a prophecy of German greatness, yet his treatise was fated to immortalize for English history the Germanic love of liberty and democratic procedures. "Some have sent us to Tacitus and as far as Germany to learn our English constitution," wrote an anonymous pamphleteer in 1689, expressing succinctly what almost a century of Gothic propagandizing had established. [1] A curve of history which indicated the continuity of English institutions since their founding and the sanctity adhering to those institutions precisely because they were continuous showed to the defenders of parliament the way to realize the impact of the national past upon their own life and thought.

England had once been free in its tribal assemblies, and the freedom of Parliament therefore should be retrieved—this was the aim and, in substance, the reasoning of those defenders of parliamentary prerogative who appear in this study as

[1] *An Answer to the Vindication of the Letter from a Person of Quality in the North* (London, 1689); cited by Keith Feiling, *History of the Tory Party* (Oxford, 1924), p. 484.

"Gothicists." The issue raised by the challenge thrown down by the Stuart monarchs to Parliament was joined on the battlefield, but the defense of Parliament was accomplished in the minds of Englishmen before they made it the work of their hands. It was accomplished by three passages in Tacitus' *Germania* which bore on one point: the king's authority is limited and is to be submitted to public control exercised in public assemblies:

VII: The authority of their kings is not unlimited or arbitrary (nec regibus infinita aut libera potestas).

XI: On minor matters the chiefs deliberate; on larger questions the whole tribe (de minoribus rebus principes consultant, de maioribus omnes).

XI: The king or chief, according to age, birth, distinction in war, or eloquence, is heard more because he has influence to persuade than because he has power to command (mox vel princeps, prout aetas cuique, prout nobilitas, prout decus bellorum, prout facundia est, audiuntur, auctoritate suadendi magis quam jubendi potestate.

"De minoribus," and so on in particular became a national rubric pointing to the seed of English parliaments in the old Saxon witenagemot. The passage summed up the source of true democratic government and, by implication, the pith of the complaint against the monarch's lust for absolute power.

The gains made by historiography in the Gothic party pamphlets are of equal importance. Because Parliament's defenders sought consciously for a cultural continuity in English life, it was inevitable that while writing history the antiquarian researchers would develop *pari passu* a theory of historiography. This intellectual discovery becomes all the more impressive when we recall that the previous period, the Renaissance, had discussed at great length the availability of history for the epic without developing at the same time a basic theory of history itself.

8

There were many on the side of the crown who quickly pointed out that political issues were affecting the character of the antiquarian researches in a way which vitiated the accuracy of their findings. Matthew Wren, for example, observed that antiquity was something which "even those who profess to slight it, make great advantage of when they imagine it is on their side." [2] The political arena, however, is not the most likely place for a dispassionate discussion of accuracy, and the Royalists themselves were not free from prejudice. Indeed, James I was overheard in the rueful remark: "Ah, if I had only looked into precedents what kings had done and might do." [3] Historiography, it seems, always reflects a contemporaneous *Zeitgeist.* The *Germania* remained even during the Victorian period of "scientific" historiography the *fons et origo* of English liberties. Turner, Freeman, and Stubbs were not defending Parliament against royal encroachment, but their contemporaneous *Zeitgeist* was invigorated by the agitation for the Reform Bill of 1832. They peered into the past through the rosy spectacles of the Reform Bill. As Charles Petit-Dutaillis, who undertook to bring Stubbs up to date, observes:

The 'Constitutional History' of Stubbs has grown out of date in yet another way. Stubbs wrote history on lines on which it is no longer written by the great medievalists of today. He belonged to the liberal generation which had seen and assisted in the attainment of electoral reforms in England and of revolutionary and nationalist reforms on the Continent. He had formed himself in his youth under the discipline of the patriotic German scholars who saw in the primitive German institutions the source of all human dignity and of all human independence. He thought he saw in the development of the English Constitution the magnificent and unique expansion of these germs of self-government, and England was for him the messenger of liberty to the world.

[2] *Monarchy Asserted* (Oxford, 1659), p. 2.
[3] Wallace Notestein, "The Initiative of the House of Commons," *Proceedings of the British Academy,* XI (1924-25), 174.

The degree to which this optimistic and patriotic conception of English history could falsify, despite the author's scrupulous conscientiousness, his interpretation of the sources, is manifest in the pages which he has devoted to the Great Charter. [4]

The ancestor of the Gothicists in England is Richard Verstegen, who stands at the head of the stream because it is his authority on Germanic antiquities which is cited with the greatest frequency throughout the seventeenth century. He is by no means the first to identify the English people as descendants of a Germanic stock, but he is the first to devote an entire book to a discussion of the historical, cultural, and linguistic proofs of his theory. [5] The success of the book is indicated by the five editions, 1605, 1628, 1634, 1653, and 1673.

Verstegen has nothing to say on tribal assemblies. Nevertheless, the *Restitution* supplied a reservoir of ideas to the defenders of Parliament, out of which they drew two of particular importance: the *dux bellorum,* and "anti-Normanism"; these are the conceptions of traditional political inheritances which aided the parliamentary cause—a plethora of other writers supplied the notion of public assemblies. In addition, Verstegen also stresses a conception of traditional racial characteristics: the Germans are invincible, courageous, and so on. Later Gothicists employ with great frequency Verstegen's racial theory to support their view of the predilection of the English, a branch of the German race, for liberty.

Verstegen brings the English within the scope of German history by calling on the authority of Tacitus, whom he hails as "a most credit-worthy writer." The opening paragraph of the treatise informs the reader that "Englishmen are descended of German race, & were heretofore generally called Saxons." [6]

---

[4] *Studies and Notes Supplementary to Stubbs's Constitutional History* (2d. ed.; Manchester, 1911), I, xii-xiii.

[5] *Restitution of Decayed Intelligence.*

[6] *Restitution* (1605 ed.), p. 1; for Tacitus, see p. 40.

Verstegen is aware that the Roman historian does not mention the Saxons, but in order to establish his own preference for tracing English origins back to Saxon origins and to make use at the same time of Tacitus' general description of the Germans, he glibly affirms that the reason why Tacitus did not call the Saxons by name is that he knew them by the name of Cambrians. [7]

The Germans, he tells us, are a people distinguished for three reasons: they have always possessed their own land, they are invincible, and they compose a pure race.

The first therefore & most memorable, & most worthy of renowne and glory, is that they have beene the onely and ever possessors of their countrey, to wit the first people that ever inhabited it, no antiquity being able to tel us that ever any people have dwelt in Germany save only the Germans themselves, who yet unto this day do there hold their habitation. Secondly, they were never subdued by any, for albeit that the Romans with exceeding great cost, losses & long trouble, might come to bee the commanders of some part there of; yet of the whole never, as of Gallia, Spain, & many other countries els, they were. Thirdly they have ever kept themselves unmixed with forraign people, and their language without mixing it with any forrain toung. [8]

The English share in the German psychological characteristics:

First then as touching their antient conditions and manner of life. They were a people very active and industrious, utterly detesting idleness and sloth; stil seeking by warres to enlarge the bounds of their owne territories: fierce against their enemies, but conversing together among themselves in great love and friendlinesse an especial cause of the augmentation of their prosperitie. [9]

---

[7] *Ibid.*, pp. 20-21.
[8] *Ibid.*, pp. 42-43.
[9] *Ibid.*, ch. iii, on "The Ancient Manner of Lyving of Our Saxon Ancestors," p. 55.

Verstegen's account of the Germanic *dux bellorum* is a concept second in importance for the Parliamentary cause only to the notion of free tribal assemblies:

For the generall government of the countrie, they ordained twelve Noble men, chosen from among others for their worthinesse and sufficiencie. These in the time of peace rode their severall circuits, to see justice and good customes observed, and they often of course, at appointed times met all together, to consult and give order in publike affaires; but ever in time of warre one of these twelve was chosen to be King; and so to remaine so long only as the war lasted; and that being ended, his name and dignitie of King also ceased; and he became as before; and this custome continued among them until the time of their warres with Emperor Charles the Great, at which time Wittikind, one of the twelve as aforesaid a Nobleman of Angria, in Westphalia, bore over the rest and authorite of King. [10]

If a king, that is, were not an hereditary *princeps* but an elective *dux bellorum* elevated in a war crisis from a military captaincy to a kingship, it followed that in times of peace the king was demotable. In short, if the people made the king they could then also unmake him. Actually, the real issue was not whether the king was a *dux bellorum* or a *princeps,* but whether the king, whatover his origin, would be content to rule under the sovereignty of law which prescribed the monarch's just claims to rule and the subjects' loyalty to the monarch. But in the confusion of events leading up to the Civil War, this basic issue was only rarely recognized. To shatter the King's claim to rule by divine appointment, Parliament's defenders seized on the concept of the *dux bellorum* and magnified it into a theory of justifiable rebellion against monarchs who were so far from divine appointment that the records of history showed they were merely of human clay, appointed by the people, with their rights strictly limited and revocable under certain conditions. Verstegen, it is to be

[10] *Ibid.,* pp. 62-63.

noted, is discussing Germany, and he indicates that the elective system is a thing of the past ever since Wittikind
established an hereditary monarchy. Similarly, in his tenth
chapter on "Titles," Verstegen defines "Cuning" in such a
way as to bring out the king's original elective status, but
both Royalists and Gothicists could read the account with
equanimity since it was equally clear that the king was
elective or, alternatively, elective only "in the beginning":

> Cuning is as much in signification as one espetially valliant
> and this beeing the title of the chief of all, expresseth him the
> most apparent in courage or valour. And certaine it is that the
> kings of most nations were in the beginning elected and chosen
> of the people to raigne over them, in regard of the greatnesse of
> their courage, valour and strength, as beeing therefore best able
> to defend and governe them. [11]

The Gothicists had to do more than to settle Parliament's
origin in the ancient tribal assembly. They had to show, in
addition, the continued growth of the public assembly, un-
interrupted by the successive Danish and Norman invasions.
Since the Gothicists sought consciously for a continuity in
English life and believed that they had found it in the unbroken
development of English parliaments, their neglect to take
account of the Norman cataclysm implied that to their minds
William had made no radical alterations. As Royalist theory
continued to press the claim for absolute monarchical power
by virtue of the King's legacy from the Norman Conqueror's
seizure of power, the problem of "Normanism" became a
paramount issue. By 1647 "anti-Normanism," as a party
slogan, appears as the title of a tract against absolutism.
Verstegen has no concern with Parliament's rights, but his
pride in England's Saxon origins impels him to assert the
continuity of Saxon culture in England in spite of invasions:

[11] *Ibid.*, pp. 313-314.

Thus I have made it plainely appear (for that some have inconsiderately believed the contrarie) that the maine corpes and body of the realme, notwithstanding the Norman conquest and the former invasion of the Danes, hath still consisted of the ancient English-Saxon people, wherein even unto this day it doth yet consist... And whereas some do call us a mixed nation by reason of these Danes and Normannes coming in among us, I answere (as formerly I have noted) that the Danes and Normannes were once one same people with the Germans, as were also the Saxons; & wee not to bee accompted mixt by having only some such ioyned unto us againe, as sometime had one same language and one originall with us. [12]

Native sources of the conception of the *dux bellorum* were available to Verstegen in Bede's *Ecclesiastical History,* Ralph Higden's *Polychronicon,* and Sir Thomas Smith's *De republica Anglorum.* [13] Not until the full stream of Gothic propaganda flows, after Verstegen, does the conception of the elective *dux* become an effective weapon against the King's pretensions to absolute power.

The rediscovery of England's ancient folkmoot as a symbol and embodiment of ordered democratic life was the work not of an amateur like Verstegen but of the scholars of the seventeenth century, the first great medievalists. Verstegen enjoyed great prestige borrowed from the scholars, rather than *vice versa.* The Society of Antiquaries of London enlisted and organized the scholarly researches into Enland's past. This society had been founded by Archbishop Parker for the express purpose of furthering research into Anglo-Saxon church charters in order to establish the rights of the native church against Rome. England's political institutions also fell within the interest of the members. The legacy of learning left to the nation by the antiquaries was equaled only by their

[12] *Ibid.,* p. 187.
[13] Bede, bk. v, ch. x, Loeb ed., II, 240; Higden, Rolls series, edited by J. R. Lumby (London, 1885-86), I, 260-261; Smith, bk. I, ch. xv, L. Alston edition (Cambridge, 1906), p. 29.

zeal for preserving England's ancient political liberties, a legacy which they left as an inspiration. The legacy and the inspiration both can be measured in an anthology or primer of Gothic ideas composed by the leading members of the society. Although not gathered and printed until 1658, the papers were prepared several decades before for oral presentation at the meetings of the society (Francis Tate, one of the authors, died in 1616); but the activities of the antiquaries falling under James's suspicion, the public meetings appear to have been discontinued in 1604. The anthology is entitled *The Opinions of Several Learned Antiquaries, viz. Dodridge, Agar, Tate, Camden, Holland, Cotton, Selden. Touching the Antiquity, Power, Order, State, Persons, Manner, and Proceedings of the High Court of Parliament in England.* [14]

Dodridge establishes that the Saxons convened legislative assemblies which remained unaltered in England during the Danish invasion and were only partially destroyed by William: "Now that substance, and forme of Parliamentary Assemblies went all along the Saxon age, held during the incursion of the Danes, and was continued by the Conqueror in part." The precise question whether the Saxon witenagemot was aristocratic or actually was attended by the people at large is covered by Dodridge, as it was throughout the Gothic movement, by the relevant passage in Tacitus, implying a democratic council. Dodridge quotes Tacitus: "The story of the Saxons and their Laws do shew, that they were of the same minde transplanted hither, as Tacitus saith the Germanes were: Nec Regibus infinita potestas; de Minoribus rebus principes consultant, de majoribus omnes." [15] Tate contributes the idea of a British or pre-Saxon Parliament and stresses the

---

[14] London, 1658, reprinted 1685; also in Thomas Hearne's *A Collection of Curious Discourses* (London, 1773). The first edition of the *Curious Discourses* appeared in 1720; the separate essays were redistributed in the later editions of 1773 and 1775.

[15] Hearne, *Curious Discourses* (1773 ed), II, 10-11.

continuity of the "gemote": "But the Assembly of the three Estates to consult for the affairs of the Commonwealth is as ancient as the Britains, and continued here in the time of the Saxons, Danes, and Normans." [16]

Agar and Camden support Tate in his notion of a pre-Saxon Parliament. Repeated reference to the anthology in the latter part of the century indicate its usefulness in disseminating knowledge of the golden age of freedom in England's past.

A second product of the Society of Antiquaries was Speed's *History of Great Britaine* (1611). Speed was aided in his writing by his colleague Sir Robert Bruce Cotton, who revised proofs for Speed's *History* in 1609. [17] Speed refers to Verstegen (p. 286) and follows him practically verbatim on the elective status of the Saxon *dux*: "For the generall government of their countries they ordained twelve Noblemen chosen from among others, for their worthiness and sufficiency...but ever in time of warre one of these twelve was chosen to be King, and so to remaine so onely as the warres lasted: and that being ended, his name and dignotie of King also ceased, becomming againe as before." [18]

Andrew Horn's *Mirror of Justice* (1285? 1290?), second in popularity among Gothicists only to Verstegen's *Restitution,* is also connected with the activities of the Society of Antiquaries. It was first printed in 1642, untranslated from the French, from a transcript belonging to Francis Tate, contributor to the "Gothic anthology." The significance of this first printing is expressed by the distinguished legal historian, F. W. Maitland: "This happened in 1642, a marvellously

---

[16] *Ibid.,* II, 65.

[17] *Original letters of Eminent Literary Men,* Camden Society, XXIII (London, 1843), 108-109.

[18] *History of Great Britaine* (3d ed.; London, 1650), p. 290. The *History* begins in all editions with book five; it was designed as a sequel to his *Theatre of Empire of Great Britain.*

appropriate date for the appearance of a book which proclaimed as the first and sovereign 'abuse' that the king is
beyond the law to which he ought to be subject." [19] The
service of Horn's Mirror to the Gothic cause lay in its
insistence, as Maitland points out, that the nation "must go
back to the 'coming of the English.' " [20] In chapter two,
entitled, "Of the Coming of the English," Horn appears to be
conscious, in a manner resembling Saint Augustine describing
the providential mission of the Goths to punish the wicked
Romans, of a heavenly vocation to justify the advent into
England of the Saxons:

After that God had abated the pride of the Britons, who had
recourse to force rather than law, He delivered the kingdom to
the humblest and simplest of all the neighbouring nations: to
wit, the Saxons, who came to conquer it from the parts of Almaine. Of which folk there were as many as forty sovereigns,
who all aided each other as fellows. They first called this land
England, which thereto was called Britannia Major. And they,
after great wars and tribulations and pains long time suffered,
chose from among themselves a king to reign over them and to
govern the people of God and to maintain and defend their
persons and goods by the rule of right. And at his crowning
they made him swear that he would maintain the Christian faith
with all his power, and would guide his people by law without
respect of any person, and would be obedient to holy Church,
and would submit to justice and would suffer right like any
other of his people. And after this, the kingdom became herit-
able. [21]

[19] Introduction to Horn's *Mirror of Justice,* edited by W. J. Whitaker, Selden Society, VII (London, 1895), x. Coke also owned a
manuscript *Mirror;* Coke was strong for the common law but he does
not figure importantly as a Gothicist; in the *First Institute,* under
"Parliament," he describes the witenagemot briefly; see Sir Edward
Coke, *The First Part of the Institutes of the Laws of England* (5th
ed.; London, 1656).

[20] Maitland, p. xxxviii; as a strict account of old English law, Maitland shows that the *Mirror* is worthless to the legal historian.

[21] *Mirror of Justice* (Whitaker ed.), p. 6.

The role of the Saxons in English history is now completely reversed. In Bede, the *Anglo-Saxon Chronicle*, Matthew of Westminster, Roger of Wendover, Henry of Huntingdon, and Florence of Winchester the Saxons appear as piratic marauders, wily and treacherous in their proposals toward Vortigern that they would remain content to be only his allies. In Horn, the Saxons are contrasted in their simplicity and democratic virtues with the sinful, autocratic Britons. The *Mirror of Justice* is significant also because it treats the Norman Conquest *sub silentio;* it implies that to Horn the Saxon democratic institutions had an unbroken development in England.

In 1646 Horn's text was translated by William Hughes. Hughes' preface places beyond doubt the importance of the *Mirror* to the Gothic movement:

Parliaments have been ancient, they were in the time of the Saxons, long before the Norman conquest (for as the proverb is) in the time of the Danes, the laws lay then in water, the people were governed rather by princes wills than public laws; for then (as one saith) "Sepultum suit jus in regno, leges et consuetudines simul sapitae, temporibus illorum prava voluntas, vis et violentia magis regnabant, quam judicium in terra." And although in the Saxons time I find the usual words of the acts to have been *edictum, constitutio,* little mention being made of the commons, yet I further find that "tum demum leges vim et vigorem habuerunt, cum fuerunt non modo institutae sed firmatae approbatione communitatis." [22]

Samuel Daniel who, as we have already seen, expresses a belief that English laws are Gothic, tells in his *History* (1621) of liberty in England "before the Romans did by strength and cunning unlocke those liberties of theirs. And such as were then termed Kings, were but as their Generalls in warre, without any other great iurisdiction." In the same passage Daniel describes the British chief, Cassevelaunus, as a *dux bellorum* "by the common councell was elected in this their

[22] "Preface," *The Mirror of Justice* (London, 1646).

publique danger." "Whereby we perceive," concludes Daniel, "it was no Monarchie... So that with what credit, the accompt of above a thousand yeers from Brute to Cassevellaunus in a line of absolute Kings, can be cleared, I doe not see." [23]

A straw in the wind, showing the quarter from which Parliament's defense of its ancient rights was arising, was the mishap of Dr. Dorislaus which deprived him of a teaching appointment at Cambridge University. Fulke Greville had long cherished an ambition to establish a history lectureship at Cambridge in honor of his family. Efforts were made to install Vossius, the celebrated Dutch historian, as the first incumbent. When Vossius proved unavailable, the post was filled by the appointment of Dr. Dorislaus, also of Leyden. Dr. Dorislaus was appointed in May 1627, but his tenure was short. A lecture on Tacitus was his undoing. The bewildered scholar protested his innocence but the charge remained standing: he spoke too much of the liberties of the people.

Two separate contemporaneous accounts survive of the affair. Dr. Samuel Ward, writing to Archbishop Usher, said:

He read some two or three Lectures, beginning with Cornelius Tacitus; where his Author mentioning the conversion of the State of Rome from Government by Kings to the Government by Consuls, by the suggestion of Junious Brutus; he took occasion to discourse of the Power of the People under Kings, and afterward. When he touched upon the Excesses of Tarquinus Superbus his infringing of the Liberties of the People, which they enjoyed under former Kings; and so, among many other things, descended to the vindicating of the Netherlanders, for retaining their Liberties the violences of Spain. In conclusion, he was conceived of by some, to speak too much for the defence of the Liberties of the People. [24]

[23] *Collection of the Historie of England* (London, 1621), p. 2.
[24] Letter dated May 16, 1628, in Richard Parr, *Life of James Usher* (London, 1688), p. 393.

Dr. Matthew Wren reported the affair to Bishop Laud:

At his coming home to Cambridge found Dr. Dorislaus, sent hither by Lord Brooke, whose domestic he now is, with his Majesty's letters to assign him a school and time to read a history lecture on the Annals of Tacitus. His first lecture passed unexcepted at, but the writer warned the Heads in private that the lecturer placed the right of monarchy in the people's voluntary submission. The second lecture contained such dangerous passages, and so appliable to the exasperations of these villainous times, that the writer could not abstain before the Heads from taking offence. The Vice Chancellor, sent for his lectures, out of which the writer privately gathered the principal passages which he encloses. The writer declined to incorporate the lecturer as a Doctor of Cambridge, but describes him as of good learning, very ingenuous, and ready to give satisfaction in any kind. It was agreed to send him to some of the Council, and await further directions. Not doubting that the Duke will consult with Bishop Laud, the writer apprizes him of the facts, but does not wish to be known as a delator. [25]

If the times were not as villainous as Wren in his agitation feels, they were rapidly becoming so. The Dorislaus mishap of 1627 showed that the King's friends were on the alert for propaganda subversive of the King's authority. But Parliament, too, was stirring restlessly. In the next year, the first ship-money case aroused Parliament to the danger in the King's demands to tax freely. On a previous occasion, when a delegation from Commons waited upon the King to plead the prerogatives of Parliament, the King is reported to have commanded a servant to bring chairs "for the ambassadors." A parliament instructed in its rights by the antiquarian researches could not be so easily swept aside. The Gothic propaganda was becoming a major issue. The year 1628 saw, for example, the composition of a treatise on Parliament's origin

---

[25] *Calendar of State Papers, Domestic, 1627-28*, p. 470; dated Dec. 16, 1627. An account of the affair is in G. Bullough, "Fulke-Greville, First Lord Brooke," *Modern Language Review*, XXVIII (1933), 1-20.

in the Saxon witenagemot which left no doubt about the extent and source of the people's power.

The tract is entitled, *The Priviledges and Practice of Parliaments in England. Collected Out of the Common Lawes of this Land. Seene and Allowed by the Learned in the Lawes. Commended to the High Court of Parliament now Assembled* (London, 1628). It traces the continuity of parliaments in England, despite the Norman invasion:

The most Common and best meanes for the preservation and Conservation as well of private or publique Tranquillitie and Societie used in all Ages, and by all Nations, is by way of lawful Assembly, and Consultation, which wee call Parliament, to looke into the necessity of publique Condition, and so to fore-see seasonable remedie. Where no Counsell is, the people fall, But where many Counsellors are, there is health, Prov. 11 and 14. Tully saith, Communis utilitatis de relictio contra naturam est. The Saxons called this Court Miclegemot, the great Assemblie, and Witenagemot, the Assemblie of wise men; The Latine Authors of those times called it Commune Consilium, magna curia generalis conventus, etc. But William the Conqueror as it seemeth changed the name of this Court, and first called it by the name of Parliament. But manifest it is, that the Conqueror changed not the frame or Jurisdiction of this Court in any point; yea, the very names which are attributed to this Court before the Conquest are continued to this day. [26]

Sir Henry Spelman's study of the origins of feudal tenures appears to raise a narrow, technical problem in land-grants, of interest solely to legal historians. But a closer study of its thesis and the spirit of democratic protest against "Normanism" which motivated Spelman's research, will reveal the importance of the Gothic ideas in awakening the nation to the dangers in the Royalist claim to absolute rule because of the Norman Conquest.

A lawsuit over a defective land-title was Spelman's opportunity to advance the cause of anti-Normanism. On the oc-

[26] Cited from the 1640 edition, pp. 1-2.

casion of an inquiry into King Charles I's title to land in certain counties of Ireland, a proclamation was published urging all parties concerned to come forward and have their claims to title validated. Several appeared including Lord Dillon whose title was declared void. Lord Dillon protested that since tenure was brought in by the Conquest and grants were by common law, his claim by common law was sounder than the King's claim by tenure. Dillon's objection was overruled on the ground that tenure was as old as common law since it existed among the Saxons before the Conquest. The King's lawyers rested their case on a passage in Spelman's legal *Glossarium* (1626) where under "Feodum" he had referred the origin of feuds in England to the Saxons. To Spelman, however, the King's interpretation of the definition was a plain perversion of what he actually wrote. In order to aid Dillon in his suit, Spelman wrote in 1639 *The Original, Growth, Propagation, and Condition of Feuds and Tenures by Knight-Service in England.* [27] (It was not the first time that Spelman had fallen foul of the royal clique. In the same *Glossarium,* Spelman's definition of Magna Charta enhanced too greatly the rights of the people over the king, and he was quickly called to account by Laud.) [28]

Tacitus and Jordanes appear as authorities in Spelman's treatise. [29] He grants that Feuds and Tenures did originate with the Saxons: "Thus it appeareth that Feuds and Tenures and the Feudal law itself, took their original from the Germans

[27] In *The English Works of Sir Henry Spelman...Together with his Posthumous Works Relating to the Laws and Antiquities of England,* edited by Edmund Gibson (London, 1723) pp. 1-46 of the *Posthumous Works,* separate pagination and two title-pages: 1723, 1727; the main title-page is dated 1723. Gibson's preface gives an account of the manuscript and the legal suit.

[28] John Aubrey, *Brief Lives,* edited by Andrew Clark (Oxford, 1898), II, 231.

[29] *Posthumous Works,* p. 3.

and Northern nations." [30] However that might be, he adds, the Tenures were not hereditary but for life only. "If we understand them to be Feuds among the Saxons, or of that nature, then are we sure that they were no more than for life, and not inheritable, nor stretching further, without further grace obtained from the Lord." [31] Hereditary tenure, in short, was an instrument of tyranny introduced by William the Conqueror on the model of Hugh Capet's conquest of France in 987:

This was a fair direction for William of Normandy (whom we call the Conqueror) how to secure himself of this his new acquired Kingdom of England; and he pretermitted not to take advantage of it. For with as great diligence as providence, he presently transfer'd his Country-customs into England (as the Black Book of the Chequer witnesseth) and amongst them (as after shall be made perspicuous) this new French custom of making Feuds hereditary, not regarding the former use of our Saxon Ancestors; who like all other nations, save the French, continued till that time their Feuds and Tenures, either arbitrary or in some definite limitation, according to the ancient manner of the Germans, receiv'd generally throughout Europe. For by the multitude of their Colonies and transmigrations into all the chiefest parts thereof, they carried with them such Feodal Rites, as were then in use amongst them; and planting those Rites and Customs in those several Countries where they settled themselves did by that means make all of those severall Countries to hold a general conformity in their Feuds and Military Customs. So by the Longobards they were carried into Italy, by the Saliques into the Eastern parts of France, by the Franks into the West part thereof, by the Saxons into this our Britain. [32]

The difference between Saxon tenure and hereditary tenure is that between nobility and slavery, and in stirring words Spelman concludes by denouncing the King's lawyers:

[30] *Ibid.,* p. 4.
[31] *Ibid.*
[32] *Ibid.,* p. 5.

It was neither my Words, nor my meaning, to say that he [i.e. William the Conqueror] first brought in either Feuds or Military Service in a general sense, but that he brought in the Servitudes and Grievances of Feuds, viz. Wardship, Marriage, and such like, which to this day were never known to other Nations that are governed by the Feodal Law. There is great difference between *Servitia Militaria* and *Servitutes Militares*: The one, Heroic, Noble, and full of Glory, which might not therefore be permitted in old time to any that was not born of free parents: no, not to a King's son (as appeareth in Virgil) wherein our Saxons were also very cautelous, and accounted a Souldiers shield to be *Insigne Libertatis*: the other, not ignoble and servile, but deriv'd even from the very Bondage. Let not this offend: I will say no more. [33]

Even as Spelman was writing, the defenders of Parliament were gathering around an *insigne libertatis* to recover their lost Saxon rights of which the King would have them deprived.

The remainder of Spelman's argument rests upon an examination of Saxon charters in order to show that such Norman terms as "tenure in capite" were non-existent in pre-Conquest history, an argument which reflects Spelman's attitude toward German law:

To come therefore to the point; if my Opinion be any thing, I think the foundation of our Law to be laid by our German Ancestors, but built upon and polished by Materials taken from the Canon Law and Civil Law. And under the capacious Name of Germans, I not only intend our Saxons. And let it not more mistake us to take our Laws from the Noble Germans, a prime and most potent People, than it did the conquering Romans their from the Greeks, or the learned Grecians from the Hebrews. [34]

Parliament's Grand Remonstrance of 1641 widened the breach between the King and the people; events were moving

---

[33] *Ibid.,* p. 46.
[34] "The Original of the Terms," p. 100. The *Posthumous Works* are included in the *English Works* but with separate pagination; the "Original of the Terms" is the fourth separate essay.

rapidly toward actual war and, finally, regicide. Driven into a tight corner by the Remonstrance, the Royalists pressed even more vigorously the "Norman" claim to unlimited monarchical power by title of conquest; William the Conqueror, they argued, had in his heirs perpetually bound the land in dominion to the royal will. Philip Hunton's *Treatise of Monarchy* (1643) affords an example of the Gothic propaganda combating the "Norman" claim. A flurry of Royalist pamphlets followed Hunton's *Treatise* in counterattack. It was a characteristic of the period that there was never a shortage of words.

Following a general discussion of the theory of title by conquest, Hunton turns in part two, chapter one, to a consideration of the theory as it particularly concerns England:

All conquest doth not put the Conqueror into an absolute right. He may come to a right by Conquest: but not sole Conquest; but a partiall, occasioning a Right by finall Agreement; and then the right is specificated by that fundamentall Agreement: Also he may by sword prosecute a claime of another nature: and in his war intend only an acquiring of that claimed right, and after conquest rest in that: Yea farther, he may win a Kingdome meerly by the Sword and enter on it by right of Conquest: yet considering that right of conquest hath too much of force in it to be safe and permanent; he may thinke conquest the best means of getting a Kingdome, but not holding, and in wisdome for himself and posterity, gaine the affections of the people by deserting that Title, and taking a new by Politique agreement, or descend from that right by fundamentall grants of liberties to the people, and limitations to his own power: but these things I said in effect before, in the first part, only here I have recalled them to shew what a *non sequitur* there is in the Argument. 35

Up to this point, Hunton has been showing that in the logic of the situation, the Conqueror must accept some limitation to his title. So much refutes the assertion that William was in reality a conqueror. The problem of the Saxon Conquest,

35 *Treatise of Monarchy* (London, 1643), pp. 34-35.

however, throws him on the horns of a dilemma. If the Saxons
entered by conquest, then by the same logic, they too must
have been forced to adapt their customary form of government
to the situation in England. But this is an absurdity because
the Saxons were free and self-governing; it is utterly inconceivable that the democratic Saxons would willingly take on
the ways of the autocratic Britons, the subjected people. Forced to eat his cake and have it, Hunton finds a way out in the
ingenious theory that the Saxon advent was an expulsion, not
a conquest—they expelled the Britons and continued in their
new home in their normal democratic ways:

> For that of the Saxons was an expulsion, not a Conquest, for
> as our Histories record, They comming into the Kingdome drove
> out the Britaines, and by degrees planted themselves under their
> Commanders; and no doubt continued the freedome they had
> in Germany: unles we should thinke that by conquering they lost
> their own Liberties to the Kings, for whom they conquered and
> expelled the British into Wales. Rather I conceive, the Originall
> of the subjects libertie was by those our forefathers brought out
> of Germany: Where, as Tacitus reports, *nec Regibus infinita
> aut libera potestas*: Their Kings had no absolute but limited
> power: and all weighty matters were dispatched by generall
> meetings of all the Estates. Who sets not here the antiquity of
> our Liberties and frame of Government? so they were governed
> in Germany, and so here to this day, for by transplanting them-
> selves, they changed their soyl, not their manners and Govern-
> ment. [36]

Having established by this ingenious argument the continuity of Saxon democracy, Hunton recapitulates the general
argument, bringing it back again to William the Conqueror:

> Then, that of the Danes, indeed, was a violent conquest: and
> as all violent rules, it lasted not long: When the English ex-
> pelled them, they recovered their countries and liberties together.
> Thus it is clear, the English liberty remained to them, till the
> Norman invasion, notwithstanding that Danish interruption.

[36] *Ibid.*, pp. 35-36.

Now for Duke William. I know nothing they have in him, but
the bare style of conqueror, which seems to make for them. The
very truth is (and every intelligent reader of the history of
those times will attest it) that Duke William pretended the
grant and gift of King Edward, who died without children; and
he came with forces into this kingdom, not to conquer, but to
make good his title against his enemies. His end of entering the
land was not to gain a new absolute title, but to vindicate the
old limited one, whereby the English-Saxon kings, his predecessors, held this kingdom. [37]

Dr. Henry Ferne, the King's personal chaplain, quickly
isolated for attack Hunton's ingenious distinction between an
expulsion and a conquest. [38] The following year Hunton
replied to Dr. Ferne in his *Vindication of the Treatise of
Monarchy*. "I fetch not the root of succession," he says,

so farre backe as the Saxons, as this Replier traduces 'to cut
off advantages which may be made from the Normans entrance,
p. 22.'... Concerning the Saxon entrance, I said it was not a
conquest, properly and simply, but an expulsion. He answers,
'This is neither true, nor greatly materiall, p. 22.' I say, it is
both true and materiall: It is true: for all the Britaines which
retained their name and Nation, were they many or few, were
expelled into Wales. All the rest in *gentem, leges, nomen,
linguamq vincentium concesserunt*; as himselfe cites for me out
of Mr. Cambden. And it is very materiall; for if they which only
remained here in *gentem & leges vincentium concesserunt*; Then
the Conquerors, as I said, kept their old forme of Government;
the Saxons came not into the condition of the conquered Brittaines; but they into the old liberty of the Saxons. Hereupon
grew there a necessity of inquiry into the Government of the
Nation, before they came hither; that so we might know what a
one they established here; and brought the remaining Brittaines
into. And a record of more unquestionable authority than Tacitus I could not imagine; nor a more expresse testimony for a
limited forme in the very potestas of it; of which sort he affirmes
the government of all the Germanes Nation was. How ever the

[37] *Ibid.*, p. 35.
[38] *A Reply unto Severall Treatises Pleading for the Armes now
taken up by Subjects* (Oxford, 1643).

Doctor is pleased to call it a 'conjecture, a dreame,' and 'uncertainty;' No, the expresse testimony of such an Author is not so: Rather that probability of these Saxons not being then a people of Germany, but did afterward breake out of the *Cimbrica Chersonesus*, is so; which himself dares call no more then a probability. I say, it is a greater probability, that they were a people of Germany before they came in hither; for the Angli which accompanied them in that invasion, were questioneless Germanes, and reckoned by Tacitus among that people, doubtlesse they were neighbours in habitation, which were joyned in that voyage and conquest. Suppose the matter were not cleare of the Saxons, yet is it of the Angli which gave denomination to the Land and people, who no doubt retained their Lawes and Governement, says Cambden; which was limited in the very royall power saith Tacitus. But this Doctor would make men believe as if I endeavored to deduce the very modell of our present Government from that Saxon ingresse: Whereas all that I ayme at, is to make it appeare that in *semine*, in the *rude beginnings* it is so ancient; and shall affirme the limited power of the English kings, and liberty of the subjects to have been from thence continued till now, unless he can bring some better proofes of its interruption, and induction of an unlimited power, then as yet he saith. [39]

James Howell holds in the continuity of parliaments in England since Saxon days, the successive conquests notwithstanding:

He that is never so little versed in the Annals of this Isle, will find, that it hath been her fate to be four Times conquered... These so many Conquests must needs bring with them many disturbances and changes in Government; yet, I have observed, that, notwithstanding these Tumblings, it retained still the form of a Monarchy, and something there was always, that had analogy with the great Assembly, the Parliament.

The first Conquest, I find, was made by Claudius Caesar... It is well known what Laws the Romans had; he had his Comitia, which bore a Resemblance with our Convention in Parliament; the Place of their Meeting was called Praetorium [*footnote*: The Senate or Parliament House]; and the Laws which they enacted,

[39] *Vindication* (London, 1644), p. 33.

Plebiscita [*footnote*: i.e. The voluntary Acts or Laws made by Representatives of the People].

The Saxon Conquest succeeded next which were the English, there being no Name in Welch or Irish for an Englishman, but Saxon to this Day. They governed by Parliament, tho' it were under other Names, as Michel Sinoth, Michel Gemote, and Witenage Mote. [40]

The Royalists who urged that the monarch had absolute power by title of conquest had no way of avoiding the plain fact, known to all, that parliaments nevertheless did meet after William's conquest. To meet this difficulty in their position, the Royalists contended that whatever liberties the Conqueror granted, such as a parliament, he donated as a favor, *ad placitum,* as a token of royal kindness. This is, in essence, the basis of Sir Robert Filmer's refutation of Hunton in his *Observations Upon Mr. Hunton's Treatise of Monarchy* (1646).

Filmer is rather restrained; a statement by Colonel Thomas Dymock of the theory of parliament's origin in a donation is more typical of indignant Royalist feelings. William enslaved the people, Dymock says; "I maintaine, therefore, that the Kings of this Isle were monarchs, and absolute, without depending any thing upon their Subjects, when the people were all at their mercy, and Parliament wanted a being." [41] Filmer has the identical idea. In *The Power of Kings* (1680), he says: "In the Parliaments of England, which have commonly been holden every Third Year, the Estates seem to have a great Liberty, (as the Northern People almost all breathe thereafter) yet so it is, that in effect they proceed not, but way of Supplications and Requests to the Kings." [42]

[40] "The Pre-eminence and Pedigree of Parliament," printed for the first time in the third edition of James Howell's *Dodona's Grove* (London, 1645), pp. 7-8.

[41] *Englands Dust and Ashes Raked Up* (London, 1648), pp. 72-73.

[42] Published together with "Patriarcha" and *Observations Upon Mr. Hunton's Treatise of Monarchy* in the same volume with his *Free-*

"Patriarcha, or the Natural Power of Kings" repeats Filmer's theory of Parliament's origin in royal indulgence:

First, We are to remember, that until about the time of the Conquest, there could be no Parliaments assembled of the General States of the whole Kingdom of England, because till those days we cannot learn it was entirely united into one Kingdom... A second Point considerable is, Whether in such Parliaments, as was in the Saxon times, the Nobility and Clergy only were of those Assemblies, or whether the Commons were also called? Some are of Opinion, that though none of the Saxon Laws do mention the Commons, yet it may be gathered by the word *Wisemen*, the Commons are intended to be of those Assemblies, and they bring (as they conceive) probable arguments to prove it, from the Antiquity of some Burroughs that do yet send Burgesses, and from the Proscription of those in Ancient Demesne, not to send Burgesses to Parliament... On the contrary, there be of our Historians who do affirm, that Henry the First caused the Commons first to be Assembled by Knights and Burgesses of their own appointment, for before his Time only certain of the Nobility and Prelates of the Realm were called to Consultation about the most Important affairs of State. If this Assertion be true, it seems a meer matter of Grace of this King, and proves not any Natural Right of the People. [43]

The year 1647 produced two determined attacks, by John Hare and Nathaniel Bacon, on the royal theory of conquest. The term "anti-Normanism" appears for the first time as a rallying-cry for the defenders of Parliament. Thus the sharpened perception of the problem of historical continuity stressed by the Gothicists exposed in a glaring light the problem of "Normanism." In John Hare's *St. Edward's Ghost or Anti-Normanism,* anti-Normanism is joined to a defense of Saxon liberties:

---

*holder's Grand Inquest* (London, The Fourth Impression, 1684), pp. 297-298. "Patriarcha" remained in manuscript until 1680 when it appeared in print in the first edition of *The Freeholder's Grand Inquest.*

[43] *Ibid.,* pp. 118-119, 120-121.

There is no man that understands rightly what an Englishman is, but knows withal, that we are a member of the Teutonick nation, and descended out of Germany: a descent so honourable and happy, if duly considered, as that the like could not have been fetched from any other part of Europe, nor scarce of the universe.

After the dissolution of the Roman empire, how did the Teutonick glory and puissance break forth and diffuse themselves? The German colonies filled all Europe; the Franks seized upon the Transalpine Gaul, since, from then, named France; the Lombards upon the other Gauls, afterwards called Lombardy; the Goths on Spain; and the Saxons, or English, our peculiar progenitors, in a more plenary way, upon the best part of Britain, which we now possess, to which we have since also added the command of the Welsh, Irish, and the Scots: So that in all the regions aforesaid, as the sovereignty and royalty, so also most of the nobility, and in England the whole commonalty, are German, and of the German blood; and scarcely was there any worth or manhood left in these occidental nations, after their so long servitude under the Roman yoke, until these new supplies of freeborn men from Germany reinfused the same, and reinforced the then servile body of the west, with a spirit of honour and magnanimity; insomuch, that, as Du Bartas hath well observed, that land may well be stiled the *equus Trojannus,* or inexhaustible fountain of Europe's worth and worthy men. [44]

It would seem that higher praises of the "free-born" Germans cannot be found, but Hare rises to greater lyrical heights:

One more flower of this our mother nation's royal garland, and a point of her prerogative above other nations (not only of Europe, but also of the rest of the world, the Scythick excepted), is her unconquerableness, her untainted virginity and freedom from foreign subjection, which from her first foundation and cradle, she hath so conserved and defended, that none can truly boast to have been her ravisher. [45]

From Hare's anti-Norman point of view, it is inconceivable that this heritage of freedom and valor would be lost to the

[44] In *Harleian Miscellany,* VI, 92, 95.
[45] *Ibid.,* pp. 95-96.

Norman conqueror: "Did our ancestors, therefore, shake off the Roman yoke, with the slaughter of their legions, and during the whole age of that empire, as Tacitus confesseth, resist the puissance thereof, that the honour and freedom of their blood might be reserved for an untainted prey to a future conqueror?" [46]

He concludes with a program of five "anti-Norman" demands:

1. That William, sirnamed the Conqueror, be stripped of that insolent title.
2. That the title of the crown be ungrounded from any pretended conquest over this nation, and that his majesty be pleased to derive his right from St. Edward's legacy, and the blood of the precedent English kings, to whom he is the undoubted heir.

Points 3, 4, and 5 are demands to purge the language, laws, and customs of Normanisms. It is interesting that Hare cites Verstegen in connection with the proposed purge. [47]

"Normanism" received another destructive blow from Nathaniel Bacon in his *Historical and Political Discourse of the Laws and Government of England* (1647). The "Advertisement" gives Bacon's reason for writing the book:

A Private Debate concerning the Right of an English King to the Arbitrary Rule over English Subjects, as Successor to the Norman Conqueror, (so called) first occasioned this Discourse. Herein I have necessarily fallen upon the Antiquity and Uniformity of the Government of this Nation: which being cleared, may also serve as an Idea for them to consider, who do mind the restitution of this shattered Frame of Policy. For as in all other Cures, so in that of a distempered Government, the Original Constitution of the Body is not lightly to be regarded; and the contemplation of the Proportion of the Manners of the Nation in a small Model, brings no less furtherance to the right apprehension of the true nature thereof (besides the delight) than the perusing of a Map doth to the Traveller, after a long

[46] *Ibid.,* p. 99
[47] *Ibid.,* pp. 103-104.

and tedious travel... Ambition hath done much by Discourse and Action to bring forth absolute Monarchy out of the womb of the Nation; but yet like that of the Philosopher's Stone, this issue is but wind, and the end misery to the undertakers: And therefore more than probable it is, that the utmost perfection of this Nether-world's best Government, consists in the upholding of a due proportion of several Interests, compounded into one temperature. [48]

Bacon's first chapter discusses "Of the Britons and their Government."

This is Britain, or rather that part thereof, in after-ages called Saxony and England, from the people's Names transplanted thither. The Britons (to lay aside all conceits of Fame) I take to be an issue of the neighbouring Nations, from the German and Belgick shores... In their civil Government they allowed preeminence to their Magistrates rather than Supremacy, and had many chiefs in a little room; the Romans called them little Kings for the greater renown of their Empire. But others of more sobriety account them no better than Lords, of Liberties not much exceeding those of a City... But that which cleareth the matter, is the testimony of Dion in the Life of Severus the Emperor, who expressly saith, that in Britain the People held the helm of government in their own power. So as these were not kings, nor their Government Monarchical, and yet might be regular enough, considering the rudeness than in those days overspread the world. [49]

Turning to the Saxons, Bacon says:

I hold it both needless and fruitless to enter into the Lists, concerning the original of the Saxons; whether they were Natives from the Northern parts of Germany, or the Reliques of the Macedonian Army under Alexander... The people were a free people, governed by Laws, and those made not after the manner of the Gauls (as Caesar noteth) by the great men, but by the people; and therefore called a free people, because they are a Law to themselves; and this was a privilege belonging to all the Germans, as Tacitus observeth, in cases of most publick consequence, de majoribus omnes. [50]

[48] *Laws and Government,* p. iii.
[49] *Ibid.,* p. 1.　　　　　　　　　　　　[50] *Ibid.,* p. 9.

The Saxon ruler was not a *princeps* but a *dux bellorum*:

A King amongst the Old Saxons in probability was anciently a Commander in the field, an officer *pro tempore,* and no necessary Member in the constitution of their State: for in time of peace, when the Commonwealth was it self, the executive power of the Law rested much in the Nobility; but in times of War, and in publick distractions, they chose a General, and all swore Obedience unto him during the War; it being finished, the General laid down his Command, and everyone lived *aequo jure, propria contentus potestate.* But in their transmigration into Britain, the continuance of the War causing the continual use of the General, made that Place or office to settle and swell into the condition of a King; and so he that was formerly *Dux* became *Rex;* there beeing no more difference in the nature of their places, than in the sense of the words; the one signifying to Lead, the other to Govern; so as he that formerly was a servant for the occasion, afterwards became a servant for life; yet cloathed with Majesty, like some bitter Pill covered with Gold, to make the service better tasted. Nor was the place more desirable, if duly considered. For first, his Title rested upon the good opinion of the Freemen; and it seemeth to be one of the best Gems of the Crown, for that he was thereby declared to be most worthy of the love and service of the people...

Secondly, this Election was qualified under a stipulation or covenant, wherein both Prince and people were mutually bound to each other; the people to defend their King, which the historian [*margin*: Tacitus] saith was *praecipium Sacramentum*; and the Prince to the people to be no other than the influence of the Law, suitable to that saying of Aethelstan, the Saxon King, *Seeing I according to your Law allow you what is yours, do you so with me*; as if the Law were the sole umpire between King and people, and unto which not only the people, but also the King must submit...

So as 'tis evident, the Saxons fealty to their King, was subservient to the publick safety; and the publick safety is necessarily dependant upon the liberty of the Laws. Nor was it to be expected that the Saxons would endure a King above this pitch. For those parts of Germany (whence they came) that had the Regiment of Kings (which these had not) yet used they their Kings in no other manner than as Servants of State, in sending them as Embassadors and Captains as if they claimed more interest in him than he in them: And the Historian [Tacitus] saith expressly, that amongst those people in Germany that had Kings, their Kings had a defined power, and were not *supra libertatem*.

And, thus, upon all the premises I shall conclude, that a Saxon King was no better than a *primum mobile* set in regular motion, by Laws established by the whole body of the Kingdom. [51]

Neither the Danish nor the Norman invasion altered old Saxon custom:

I have endeavoured to refresh the Image of the Saxon Commonwealth, the more curious lineaments being now disfigured by time. Afar off it seems a Monarchy, but in approach discovers more of a Democracy... The first great change it felt was from the Danes that stormed them, and shewed therein much of the wrath both of God and Man. And yet it trenched not upon the fundamental Laws of the people's Liberty. [52]

Bacon refutes the theory that Duke William acquired a title to absolute power by conquest:

Some there are that build upon passionate notes of Angry Writers, and do conclude that the Duke's way and Title was wholly by Conquest, and thence infer strange aphorisms of state destructive to the government of this Kingdom. Let the reader please to peruse the ensuing particulars, and thence conclude as he shall see cause. [53]

Bacon's refutation depends on the evidence he adduces that William's "coronation questionless was the same with that of the Ancient Saxon kingdom," "that the government of the Normans proceeded upon the Saxon principles, and first of Parliaments," that there remained "the immunities of the Saxon free-men under the Norman Government," and that "the entry of the Normans into this Island could not be by conquest" for these several reasons. [54]

[51] *Ibid.*, pp. 29-31.
[52] *Ibid.*, p. 69.
[53] *Ibid.*, p. 72.
[54] *Ibid.*, chapters xlv-l, inclusive.

Summarizing, Bacon declares: "And thus I have brought the shape of English Government (rude as it is) from the first off-spring of the Saxons, through the rough waves of the Danish tempests, the rocks of Norman invasion, and of the Quicksands of Arbitrary government under Popes and Kings to the Haven." [55]

Bacon's comprehensive study of Anglo-Saxon antiquities is a landmark in the growth and development of the Gothic tradition in England. The sentence which closed his book uttered a hope which, no doubt, was being silently expressed in the hearts of many Englishmen now that they had been taught to know their ancient liberties: "I now conclude... if we may attain the happiness of our Forefathers, the ancient Saxons, Quilibet contentus sorte propria." [56]

Recalling Bacon's statement, "Nor can any Nation upon earth shew so much of the ancient Gothique law as this Island hath," the six editions of the *Historical Discourse* [57] firmly implanted in English minds the association of the Goths with a native tradition of democratic liberties.

John Sadler's distinction between the merely judiciary power of the House of Lords and the legislative function of Commons is a new development in democratic theory. Sadler cites the combined evidence of Verstegen and Tacitus:

That the Commons, should have Most Right, to the Power Originall, or Legislative, in Nature; I shall leave to be disputed by others. I shall only touch some few particulars, which have sometimes made me to suspect that by our Laws, and Modle of this Kingdom, it Both was, and should be so. How the Roman Historian found the Judiciall Power, given to the Lords, by our old Ancestors, I did observe before: He is as plain, for the Legislative in the Commons. Nay, to the Lords, themselves, he saith, in Judging, was adjoyned by a Committee of Commons,

---

[55] *Ibid.*, p. 199.

[56] *Ibid.*, p. 178, "The Second Part" (separate pagination).

[57] 1647, 1672 (the government seizes and burns copies, the publisher prosecuted), 1682, 1688, 1739, 1760.

Both for Counsle, and Authority: Ex Plebe Comites; Consilium simul et Authoritas. And again, he sheweth, how the Lords did sit in Councell, about the Less Affaires; but of Greater, All, Both Lords and Commons. [58]

The sources of Sadler's Gothic ideas are Verstegen, Horn, and a "Roman Historian" who can be none other than Tacitus, judging from his translation of the passage "de minoribus..."

And of our Saxon Ancestors, the *Miror* is very plain, that they did Elect, or chuse, Their King from among themselves... In this, we might appeal to Tacitus, of our Ancestors, or Theirs: Who did both Elect, and Bound Their Kings and Generalls: but Most of all, their Kings. Reges ex Nobilitate, Duces ex Virtute sumunt: and of their Kings (he saith) the Power was so Bounded, that he could not call it Free. Nec Infinita, aut Libera Potestas. And that, in Concilis, Their Kings Authority, was in perswasion, rather then Command. Suadendi potius quam Jubendi potestate. [59]

Sadler repeats the pivotal passage from Tacitus: "None doubt, Tacitus speaketh of our Saxon Ancestours (or rather Theirs); in that, of their Choosing Kings and Generalls (Reges ex Nobilitate, Duces ex virtute); by Common Councell in ijusdem Conciliis, Eliguntur & Principes, de Majoribus, Omnes Consultant." [60]

Marchamont Nedham also finds in the past tribal assemblies, regulating the affairs of the nation and electing a *dux bellorum* to serve in time of war. Nedham is obviously following Samuel Daniel, even to the extent of actual phrasing:

In our Country here, before the time that Caesar's Tyranny tooke place, there was no such thing as Monarchy: For, the same Caesar tells us, how the Britains were divided into so many severall States; relates how Cassevelaunus was, by the Common Councell of the Nation, elected in this their publique danger, to

[58] *Rights of the Kingdom; or, Customs of Our Ancestors: Touching the Duty, Power, Election, or Succession of Our Kings and Parliaments* (London, 1649), p. 88.

[59] *Ibid.*, p. 35.

[60] *Ibid.*, p. 79.

have the principall administration of the State with the businesse of Warre...And now we see all the Westerne World (lately discovered) to bee, and generally all other Countries are, *in puris naturalibus,* in their first and most innocent condition, setled in the same Form, before they came to be inslaved, either by so predominant power from abroad; or some are among Themselves more potent and ambitious than his Neighbors. And such was the State heretofore, not onely of our Nation, but of Gaule, Spaine, Germany, and all the West parts of Europe, before the Romans did by strength and cunning unlock their Liberties. And such as were then termed Kings were but as their Generalls in War, without any other great Jurisdiction. [61]

The wide dissemination of the Gothic propaganda for the freedom of old English institutions is reflected in Hobbes's political theories. The position which Hobbes took on the elective Saxon *dux bellorum* is thoroughly consistent with the doctrine of absolute monarchical supremacy which he expounded in his political writings. The identical naturalistic basis which he provided for social ethics by reducing human nature to the simple qualities of egotism and self-preservation is reflected in his conception of the Saxon brought together out of fear and weakness to form a state. Unlike the Gothicists, however, he draws radically different conclusions from the fact of the Saxon liberties. His argument is developed in a dialogue:

*B.* Before you go any further, I desire to know the Ground and Original of that Right, which either the House of Lords, or the House of Commons, or both together, now pretend to.
*A.* It is a question of Things so long ago past, that they are now forgotten. Nor have we any Thing to conjecture by, but the Records of our own Nation, and some small and obscure Fragments of Roman Histories: And for the Records, seeing they are of Things done only, sometimes justly, sometimes unjustly, you can never, by them, know what Right they had, but only what Right they pretended to.

[61] *The Case of the Common-Wealth of England Stated* (London, 1650). pp. 83-84.

*B.* However, let me know what Light we have in this Matter from the Roman Histories.

*A.* It would be too long, and a useless Digression, to cite all the ancient Authors that speak of the Forms of those Commonwealths, which were amongst our first Ancestors, the Saxons, and other Germans, and of other Nations, from whom we derive the Titles of Honour now in use in England; nor will it be possible to derive from them any Argument of Right, but only Examples of Fact, which, by the Ambition of potent Subjects, have been oftener unjust than otherwise. And for those Saxons or Angles, that in ancient Times by several invasions, made them Masters of this Nation; they were not in themselves one Body of a Commonwealth, but only a League of divers petty German Lords and States, such as was the Grecian army in the Trojan War, without Obligation, than that which proceeded from their own Fear and Weakness. Nor were those Lords, for the most part, the Sovereigns at Home in their own Country, but chosen by the People for the Captains of the Forces they brought with them. [62]

Despite his admission, which would bring him into agreement with the Gothicists, that the Saxon ruler was not a *princeps* but a *dux bellorum,* it is interesting to see how Hobbes finds in this admission proof of his theory of royal absolutism.

He is utterly consistent in his thinking. We recall that in the *Leviathan* Hobbes argued that the monarch derived his absolute power from the transfer to him of the natural rights of the people. In Hobbes's analysis, the people had fled from the brutish state of nature in order to secure the safety afforded by society. In order to compose the social state the people drew up a compact in which they willingly gave up certain rights in exchange for the protection that the compact guaranteed. These rights were then transferred to the monarch who

[62] *Behemoth: The History of the Causes of the Civil War of England...from the Year 1640 to the Year 1660* (published 1679), in Francis Maseres' *Select Tracts Relating to the Civil Wars in England* (London, 1815), p. 528.

can rule efficiently because he unites in his person all the rights. Hobbes argues, therefore, that the Saxons had made an incomplete transfer of their rights to their ruler as shown by two facts: they elevated the ruler only to the status of a *dux bellorum*; and they reserved some of the power by insisting on a right to oppose the ruler's decisions by force if necessary. It is little wonder, then, that Hobbes scorns the Gothic conception of limited authority. To a thinker like Hobbes, monarchical sovereignty is meaningless unless the transfer of power to the king is complete. Hobbes revives the Royalist theory that parliaments exist only as a favor, *ad placitum,* bestowed by a gracious king. That is, he is willing to allow some mark of favor to be bestowed on those who aided the Saxon *dux bellorum* in their migrations, but the favor must not be taken for a right:

And therefore it was not without Equity, when they had conquered any part of the Land, and made some one of themselves King thereof, that the rest should have greater Privileges than the common People and Soldiers. And amongst these Privileges a Man may easily conjecture this to have been one. That they should be made acquainted, and be of Council, with him that hath the Sovereignty, in matters of Government, and should have the greatest and most honorable offices, both in Peace and War. *But because there can be no Government where there is more than one Sovereign,* it cannot be inferr'd, that they had a Right to oppose the King's Resolutions by Force, nor to enjoy those Honours and Places longer than they should continue good Subjects. And we find that the Kings of England, did, upon every great Occasion, call them together, by the Name of discreet and wise men of the Kingdom, and hear their Counsel, and make them Judges of all Causes that, during their setting, were brought before them. But, as he summon'd them at his own Pleasure, so had he also ever the Power, at his own Pleasure to dissolve them. [63]

An interesting sidelight on historiography, as Hobbes under-

---

[63] *Ibid.,* p. 528.

stands it, and as it contrasts with the point of view of the Gothicists, is his disparagement of the historical account of the Goths. He finds the historical record unsatisfactory for the surprising reason that it is based on "only examples of fact" without "any Argument of Right." This rather cryptic statement becomes clearer when seen from the naturalistic viewpoint which Hobbes held in establishing his system of ethics. He tells us how deeply he was impressed by his discovery of Euclid's *Geometry* and of his resolve to develop a comprehensive system of thought based on similar a priori, self-evident principles. He consequently disparages the "examples of Fact" in the Gothic histories because they do not tell of what should have been, according to a priori principles of right, but only of what actually was. Contrariwise, the belief of the Gothic pamphleteers that they were telling only the facts of past history, as they found them, was their claim to receive a hearing.

Milton's contemptuous treatment of the Britons and Saxons in the *History of Britain* (first four books completed by 1649) would appear to exclude Milton immediately from among those defenders of democracy called in this study "Gothicists." Actually, however, the *Pro populo Anglicano defensio,* written approximately one year later, reveals Milton upholding the same doctrine of Gothic freedom which we have seen being asserted by a large number of writers on the basis of arguments drawn from implications of England's traditional political inheritances from the past.

The facts of the publication of the *Defence* are well known. Claudius Salmasius had been commissioned to write a treatise attacking the regicides, and produced the *Defensio regia pro Carolo I*; Milton's *Defence* was Cromwell's official reply. All of the usual Royalist arguments are in Salmasius' tract. He asserts the King's absolute power by title of conquest and by the patriarchal theory. By citations drawn from the Old Testament describing the Hebrew example, he demands passive obedience to the King. From the example of the bee kingdom, he argues that divine right is grounded in the "law of nature." Finally, Salmasius asserts that Tacitus, properly read, is on the side of royal absolutism. [64] Abusive and even gross with his enemy, Milton is never so effective in the *Defence* as when he ridicules Salmasius' scholarship:

But, Tacitus, say you, that lived under the government of a single person, writes thus: 'The gods have committed the sovereign power in human affairs to princes only, and have left to subjects the honor of being obedient.' But you tell us not where Tacitus has these words, for you were conscious to yourself, that you imposed upon your readers in quoting them; which I presently smelt out, though I would not find the place of a sudden: for that expression is not Tacitus' own, who is an approved writer and of all others the greatest enemy of tyrants; but Tacitus relates that of M. Terentius, a gentleman of Rome, being accused of a capital crime, amongst other things that he said to save his life, flattered Tiberius in this manner. It is in the Sixth Book of his Annals [*Annals* 6, 8, 7]: 'The Gods have entrusted you with the ultimate judgment in all things; they have left us the honor of obedience.' And you cite this passage as if Tacitus said it himself; you scrape together whatever seems to make for your opinion, either out of ostentation, or out of weakness; you would leave out nothing that you could find in a baker's or a barber's shop; nay, you would be glad of anything that looked like an argument, from the very hangman. If you had read Tacitus himself, and not transcribed some loose quotations out of him by other authors, he would have taught you whence that imperial right had its original. 'After the conquest of Asia,' says he, 'the whole state of our affairs was turned upside down: nothing of the ancient integrity of our forefathers was left amongst us; all men shook off that former equality which had been observed and began to have reverence for the mandates of princes.' This you might have

[64] The folio Elzevir edition (Lugduni Batavorum, 1649), pp. 150, 181, 335. For a complete bibliography of the numerous editions of Salmasius' work and the thirteen editions of Milton's reply, see F. F. Madan, "Milton, Salmasius, and Dugard," *Library*, IV (1923), 119-145.

learned out of the Third Book of his Annals [*Annals*, 3.26, 5-6], whence you have all your legal right. 'When that ancient quality was laid aside, and instead thereof ambition and violence took place, tyrannical forms of government started up, and fixed themselves in many countries.' [65]

Instead of Salmasius' forged Tacitus, Milton produces the now familiar passage from the *Germania* describing the Germanic tribal assembly: "Neither is the regal power among the Germans absolute and uncontrollable; lesser matters are disposed and ordered by the princes; greater affairs by all the people. The king or prince is more considerable by the authority of his persuasions, than by any power that he has of commanding. This is out of Tacitus." [66]

Milton's description of the Saxon witenagemot assimilates the *Germania* to English political history in the manner of all the Gothic propaganda for Parliament's privileges:

You say that 'there is no mention of parliaments held under our kings that reigned before William the Conqueror.' It is not worth while to jangle about a French word: the thing was always in being: and you yourself allow that in the Saxon times, Concilia Sapientum, Wittenagemots are mentioned. And ther are wise men among the body of the people as amongst the nobility... Remember that the Saxons were of a German extract, who never invested their kings with an absolute, unlimited power, but consulted in a body of the more weighty affairs of Government; whence we may perceive, that in the time of our Saxon ancestors parliaments (the name itself excepted) had the supreme authority. The name they gave them was 'counsels of wise men.' [67]

The *History of Britain,* however, is cut from another piece of cloth: "The Saxons were a barbarous and heathen Nation, famous for nothing else but robberies and cruelties to all

---

[65] *Defence of the People of England,* edited by J. A. St. John, in the Bohn edition of Milton (London, 1848), I, 128-129.

[66] *Ibid.,* I, 134; see *Germania,* vii, xi, in *Complete Works of Tacitus,* edited, with an introduction, by M. Hadas (New York: The Modern Library, 1942).          [67] *Defense,* I, 167ff.

thir Neighbors, both by Sea and Land." Their predecessors, the Britons were equally bad: "Britains never more plainly manifested themselves to be right Barbarians; no rule, no foresight, experience or estimation, either of themselves or their enemies." [68] The contrast between the *Defence* and the *History* is complete. The faith declared in the one document in old English virtue and capacity for self-rule is unequivocally denied in the other.

While the *Defence* is interesting because it reflects the use being made of Tacitus throughout the seventeenth century in behalf of democracy, the *History* is of far greater importance. The *History* brings to light, as no other document in the Gothic tradition does, that as between the two elements in the tradition—political inheritances, and racial inheritances—there was an essential opposition.

The real theme of the opening books of the *History,* dealing with the Britons and Saxons, is not so much their barbarism, intractability, and so forth, as it is their racial psychology. Their barbarism, that is, is a result not a cause. Milton sees the British as a people with a special predilection for liberty, but, he adds, the defect of their racial quality is such that their liberty speedily degenerates into license:

For Britain, to speak truth not often spoken, as it is a land fruitful enough of men stout and courageous in war, so it is naturally not over-fertile of men able to govern justly and prudently in peace, trusting only in their mother-wit; who consider not justly, that civility, prudence, love of the public good, more than money or vain honour, are to this soil in a manner outlandish, grown not here, but in minds well implanted with solid and elaborate breeding, too impolitic else and rude, if not headstrong and intractable to the industry and virtue either of executing or understanding true civil government. Valiant indeed and prosperous to win a field; but to know the end and reason of winning, injudicious and unwise: in good or bad success, alike unteachable. [69]

[68] *History of Britain,* in Bohn edition, V, 211.    [69] *Ibid.,* V, 240.

It is significant that Milton is subsuming the British instance under a general observation on liberty: "For libertie hath a sharp and double-edge, fitt onlie to be handl'd by just and vertuous men, to bad and dissolute, it becomes a mischief unwieldie in thir own hands." [70] This holds true for all people (actually he has been describing the decay of Rome), but the problem is especially aggravated in England because of the unusual endowment of strength and valor in the English national character. [71] It is especially true of the English that having a double capacity for freedom, a double amount of prudent restraint would be necessary:

For although at first greedy of change, and to be thought the leading nation to freedom from the empire they seemed awhile to bestir themselves with a shew of diligence in their new affairs, some secretly aspiring to rule, others adoring the name of liberty, yet so soon as they felt by proof of the weight of what it was to govern well themselves, and what was wanting within them, not stomach or the love of licence, but the wisdom the virtue, the labour, to use and maintain true liberty, they soon remitted their heat, and shrunk more wretchedly under the burden of their own liberty, then before under a foreign yoke. [72]

Two conclusions may be drawn from this evidence. In the first place, Milton is echoing the racial ideas in the *translatio* thought-complex. He clearly has in mind the conception of the German humanist-reformers which stressed the distinctive

[70] Columbia *Milton,* "The Digression," X, 324. For the place of the "Digression" in the *History,* see the editorial notes at the end of this edition.

[71] There is undoubtedly a climate theory affecting the argument here, as Prof. Z. S. Fink has shown in his "Milton and the Theory of Climatic Influence," *Modern Language Quarterly,* II (1941), 67-80; Fink, however, exaggerates its importance, since the Romans do not fall in the category of a northern people, valorous in character but with the accompanying defect of imprudence in managing the liberties they have won. The *translatio* is the effective idea here.

[72] *History,* Bohn edition, V, 241.

entity of the German folk by virtue of their invincibility, manliness, and so forth. In the *Defensio secunda* (1654), written to answer the critics of the *Defensio prima*, the prophetic mood engendered by the *translatio* theory is explicit: "I seem to survey, as from a towering height, the far extended tracts of sea and land, and innumerable crowds of spectator betraying in their looks the liveliest interest, and sensations the most congenial with my own. Here I behold the stout and manly prowess of the Germans disdaining servitude." [73]

In the second place, the Miltonic genius, revealed grandly in the poems, is impressed on these passages describing the failure of democracy—for racial reasons—in old English life. Milton, as is very well known, began as a champion of the people; but he became progressively disillusioned about the capacity of the people to rule themselves. Toward the end, with increasing bitterness, he even sponsored the far from democratic idea that only the godly should rule and impose from above their moral enlightenment on the unregenerate sinners who compose the "mob." He saw the prize of liberty within the grasp of the Long Parliament, but he saw too the prize running quickly through its fingers, lost through lack of prudence:

> License they mean when they cry libertie;
> For who loves that first must be wise and good. [74]

[73] Bohn edition, I, 219-220. My opinion is that the famous eagle passage in the *Areopagitica* (in II, 94, of the Bohn edition) was written with Brant's poem on the falcons in mind, not only because of the bird imagery but because of the underlying conception of a glorious destiny awaiting the Germanic peoples. Not to Hebrew prophetic sources but rather to the same *translatio* theory, I would also relate those Miltonic utterances expressing his belief that God had revealed himself first to the English.

[74] "On the detraction which followed upon my writing certain treatises," second poem entitled, "On the same," in Columbia *Milton*, I, 63.

The lesson which Adam and Eve learn is "liberty rightly used." The problem facing Milton's matured intellect in *Samson Agonistes* was the need for a double amount of restraint to insure the wise use of a double amount of strength. From Gildas onward, all English historians harped on the theme of British sinfulness. Milton, at first glance, may seem merely to have picked up the burden of the song. Actually, however, from the viewpoint of the Gothic tradition, his diatribe on old English immorality has a deeper significance since it is allied so closely with a national apotheosis of democracy and a prophecy of a special destiny of "better things to come" for the English nation.

Milton sees old English immorality not as ordinary sinfulness but specifically as the folly of a people who have an exceptional genius for liberty but who lack the requisite wisdom to reap its fruits in a democratic government. Milton's erudition was massive in the classics, Hebrew literature, contemporary Reformation tracts, and so forth; but perhaps as no other doctrine or dogma could, Milton's bifurcation of the two elements in the Gothic tradition (the racial inheritances which prevent the English from achieving the political inheritance of democracy) sharpened his perception of the crucial philosophic problem facing his poetic maturity. For the sake of a brawl with Salmasius it may have been satisfactory to assert the Englishman's tradition of democratic self-rule. But looking backward to the *History,* the passages in the *Defence* praising Saxon parliaments are pure nostalgia. Almost all Milton commentators agree that there is a causal relationship between Milton's rejection of the national themes listed in the commonplace book and his decision to write instead a religious epic. In this connection, the importance of the passages in the *History* on the national apotheosis of democracy (or rather the national failure—for racial reasons—to achieve a democracy) has been overlooked or, inter-

preted outside of the Gothic tradition of liberty and enlightenment to which they belong, has been misunderstood.

The Gothic doctrines were attacked on both wings, by the
Royalists on the right, by the Levellers on the left. [75] The
Levellers went back to an even more venerable antiquity than
did the Gothicists, for they went back to the Biblical paradise.
There the Levellers found evidence of a natural law anterior
to and of higher validity than the secular law preserved in
parliaments. As a result of the Leveller pressure from the left,
we find a new development or change of emphasis in the
Gothic tracts written after 1649. The Gothicists now defend
the idea of an "organic Parliament." They resist simultaneously republicanism, Leveller left-wing ideas, and conquest theories of Royalism by affirming steadfastly that King
and Commons together compose a valid government. Against
Royalists, the argument remained that the king never held
by conquest, he must rule under the sovereign law as enacted
by parliaments ever since the days of the Saxons. Against
Levellers, the argument is to the effect that the "natural law"
is a chimaera—the venerable tradition of tribal assemblies
and parliaments is a surer foundation on which to build.

William Prynne, for example, singles out for attack Lilburne
and Cannes of the Leveller faction. He condemns their repudiation of the past in favor of a "natural law." He names
them among the party "who are grown so desperately im-
pudent, as not only to write, but publikely to assert in print,
in Books printed by Authority (even in Capitals in every Title
page) That the Freemen and People have no such unalterable
Fundamental Laws and Liberties left them by their forefathers." [76]

[75] See Appendix B, "The Levellers: Climax and Crisis in the Gothic
Tradition."

[76] *The first and Second Part of a Seasonable Legal, and Historical
Vindication and Chronological Collection of the Good, Old, Fundamental Liberties* (London, 1654-55), p. 3.

The Presbyterian majority in Parliament had for some time been working for the return of the King, without granting, however, the Royalist thesis that the King had absolute power. Although the radicals in the New Model Army accused them of turning the tradition of parliamentary liberalism into a mockery, in their pamphlets the Presbyterians still argued for an organic Parliament under sovereign law which would restrain the King. Prynne gave expression to these ideas on the basis, curiously, of the myth of Brutus, the founder of the nation. He argues the point that English kings are not elective and subject to popular recall by asserting Brutus to have been the first of a line of hereditary monarchs. But he also establishes parliamentary privileges in the claim that Brutus' first act was to convene a parliament: "An Hereditary Kingdome and Monarchicall Government by Kings, was the original Fundamentall Government setled in this Island by Brute." [77]

He sums up his position:

In this History of our first British King, Brute, we have these 5 remarkable particulars.
1. A warre to shake off Slavery, and recover publick Liberty.
2. A kinde of Generall Parliamentary Councill summoned by Brute, of all the elders of Briton, to advise of Peace, Warre, and of their common safety and affaires.
3. A resolution against killing even a Tyrannical oppressing King, taken in the field of Battle, out of Covetousnesse to enjoy his Crown and Dominions, as a most wicked Act.
4. A setling of an hereditary Kingly Government in this Isle upon the very first plantation of the Britons in it.
5. Lawes made and given to the people, whereby they might live peacably without injury or oppression. [78]

It is noticeable that Prynne manages to combine a belief in the legend of Brutus with an admiration for Verstegen, to whom he refers as "our great antiquary Richard Verstegen

[77] *Ibid.*, p. 4.          [78] *Ibid.*, p. 6.

in his *Restitutions of Decayed Intelligence,"* who scoffed at the legend. [79]

Marchamont Nedham, like Prynne, also combines an attack on the Levellers with pro-Gothicism. He describes the Levellers as those who "by placing the supreme power of making and repealing Lawes in the People, do aime to establish a meere popular Tyrannie, which they will assure unto themselves, under the Notion of the People, to the destruction of our Laws and Liberties." [80] But in another tract which exploits ideas in the Gothic tradition, Nedham, as we have seen, seeks to establish that the king originally was not a *princeps* but a *dux bellorum*. Nedham's theory of the limited elective monarch, depending as it does upon the conception that the law is sovereign and restrains the king within his prerogative, is entirely in harmony with his denunciation of Leveller "popular Tyrannie" as subversive of the law. His political theories are, like Pyrnne's, typical of the Commonwealth period in that they had to contend with the radicalism of the Levellers.

The Gothicism of James Harrington, author of *The Commonwealth of Oceana* (1656) is another typical product of the revolutionary decades in that it proposed an economic solution to the problem of settling the "interests" of the nation raised by Levellers when they proposed that the "people's interest" should be dominant in the nation as the only guarantee of permanent peace. Harrington's originality consists in his ingenious adaptation of the facts of Gothic history to his economic solution of the problem.

The main idea which Harrington proposed was a settling of what he called the "orders" in the state. His originality consisted in his contention that a state regardless of its form —monarchical, aristocratic, or democratic—is stable in the

[79] *Ibid.,* p. 386.
[80] *A Plea for the King and Kingdome* (London, 1648), pp. 24-25.

degree that the landed interest coincides exactly with the public or common interest. Practically, this would mean that the property in land be divided equally so that a mutual public interest or establishing of "orders" would follow automatically. Conversely, according to Harrington, too large a property interest within one small class would aggrandize the real political power of that class and create stresses and strains in the state. Harrington worked out his economic interpretation of the causes underlying the creation of states by a demonstration that the Gothic invasion of Rome was the original source of the unsettling of "orders" in the modern state. He thus created a new role for the Goths in history. Gothicism, in this interpretation of history, becomes a principle of economic disequilibrium in the state. It is, however, important to see that "Gothicism" may characterize any class in the state, not only the "people," when that class has an undue amount of power through undue accumulation of landed property. Actually, however, the sweep of history which Harrington takes in points to the "people" as the Goths of history, since all tendencies showed the gradual aggrandizement of power in the hands of the "people." Harrington would check this power by restraints imposed by members of the aristocracy.

Underlying Harrington's analysis was Aristotle's well-known treatment of the three forms of state—monarchical, aristocratic, and democratic—and the characteristic defects of each. In the Utopian state of Oceana which Harrington projected, there was first of all no monarch. Harrington was a Republican who was convinced that monarchy, reaching the perfection of its kind, must necessarily cause an undue acquisition of power to the king or to his favourites whom he would bribe with gifts of land. If monarchy is ruled out, the remaining alternatives are aristocracy and democracy. In his account of English history, Harrington's charge against Henry

VIII was that his confiscation of the abbey lands and their sale to the middle classes caused a shift of political power to the people. As a direct result, the King eventually lost his throne to the people in the 1640's. In *Oceana,* Harrington proposed a remedy. In a senate there would be active collaboration between the aristocrats and people by a division of functions or checks and a system of balances, resting upon an economic base of equally divided landed property, which would insure, as Harrington saw it, a settling of "orders" in the state or a public interest congruous with the interest of each class in the state. Harrington naturally ridiculed the theory of social compact since he could see in it only a political sophistry which ignored the essential economic fact that political supremacy always followed ownership of land; the propertyless class, he pointed out, has no interest in joining a compact—it has only an interest in gaining property as quickly as possible, and that means political unrest.

Harrington divides universal political history into two periods, the ancient and the modern, the latter instituted by the Goths:

Janotti, the most excellent describer of the Common-wealth of Venice, divideth the whole Series of Government into two Times or Periods. The one ending with the liberty of Rome, which was the course or Empire, as I may call it, of antient prudence, first discovered unto mankind by God himself, in the fabrick of the Commonwealth of Israel, and afterwards picked out of his footsteps in nature, and unanimously followed by the Greeks and Romans. The other beginning with the Arms of Caesar; which extinguishing liberty were the Transition of ancient into modern prudence, introduced by those inundations of Huns, Goths, Vandalls, Lombards, Saxons, which breaking the Roman Empire, deformed the whole face of the world, with those ill features of Government, which at this time are become far worse in these Western parts, except Venice, (which escaping the hands of the Barbarians, by vertue of her impregnable situation, hath her eye fixed upon ancient Prudence; and is attained to a perfection even beyond her Copy). [81]

He then proceeds to the definitions of absolute monarchy, mixed monarchy, and popular government:

If one man be sole Landlord of a Territory, or overballance the people, for example, three parts in four, he is Grand Segnior: for so the Turk is called from his Property; and his Empire is absolute Monarchy.

If the Few or a Nobility, or a Nobility with the Clergy be Landlords, or overballance the people unto the like proportion, it makes the Gothick ballance (to be shewn at large, in the second part of this Discourse) and the Empire is mixed Monarchy, as that of Spain, Poland, and late of Oceana. [Oceana here is not the projected utopia but the historical England.]

And if the whole people be Landlords, or hold the Lands so divided among them, that no one man, or number of men, within the compasse of the Few or Aristocracy, overballance them, the Empire (without the interposition of force) is a Commonwealth. [82]

Harrington is an aristocrat Republican, as he presently makes clear. That is, he condemns that phase of English history characterized by a "Gothick ballance" because the nobles had undue influence; but a collaboration of nobles and people is his ideal: "Wherefore as in this place I agree with Machiavell that a Nobility or Gentry overballancing a popular Government, is the utter bane and destruction of it; so I shall shew in another, that a Nobility or Gentry in a popular Government not overballancing it, is the very life and soul of it." [83]

While controverting Hobbes, whom he calls Leviathan, Harrington again attacks the Gothic system:

Let me invite Leviathan, who of all other Governments giveth the advantage unto Monarchy for perfection, to a better disquisition of it, by these three assertions:

The first, That the perfection of Government lyeth upon such

[81] *Oceana* (Liljegren ed.), p. 12.
[82] *Ibid.,* p. 15.
[83] *Ibid.,* p. 18.

libration in the frame of it, that no man or men, in or under it, can have the interest; or having the interest, can have the power to disturb it with sedition.

The second, That Monarchy reaching the perfection of the kind, reacheth not unto the perfection of Government, but must have some dangerous flaw in it.

The third, That Popular Government reaching the perfection of the kind, reacheth the perfection of Government; and hath no flaw in it. [84]

The first assertion, Harrington says, "requireth no proof"; but in proof of the second, he remarks:

Monarchy, as hath been shown, is of two kinds, the one by Arms, the other by a Nobility [the Turkish, he says, was a monarchy by arms, and for an example of a monarchy by Nobility he refers to Oceana, meaning not the utopia but England.] And for a Monarchy by a Nobility, as of late in Oceana... it was not in the power or wit of Man to cure it of that dangerous flaw, That the Nobility had frequent interest and perpetual power by their Retainers and Tenants to raise Sedition... Wherefore Monarchy by a Nobility is no perfect Government;

Continuing, Harrington says that there never have been but two forms of monarchy, the Gothic example notwithstanding:

And there is no other kind in art or nature: for if there have been anciently some Governments called Kingdoms, as one of the Gothes in Spain, and another of the Vandals in Africa, where the King ruled without a Nobility, and by a Councill of the people only; it is expressly said by the Authors that mention them, that the Kings were but the Captains, and that the people not only gave them Lawes, but deposed them as often as they pleased; nor is it possible in reason that it should be otherwise in like cases: wherefore these were either no Monarchies, or had greater flawes in them then any other. [85]

Harrington, as has already been remarked, was an aristocrat Republican. He has a strong belief, as he expressed it, in "the genius of a gentleman," and he could see in the advisory senate composed of gentlemen a valuable reservoir of the ripe

---

[84] *Ibid.*, p. 30.          [85] *Ibid.*, p. 31.

wisdom which only a gentleman could give. Consequently, he is strongly denunciatory of the Gothic example wherein the king was not a *princeps* at all but a *dux bellorum,* deposable by the people, and further hampered by the absence of a noble class.

The second part of *Oceana* begins the historical account of governments, and Harrington says, "I shall endeavour to shew the Rise, Progresse, and Declination of Modern Prudence." He begins: "The date of this kind of Policy is to be computed, as was shewn, from those inundations of Goths, Vandals, Hunnes, and Lombards that overwhelmed the Roman Empire." [86] The essence of his historical account is the shift in landownership, which also caused a shift in power to the Goths and hence their seditious activity against the Romans. Beginning the account with the decline of the Roman republic, Harrington shows how the corrupt emperors tried to uphold their tottering power by bribing soldiers with gifts of land. This was the beginning of the upset in the land balance. When political unrest continued, the emperors hit on a new idea:

this was by stipendiating the Gothes, a people, that deriving their Roots from the Northern parts of Germany, or out of Sweden, had (thro their Victories obtained against Domitian) long since spread their Branches unto so near a Neighbourhood with the Roman Territories, that they began to overshade them. For the Emperors making use of them in their Arms (as the French do at this day of the Switz) gave them that, under the notion of a Stipend, which they receiv'd as a Tribute coming (if there were any default in the payment) so often to distrein for it, that in the time of Honorius they sack'd Rome and possesst themselves of Italy. And such was the transition of antient into modern Prudence; or that breach which being follow'd in every part of the Roman Empire with inundations of Vandals, Huns, Lombards, Franks, Saxons. [87]

Thus, as Harrington sees it, the shift in landownership to the Goths gave them undue power. Beginning his account of

[86] *Ibid.,* p. 39.          [87] *Ibid.,* p. 42.

English history, he traces the Teutonic influence on English political institutions in the feuds, or a characteristic aggrandizement of power within the nobility leading in time to the king's loss of power altogether. Previously, the people limited the monarchical power by exercising their influence in the "Weidenagamoots":

To open the ground-work or ballance of these new Politicians. Feudum, saith Calvine the Lawyer, is a Gothick word of divers significations: for it is taken either for War, or for a possession of conquered Lands, distributed by the Victor unto such of his Captaines and Souldiers as had merited in his wars, upon condition to acknowledge him to be their perpetuall Lord, and themselves to be his Subjects. [88]

Harrington then describes the feuds of three orders: Dukes, Barons, and Vavasors. Dukes are created by the Monarch, Barons by Dukes, and Vavasors by Barons; taken together, there is an interlocking system which nevertheless is chronically prone to sedition because of the shift in land power through land grants made by each of the feuds to the other in order to gain their loyalty. "This," says Harrington, "is the Gothick ballance by which all the Kingdoms this day in Christendome were at first erected."

The Teutons had the identical system of feuds but under different names:

The Romans having govern'd Oceana Provincially, the Teutons were the first that introduced the form of the late Monarchy: to these succeeded the Scandians, of whom (because their Raign was short as also because they made little alteration in the Government as to the Form) I shall take no notice. But the Teutons going to work upon the Gothick Ballance, divided the whole Nation into three sorts of Feuds, that of Eoldorman, that of Kings-Thane, and that of Middle Thane. [89]

The Saxon witenagemot becomes an important element in his argument. Of the "Weidenagamoots," he says:

---

[88] *Ibid.*  [89] *Ibid.*, p. 43.

I shall not omit to enlighten the obscurity of these times, in which there is little to be found of a Methodicall constitution of this High Court; by the addition of an Argument, which I conceive to bear a strong testimony unto it self, though taken out of a late Writing that conceals the Author: 'It is well known (saith he) that in every quarter of the Realm a great many Boroughs do yet send Burgesses unto the Parliament which neverthelesse, be so anciently and so long since decayed and gone to naught, that they cannot be shew'd to have been of any reputation since the Conquest, much lesse to have obtained any such priviledge by the grant of any succeeding King: wherefore these must have had this right by more ancient usage, and before the Conquest; they being unable now to shew whence they derived it.' This Argument (though they be more) I shall pitch upon, as sufficient to prove; First, that the lower sort of the people had right unto Session in Parliament during the time of the Teutons. [90]

Harrington is thus consistent throughout. The same opportunity which the Gothicists saw in the witenagemot for the free expression of the people's will, Harrington recognizes but condemns as the encroachment of a power in the state over the landed interest. Similarly, he condemns the feuds as inherently incapable of settling an established order as a result of its faulty manipulation of the landed property.

The *Oceana* was written in the lurid light of the recent events of the Commonwealth. Harrington continues the account of English history down to Henry VIII's misguided policy of arming the lower classes with political power through their purchases of the confiscated abbey lands. But Harrington was especially denunciatory of the new threat raised by the radical democrats. In *The Art of Law Giving,* published in 1659, he criticized the Leveller *Agreement of the People,* citing from it:

That these Representatives have Soveraign power, save that in some things the people may resist them by arms. Which first is a flat contradiction, and next is downright Anarchy. Where

[90] *Ibid.,* p. 45.

the Soveraign power is not intire and absolute as in Monarchy itself, there can be no Government at all. It is not the limitation of soveraign power that is the cause of a Commonwealth, but such a deliberation, or poyse of Orders, that there can be in the same no number of men having the interest, that can have the power; nor any number of men having the power that can have the interest to invade or disturb the Government. [91]

The *Oceana* is evidence of the extent to which the account of the Gothic invaders of Rome fertilized and guided the political thought of the period. Even in attacking the Gothic propaganda, Harrington put it to his service in making clear his guiding principle of politics—the economic basis upon which the superstructures of states are to be erected. Within the Gothic tradition which we are surveying, the *Oceana* takes on a new significance. It is testimony also of the passionate desire of the seventeenth century for a continuity, or a "poyse of orders" as Harrington expressed it, in political life. The Gothicists found the continuity in free parliaments and a constitutionally limited monarch, but in Harrington's economic interpretation of history Gothicism appears as the fatal flaw, the cause, in fact, of chronic strife. Finally, it may be worthwhile repeating the semantic problem: Harrington describes the land reforms brought about by Huns, Vandals, Burgundians, and so on, yet he describes the new land system as the "Gothic balance."

A tract by Sir Roger Twysden registers the readjustment of post-Leveller Gothic speculation to the extreme claims made for parliamentary sovereignty during the hectic 1640's. Peering into the past, Twysden also sees parliaments evolving out of the primitive tribal assemblies; but he sees an organic Parliament, a Parliament composed, that is, of the people and of a presiding chief. The vision of King-in-Parliament is constantly before Twysden's eyes. Consequently, Gothicism to Twysden means the old tribal assembly but an assembly which is in-

[91] *Art of Law Giving* (London, 1659), p. 8.

valid unless a chief presides. What is paramount in such a
view is the law prescribing the limits of King and Parliament
both.

We may even say of Sir Roger Twysden that he led a
"Gothic" life. He had been bullied by two kings and by
Parliament, but he refused to give up his faith. He refused to
pay Charles I ship money, but he also refused to pay the Long
Parliament an illegal tax for maintenance of troops. Alienated
from both a king and a parliament which had exceeded their
legal rights, he found in Charles II a new enemy. His last
political act as a servant of Charles II was typical. He resigned
his commission as a deputy lieutenant rather than aid in
squeezing from the people taxes to furnish uniforms and arms
for the militia. It was illegal, and he was against it.

Twysden's *Certaine Considerations Upon the Government
of England* finds that England of old had a limited monarchy:
"Our auncestors made choice of regall dominion, this island
having beene ever governed monarchically, before the Romans, and since; sometymes by many kings, and of late by
one; but allwayes soe temperd, as the Commons were ever
esteemed a free people." [92]

Chapter two, "Out of what respects the King is called a
Monarch," attacks "a learned treatise I have met with...which
would prove every monarch illimited. Monarchy is limited
by law." [93]

Chapter three, "Of the Kings of England, their Tytle by
Conquest," is the beginning of a historical attack on royal
absolutism: "I have resolved heere to sett downe historically
what I have met with concerning either of these." By either
of these, Twysden means the royal claim to absolutism and
the people's claim to absolutism; he is a scrupulously accurate

[92] *Certaine Considerations*, edited from the manuscript by J. M.
Kemble, Camden Society Publications, no. xlv (1849), p. 13.
[93] *Ibid.*, p. 15; in a note, the treatise is identified as Filmer's *The
Anarchy of a Limited or Mixed Monarchy* (London, 1648).

Gothicist who does not find in the tradition of free parliaments the right to depose kings claimed by the more extreme democrats as the corollary to the people's right to elect kings. Twysden is quite aware that he will be hanged by the Royalists and shot by the people's party: "I am confident," he says ironically,

I shall displease such as hold it altogether by descent or inheritance brought in by conquest, and not satifie the others, who hold it a right in the people so inherent to elect their kings, that the English nor any other monarch whatsoever can have any other title to the crowne originally but from the free consent of the people. [94]

With this preparation, Twysden says: "I shall now addresse myself to the matter: and first touching the Saxons."

The Saxons who transplantinge themselves hither, expelling the natives into Cornwall and Wales (excepting some few they might permit to live amongst them) must bee thought to have reteyned the usages they had in Germany; and indeed, as the affinitie yet in language betweene some of the Welsh and those in Britannia Armorica doe prove the one descended from the other, so mee thinkes wee see many dark draughts of the ould German manners with us yett remaininge; as that rejecting 'Fremitur' of which Tacitus [cites *Germania*] speaks is not so unlike the refusall by noes to this day used in the House of Commons. [95]

Chapter four sets out to prove "That the Saxon heere had not an absolute but only a limited power." Twysden says,

"Having shewne how the Saxons here did follow their owne manner in making a king, another thing Tacitus notes of them is, that in Germany kings had not 'infinitam aut liberam potestatem' [*Germania*, vii] and that in their publique councells they were indued 'auctoritate suadendi magis quam jubendi potestate' [*Germania*, xi]."

Twysden next surveys the Danish and Norman conquests

[94] *Ibid.*, p. 22.　　　　　　　[95] *Ibid.*, p. 26.

and denies that the kings gained title to absolute power by
these conquests. He thinks it illogical that had he claimed
absolute power he would have had peace. [96]

Twysden contends that the law is ample protection of the
people's liberties, and he is profoundly suspicious of attempts
to regain liberty by force of arms:

> First, I never yet read of any tooke them up who if they
> prospered did conteyn themselves within those boundes they at
> first held out; that is, the secret aime in all such warr is for
> other then what at the beginning they pretend unto; the open
> professions beeing ever the restoring justice to the oppressed
> people, but the secret, of those who carry on the designe, to
> rayse themselves by others' losse and ruine. [97]

It is not known when Twysden composed his manuscript,
which was never published in his lifetime, but it was patently
written with the events of the 1640's in mind. Twysden
retained faith in the Gothic doctrine of the "King in Parliament" and, like Montrose, really feared for the common people
if kingship were destroyed. Montrose appealed to the people:
"Do you not know, when the monarchical government is
shaken, the great ones strive for the garlands with *your* blood
and *your* fortune? Whereby you gain nothing...but shall
purchase to yourselves vultures and tigers to reign over
you." [98]

In chapter eleven, Twysden treats the history of parliaments:

> I conceive parlyaments brought hither from Germany, and so
> as old as the name of England hath belonged to this nation.
> That the Germans had it, their dyats doe at this day shew,
> which have little alteration from what was in Tacitus his tyme
> when 'de minoribus rebus principes consultant, de magnibus
> omnes,' ita tamen ut ea quoque penes plebem arbitrium est apud
> principes pertractentur. Which being in substance the same is
> held in such assemblies by them and us, I see no reason why

wee should assigne other beginning to either then the auntient custome of the Germans brought hither by the Saxons. [99]

Matthew Carter, author of *Honor Redivivus,* a kind of almanac of royalty and heraldry, describes the Saxon witenagemot:

The great Council did arise from the auntient custom of not only the Saxons, but all Nations in the world almost, who have had examples of their King's summoning the chief Peers and Nobles to consult in weighty affairs. Which Councel among the Saxons was called Wittenagemote, which was a meeting of the chief Prelates and Peers, to deliberate about, and to consent to, what new Laws the King should enact. [100]

Thomas Sheridan, author of *A Discourse on the Rise and Power of Parliaments* (1677), was a Royalist, remarkably fertile in progressive ideas. He proposed a milder criminal code, wished to extend poor relief and religious toleration, urged the need for vital statistics, and proposed the financial reforms which led in time to the founding of the Bank of England. Yet his *Discourse* stresses William's successful conquest. He says in part:

To omit the British times, of which we have but very thin gleanings of the Druids, their oracles of learning, law, and religion; and to skip over that of the Romans, who were never able perfectly to introduce their manner of commonwealth, we shall find that in the time of the Saxons a people of West Friesland, (so called from the shape of their sword, a kind of scimitar) and in that of the Danes, the manner of Government was as now in substance, though not in form or name, by king and parliament; but whether the Commons were called to this great assembly or no, I cannot find from the imperfect registers of elder times. One may guess they were originally members of it because the same people in West Friesland, do at this day

[99] *Ibid.,* p. 119.
[100] *Honor Redivivus, or, The Analysis of Honor and Armory* (3d ed.; London, 1673), p. 147.

continue a form of government, different from all the rest of the provinces, not unlike this. [101]

Sheridan, however, is willing to concede the Commons a small measure of power before the Conquest in order to bring out in contrast the Conqueror's complete subjection of the natives and his destruction of the older, free institutions:

Whatsoever the power of the Commons was before the Conquest, it plainly appears that for some time afterward their advice was seldom desired and as things were then ordered, their consent was not thought necessary, being always included in that of the Lords: for the Conqueror having subjected the natives to an entire vassalage, seized upon all their possessions, reserved to the crown large proportions in every county, gave part to the Church in frank almoigne, and the residue to his fellow adventurers in the war, to be held by knight service. [102]

Such Royalist attacks as Sheridan's on the power of Commons are backslidings to pre-Cromwellian theories of conquest. The Gothic arguments for free parliaments were, then, still useful. In dedicating his book to the Earl of Essex, William Petyt says:

There have been Authors of modern times, who have in their Writings, concerning the Government of this Kingdom, published to the World, That the Commons of England (as now phrased) were no part of the antient Commune Concilium, or Parliament of this Nation, before the forty ninth Year of H. 3. and then introduced by Rebellion.

A Position when seriously weighed, equally wounds the Peerage of England, since the same Authors say, that there is no formal Summons of the Lords to Parliament, found upon Record before that time.

After I had often considered so great a point, and having often read of the freedom of this Nation, that no Englishman could lose his right or property but by Law, the Life and Soul of this so famous and so excellently constituted Government, the

[101] *A Discourse on the Rise and Power of Parliaments* (London, 1677), printed in *Some Revelations in Irish History,* edited by Saxe Bannister (London, 1870), p. 18.

[102] *Ibid.,* pp. 20-21.

best polity upon Earth (which when united in all its parts by prudent Councils, made always the people happy at home in Peace, and the Crown ever Victorious abroad in War). I did resolve to take pains to search, if matters thus represented to the highest disadvantage and prejudice of the people were true or false, which I have industriously and impartially endeavoured with that clearness, that will evidence to all unbiased judgments, the unsoundness of those Opinions. [103]

Petyt then offers the evidence:

The Histories of our Country (if there were any) are not to be found, being either burnt by the Enemy, or carried beyond the Seas by the banished Brittons. Yet this is certain, and not to be denied, that in their elder time, the People or Freemen, had a great share in their publick Council and Government For Dion Cassius, or Xiphiline out of him in the Life of Severus assures us Apud hos i.e. Britannos populos magna ex parte principatum tenet. [104]

Turning from the Britons to the Saxons, he says:

It cannot be doubted that the Saxons who made themselves Masters of the British Nation, brought with them their Country Laws and Government; and that the Commons were an essential and constituent part of their Commune Concilium, Tacitus tells us De minoribus rebus Principes consultant, de majoribus omnes, ita tamen ut ea quoq; quorum penes plebum arbitrium est, apud Principes praetractentur. After the Saxon Government became united and fixed under a sole Christian Monarch they still continued and kept their antient Wittena Gemots, or Parliaments, as now phrased, wherein they made Laws and managed the great affairs of the King and Kingdom, according to the Plat-form of their Ancestors. [105]

He passes over the Danish government because he does not find "that there was any great mutation, either of the Council or Laws of the English Nation," [106] and deals with the Normans:

[103] *The Antient Right of the Commons of England Asserted. Or, A Discourse Proving by Records and the Best Historians, that the Commons of England were even an Essential part of Parliament* (London, 1680).

[104] *Ibid.*, p. 5.  [105] *Ibid.*, pp. 6-7  [106] *Ibid.*, p. 13.

Though William the Conqueror got the Imperial Crown of England, and introduced several Arbitrary Laws, as new Tenures, etc. yet did he never make such an absolute Conquest, nor did the Kingdom receive so universal a change, as our English modern Authors (as it were by a general Confederacy without examination of Truth) have published to the World, who father upon this revolution all the alterations which their conceits or fancies can imagine and suppose... The word Conquestor or Conqueror, did not in that Age import or signifie what our late Authors by flattery have since made it; nor did it carry with it the enslaving of the Nation; [107]

Petyt concludes with a spirited attack on "the late Authors" whom he now names:

And therefore I may with good reason and warranty conclude that our Ancestors, the Commons of England, the Knights Gentlemen, Freeholders, Citizens and Burgesses of a great and mighty Nation, were very far from being in former times such vassals and Slaves, or so abject, poor and inconsiderable, as the absurd and malicious ignorance and falsities of late Writers have been pleased to make and represent them, especially the Author of the *Grand Freeholders Inquest,* and Mr. James Howel, as if they were only Beasts of carnage and burden, ordained to be taxed and talliated, and have their Lives, Estates, and Liberties given away and disposed of without their own assents, under a novel opinion and conceit, that they were no part of the Commune Concilium Regni, or Parliament, before 49 H.3. [108]

Filmer's defense of royal absolutism brought down upon his head still another rebuttal, reasoned from the Gothic point of view. James Tyrrell, friend of Locke, author of *Patriarcha non monarcha,* wrote a large number of tracts which reflect much reading in the Gothic literature. He says, in reply to Filmer,

As for the Original of the Saxon Government, it is evident out of Tacitus and other Authours, that the Ancient Germans, from whom our Saxon Ancestors descended, and of which Nation they were a part, never knew what belonged to an absolute despotick

[107] *Ibid.*, pp. 17-18.
[108] *Ibid.*, p. 123.

power in their Princes. And after the Saxons coming in, and the Heptarchy having been erected in this Island, the Ancient form of Government was not altered, as I shall prove by and by; therefore though the Monkish Writers of those times have been short and obscure, in that which is most material in a History, viz. the form of their Government, and manner of succession to the Crown amongst them; stuffing up their books with unnecessary stories of miracles, and foundations of churches, and Abbeys: Yet so much is to be pickt out of them, that the Government of the West-Saxons which was that on which our Monarchy is grafted, was not despotical, but limited by Laws, that the King could not seise mens lands or goods without Process; that he could not make Laws without the consent of his Wittena Gemote or Great Councel: Nor take away mens lives, without a Legal trial by their Peers, and that this Government hath never been altered, but confirmed by their Successors both of the Danish and Norman Race. [109]

Replying to Filmer's argument that common law is but custom which came after government and therefore has not the same authority as government, Tyrrell points out that some parts of common law are coeval with government, as for example, councils; "So likewise Fundamental Constitution of ordering all publick Affairs in General Councils or Assemblies of the Men of Note, and those that had a Share in the Land. de minoribus rebus Principes consultant, de majoribus omnes, ita tamen ut ea quoque quorum penes plebem arbitrium est, apud Principes praetractentus." [110]

Under the general title *Bibliotheca Politica,* Tyrrell composed a series of thirteen dialogues, most of which reflect the Gothic arguments, and all of which combat Royalist theory. The dialogues were published separately in quarto from 1692 to 1694 and were reprinted together in folio in 1727. The first dialogue, entitled *A Brief Enquiry Into the Ancient Constitution and Government of England,* is a good indication of the general contents of the *Bibliotheca.* In the dialogue, F stands

[109] *Patriarcha non monarcha* (London, 1681), pp. 149-150.
[110] *Ibid.,* pp. 220-221.

for an understanding Freeholder and J for a Justice of Peace. F asks: "Pray whence do Kings now-a-days derive their Power (since God hath long since left off making any Kings by Divine Precept)? Whether it is from God, or from the People?" J replies: "I told you before, that all Power is from God and consequently Kingly Power must be too: yet this is so to be understood, that this Power cannot Rightfully be acquired without the People's Consent." [111]

An argument ensues concerning the King's title by conquest which is refuted to F's complete satisfaction. Whereupon F proceeds on a new line of questioning: "Pray satisfy me in the next place concerning the Government of England; you said it was a Limited Monarchy, and I have never heard that questioned; but how did this Limitation begin? Whether from the very first Institution of the Government, or else by the gracious Concessions of our Kings?" J replies:

Without doubt, Neighbour, from the very Institution of the Government; for our first English Saxon kings were made so by Election of the People, in their great Councils, or Parliaments (as we now call them) and could do nothing considerable either as to Peace or War without its Consent; and this Council was to meet of course once a year, without any Summons from the King, and oftner by his Summons, if there was any occasion for it; and it is certain that the Freemen of England have always from beyond all times of memory enjoyed the same Fundamental Rights and Privileges (I mean in substance) that they do at this day. [112]

Tyrrell also composed a *General History of England* (1698). In the introductory essay he identifies the Saxons:

And tho the English-Saxons were not immediately derived from the Germans but Goths, as you will find in the third Book of this Volume; yet since even the Germans themselves were derived from the same Gothick Original, with all the rest of those Northern People, as the Swedes, Danes, and Norwegians,

[111] *A Brief Enquiry* (London, 1694), p. 5.
[112] *Ibid.*, p. 107.

as appears by the Agreement of their Language, Customs, and Laws; I shall therefore suppose that in the main likewise they agreed with the antient Germans, as they are described by Tacitus in their Laws, Manners, and Religion; and therefore I shall from him give you some of the most considerable of them, as they are collected by Mr. Selden in his Learned Treatise, called *Jani Anglorum Facies Altera.*

The first of which is, In conciliis Rex Vel princeps, prout Aetas cuiq; prout Nobilitas, prout Decus Bellorum, prout Facundia est, audiuntur, Auctoritate suadendi magis quam jubendi potestate. Si displicuit Sententia fremitur aspernantur; sin placuit, frameas concutiunt. Honoratissimum assensus Genus est Armis laudare. Which for the Benefit of the Common Readers, I will take upon me to translate into English, viz.

In their Councils the King, or some Principal Person, according to every one's respective Age, Nobility, Reputation in Arms, or Eloquence, are heard, rather by the Authority of Perswading, than the Power of Commanding: if their Opinions displeased them, they shewed their dislike by their clamour; but if they approved of what was spoken, they struck their Launces one against another. This was taught the most Honorable way of giving Assent to approve by Arms. [113]

Tyrrell returns to the subject of the Saxon racial origins in book three, as he promised in his introduction:

As for the Original of these Saxons that now come into Britain, there is a much greater Dispute. Cluverius in his ancient Germany, as also our Country-Man Verstegan, in his Treatise, called *A Restitution of Decayed Intelligence,* Chap. 2. would needs have them to be derived from the Germans, which is denied by the Learned Grotius in his Prolegomena to the Gothic History, as also by Mr. Sheringham, in his Treatise *De Anglorum Gentis Origine,* where he undertakes to prove, that they were a Branch of the ancient Getae, who were the Posterity of Japhet: and coming out of Scythia into Europe, first fixt themselves under the conduct of one Eric their King in the ancient Scandinavia or Gothland, which is now called Sweden and Norway; and from thence some Ages after, under the Conduct of Berig, another of their Kings, sent out Colonies into all the Isles of the

[113] *General History of England* (London, 1698), pp. xxxv-xxxvi.

Baltick Sea, and the Northern Coasts of Norway, as far as Cimbric Chersonese, now Jutland; so that the Swedes, Danes, and Saxons, had one and the same Scythic Original, as the Learned Grotius in his said Prolegomena hath fully proved; as also Mr. Sheringham in Chap. 7. of his last-cited Treatise, as well as from the ancient Gothic Chronicles written in that Language, both in Prose and Verse; also from Jornandes de Rebus Geticis, Chap. 4. that these Getae or Goths multiplying more than these Countries would well bear, in the time of Filemar the 5th King after Berig, great multitudes of them under his Conduct removed their Dwellings into the Asiatic Scythia, called Oudin in their Language. [114]

The roster of authorities to whom Tyrrell refers or quotes indicates those writers who had established themselves as the key writers in the Gothic movement.

That the Saxons established democratic institutions and that William was not a conqueror are the theses of a tract entitled *Nil dictum quod non dictum prius or The Case of the Government of England established by Law* (1681), written by W. Disney. The Saxons were a "free people," asserts Disney:

The Roman Western Empire doomed to ruine, left the Brittish state in so weak a posture, it had not force sufficient to defend it's liberty, or secure it's safety, resolves to venture for a Cure which perhaps proved worse than the disease. Invites the Saxons to their succor (who made the weakness of their Hosts the argument for their usurpation of the Government) they were a free People governed by Laws and those made by their Voluntary Voting and Consent, not subject to any Arbitrary Power, and thereupon were call'd free. [115]

"William," says Disney, "was not a Conqueror" for he took the coronation oath "in the antient manner," the people's agreement with him "agreed with the tenor of the Saxon fealty." [116] Concluding his treatise, Disney finds that the Saxon institutions were free under the sovereign written law:

[114] *Ibid.,* p. 121.
[115] *Nil dictum quod non dictum prius* (London, 1681), p. 27.
[116] *Ibid.,* pp. 29-30.

So that when we reflect upon the foregone Discourse, and satisfie our selves, our Ancestors, whether we resolve our selves into the Brittish or Saxon Original, were Freemen, they were not otherwise so, then as they enjoyed the Liberty of their Laws, under their Governours or Kings, during the successive Continuance of those Powers. And it was an acknowledg'd Maxim in the Saxon Rule, That no great man nor any other within the whole Kingdom, may abolish the written Laws. [117]

Henry Neville, author of *Plato Redivivus: Or, A Dialogue Concerning Government* (1681) declares the institution of limited monarchy to be a peculiar creation of Northern and Gothic people:

I come to the limitted Monarchies. They were first Introduced (as was said before) by the Goths, and other Northern People. Whence those great swarms came, as it was unknown to Procopius himself, who liv'd in the time of their Invasion, and who was a diligent searcher into all the circumstances of their concernments; so it is very needless for us to make any enquiry into it, thus much being clear, That they came Man, Woman, and Child, and conquer'd and possesst all these parts of the World, which were then subject to the Roman Empire. [118]

The remainder of Neville's tract is an attack on episcopacy, and investigation of the feudal land tenure set up by the Goths. He finds that the division of lands among his followers by the Gothic leader resulted in a system of checks and balances which prevented an undue amassing of political power within the hands of either the nobility or commonalty. Like Harrington, Neville takes as a basic factor in political science the relation between land tenure and political power, "for there is no maxim more Infallible and Holding in any Science, than this is in the Politicks, That Empire is founded in Property: Force or Fraud may alter a Government; but it is Property that must Found and Eternise it: upon this undenyable Aphorisme we are to build most of our subsequent

[117] *Ibid.,* p. 69.
[118] *Plato Redivivus* (London, 1681), p. 92.

Reasoning." [119] Unlike Harrington, however, Neville finds the Gothic polity to be salutary; the division of land among the Goths established order securely.

Neville's Gothic ideas were subjected to a lengthy and elaborate attack by Thomas Goddard, who poured his scorn on the Gothic writers who "run a wool-gathering after the Gothic princes." Goddard's *Plato's Demon* is written in the form of a dialogue between a merchant and a traveler. The merchant asks the traveler for "some account of the Gothick Government," and gets this reply:

Sir, I have no greater pleasure than in obeying your commands, nor have I lost thereby the advantage of this fine evening.

The Goths therefore, if we may believe Jordanes, who was himself of that race, and whom Procopius (writing only of the latter Goths) no where contradicts, broke out of the Island Scanzia or Scandinavia, and with all their substance, men, women and children, advanc'd south-east. And after several skirmishes and Victories by the way, they at last sat down about the *polus Maeotis.*

Here they inhabited many years, and following the warmth of the Sun, spread Eastwards, toward the south of Scythia, and the lower Asia. Their Government all this while, which lasted many hundreds of years, was an absolute Monarchy, and the Tenth part of the lands were generally appropriated to the support of their Prince, who descended from father to son, as at this day amongst us, and in Ottofrising: You have a long catalogue of their names, and an account of their memorable actions.

But in process of time (those Northern people, propagating very much under a warmer climate than their own) a great detachment past over into Europe, whence came the distinction of the Visigoths and Ostrogoths, which is as much as to say, the Southern and the Western Goths.

The latter spread themselves over Germany and France, and erected several Kingdoms. Their Government was Arbitrary enough, and somewhat more than that of the Germans. 'Paulo jam addictus regnantur quam caeterae Germanorum gentis,' saith Tacitus de moribus Germ. Yet we find the Germans themselves under a Kingly Government, the lands divided, and yet neither Noblemen nor people, had any other share in the Government than by way of Council, or a subordinate authority for the Administration of Justice, which is much different from a right of Power or Command. [120]

Goddard was unwilling to cease the attack on Neville without imparting a lesson on the dire results of a democracy when it is established:

*Traveller:* Now if *Plato Redivivus* will needs produce ancient customs among the Goths and impose them, without any farther consideration upon us, I hope he will give me leave also to offer the example of these Loyal Ostrogoths, which I am sure, if duly followed, would prove a better cure for us, whatever our disease be, than our Doting Mountebank impudently proposed.

*Merchant:* Pray what kind of Government did they settle amongst themselves?

*Traveller:* The most popular that could be contrived. For hating the Roman Emperors, from whom they had usurped those Lands, which they did possess (as the offender is oftentimes the last reconciled) they set up a Government as contrary to Monarchy as they could invent. For, obtaining leave to use their own form under certain conditions, and restrictions, they chose to be governed under Consuls, which they elected annually, for the most part, out of three orders, which they distinguished into Captains, Vaivods, and the Commonalty...

*Merchant:* What was the effect of this their Popular Government?

*Traveller:* The same which generally happens in all such low irregular constitutions, that is to say, defection from their soveraign and division amongst themselves; so that every Town became a different Commonwealth, and were never united or friends, but when they were to oppose the Emperor, and that they seldom fail'd to do so, as often as occasion happened. [121]

---

[120] *Plato's Demon: Or, the State-Physician Unmask't; Being a Discourse in Answer to a Book called Plato Redivivus* (London, 1684), pp. 291, 211.      [121] *Ibid.*, pp. 216ff.

Goddard would appear to be following Hobbes in his admission that the Gothic ruler was no *princeps* but a *dux bellorum*; like Hobbes, he foresees only dangerous consequences: "Now, Cousin, you must observe, that though both these Goths and Vandals instituted a kind of Kingly government, yet their Prince was rather a General than a Monarch, and their affairs were for the most part so turbulent that they were in a continuall state of war." [123]

Goddard's next tactic is an attempt to annihilate the Gothic argument by tearing the ground from underneath the Gothicsts:

And first for these Goths, I cannot find in any History, when it was they came over into England, nay I am confident that all Learned Men will agree, that there is no probable conjecture from any Author, that they ever have been here, or crost our Seas, or came nearer us than Normandy; And yet our politick Author tells us positively, according to his usual method, that they establish'd their Government in these parts after their conquest, p. 93. And endeavoring to prove it p. 46 and p. 97 that according to their institutions, the people had an influence upon the Government, he tells us that the governments of France, Spain, and England by name, and other countries, where these people setled, were fram'd accordingly.

Here we see our Country conquer'd and an excellent form of Government establish'd by the Goths, so good and admirable just, that we in this age must quit our happy Monarchy, which hath subsisted most gloriously many Hundreds of years, only to run a wool-gathering after these precious Gothic Princes, and yet no man can ever tell us when this conquest happen'd nor by whom, nor what became of them, nor indeed any thing more, than what the extravagant fancy of our Author hath imagin'd. As for the Romans who conquer'd us, sure they were neither Goths, nor Northern people, and so nothing can be pretended from that Conquest nor are the Saxons, who next invaded us, to be called Northern people, by us at least, who lye so much North to them ourselves.

But forgiving Plato all his absurdities and incongruities, the

[122] *Ibid.*, p. 222.

rather that we may find out the Truth, and confound him with it, we will suppose that by his Goths and Northern people, he means the Saxons, for the Danes were but a very little while, I think not thirty years, masters of England, and so, what may be gather'd in favour of his popular Government from them, if any thing could, would not be so much material. We will imagine then that our Saxons were of the race of the Goths, and that (retaining their customs) They introduced many of them amongst us, such as might be the division of the lands, into several Feuds, which they called Thane lands (and were like our Mannors or Lordships) under certain Tenures or Services. Many also they might have found amongst the Britaines, and retain'd them under their own Government: for it is certain the Britains held land by several Tenures, but whether they were originally of their own Institution, or the remains of the Roman Clientela's and Praeda militaria, I will not determine.

I have already told you, that the Goths upon their first Transplantation, and after they were setled in their new possessions, were govern'd by Kings, whose power increased despotically, according as the people grew secure and civiliz'd, and so they continued above a thousand years; nor do I find that the people in all this time pretended to any other share in the government than to meet in General Councils, when the affairs of the Kingdom oblig'd their King to assemble them. An truly I ever thought such National Assemblies, when well regulated, very conducible to the security, and happy subsistence of all Governments, and such our antient Monarchs, have thought to make us of, and have transmitted the custom of convoking such Councils, which we now call Parliaments, even to our days. But that these Counsellors should have any right of command, is so contrary to the design of their Institution, that this must needs be dangerous to the government itself, so they make their Good Institution useless, by rend'ring themselves suspected to the King who alone hath the right to assemble them. For what wise Magistrate, would by his own authority raise a power, which he apprehends might shock his own.

The sad effects of this we have seen of late days among our selves, when our Commoners in Parliament, who were meer Counsellors, and no more, or Representatives with a power to consent, have arrogated to themselves a Soveraign authority

and under that pretence, have forceably and violently, sub-
verted our antient Government. [123]

In concluding, Goddard is confident that he has crushed
Neville:

Now Cousin, you see what is become of those great expecta-
tions which we might have had, from the noise and bustle,
which our Author makes of the Northern polities, and their
exact rules of Government, but so it falls out that in our days,
Mountains are no less apt to bring forth mice, than formerly.

*Merchant:* But believing that you are clearly in the right, I shall
not trouble you any farther concerning those Northern polities,
but desire that you would proceed, and let me know what you
mean by the rational past.

*Traveller:* By the rational past, I mean this, that granting all to
be true, which our Author hath affirmed, concerning those
Goths and Northern people, and that in the original constitution of our Government, the people had a share in the
Supreme Authority, and that the prerogative, which our King
at present lawfully possesses hath been by degrees gained
from the people. (All of which is so notoriously false, that on
the contrary, the people have lately encroached upon the
prerogative) Yet I say at this time, and as our present circumstances stand, it is more rational, that all honest and
sober men, who laying aside ambition and malice, consider
impartially the just rights and liberties of the people, together
with the preservation of our Government, and the General
happiness of the Nation, should rather endeavor by all lawful
means, to increase the power of his present Majesty, than
diminish it. [124]

*Antidotum Britannicum: Or a Counter-Pest Against the
Destructive Principles of Plato Redivivus* (1681) written by
"W. W.," is another attempt to refute Neville. The tract does
not attack the Gothic arguments directly, but it does make its
point effectively in a taunt that judging from the Civil War
the people could not benefit from their victory over the King,
"but went from one Tyranny to another, from Barebone's Par-

[123] *Ibid.,* pp. 291 ff.
[124] *Ibid.,* pp. 301-302.

liament to Cromwell's reign, from that to a Committee of Safety," and so on. [125]

The anonymously authored *Vox Populi: Or The Peoples Claim to their Parliaments Sitting to Redress Grievances and Provide for the Common Safety* (1681) traces briefly the antiquity of parliaments and their continuity despite the conquests: "The Antiquity of Parliaments in this Nation, which have been so ancient that no Record can give any account of their Beginning, my Lord Coke thus tracing them from the Brittans through the Saxons, Danes and Normans to our days." [126]

Henry Care's *English Liberties: Or, the Free-Born Subject's Inheritance* (1682) prints Magna Charta and comments upon it. In a "Digression touching the Antiquity, Use, and Power of Parliaments," Care points out:

The word Parliament is French, derived from the three words Parler la ment, to speak ones mind, because every Member of that Court should sincerely and discreetly speak his mind for the general good of the Common-Wealth and this name (saith Coke I, Instit. fo. 110) was used before William the Conqueror, even in the time of Edward the Confessor. But most commonly in the Saxons time, it was called Michegemote or Witenage Mote, that is, the Great Mote (Meeting or Assembly, whence our Ward-Moates in London receive their name to this day) or the Wise-Moate, that is, the Assembly of the Wise men and Sages of the Land. [127]

John Selden, the great lawyer and antiquary, employs Tacitus effectively in support of his liberal beliefs. Selden says:

For though he [Tacitus] treat in general of the Germans, yet nevertheless without any question, our Saxons brought over along with them into this Island very many of the things, which are delivered to use by Those who have wrote concerning the Customs of the Germans. Among which take these following. In Councils or publick Assemblies, the King or Prince (i.e. a chief

---

[125] *Antidotum Britannicum* (London, 1681), p. 216.
[126] *Vox Populi* (London, 1681), p. 5.
[127] *English Liberties* (London, 1682), p 78.

person) according as every ones Age is, according to his Nobility, according to his Reputation in Arms, according to his Eloquence, has audience given him, where they use the authority of perswading, rather than the power of commanding. If they dislike what he sayes, they disapprove it with a Hum and a rude Noise. If they like the Proposal, they shake and rustle their Spears or Partisans together. It is the most honourable kind of Assent, to commend the Speaker with the clattering of their Arms. [128]

Tacitus is also the source of the statement concerning the witenagemot:

Whilst the Saxons governed, the Laws were made in the General Assembly of the State or Parliament... The Assemblies were termed by the Saxons, Witena-gemot, i.e. Meetings of the Wise Men and Micil gemot, i.e. the Great Assemblies. At length we borrowed of the French the name of Parliaments, which before the time of Henry the First, Polydore Virgil sayes, were very rarely held. An usage, that not without good reason seems to have come from the ancient Germans. So Tacitus sayes of them, Concerning smaller matters the Princes only, concerning things of greater concern, they do all the whole body of them consult. [129]

Two other tracts by Selden, *Englands Epinomis* and *Titles of Honour*, repeat substantially the same ideas. [130]

John Nalson, defender of the Crown, sweeps away all the Gothic arguments with a light wave: "Whether the English imbib'd their love of Liberty from their ancient Ancestors the Danes is not material here to discuss." [131] Despite his cavalier gesture, Nalson was a thoughtful Royalist. He fears democracy because it upsets what he calls "Equilibrium" of govern-

---

[128] *Jani Anglorum facies altera* (1610), translated by Redman Wescott [*i.e.*, Adam Littleton] in *Tracts Written by John Selden* (London, 1683), p. 32. The original Latin text is available in Selden's *Opera omnia*, edited by David Wilkins (London, 1726), II, 969-1032.

[129] Wescott translation, pp. 93-94.

[130] *Ibid.*, p. 8, and Wilkins' edition, III, 6-43, 650.

[131] *The King's Prerogative and the Subject's Privileges Asserted According to the Laws of England* (London, 1684), p. 48.

ment which is a matter of a strong central authority in the shape of a monarch, but of one who rules under law:

> So that it is apparent that the Romans lost their Liberty for want of the Tribunes prudent management of the Ballance which was put into their hands, whereas the Ephori knew the Limits of their own Authority, as well as the Bounds of that Power to which they were appointed as Assistants and Moderators. Nor is this Equilibrium in Government any airy Notion or Idea. [132]

Nalson is even willing to grant that English political institutions were continuous despite the conquests, but they were continuous under the sovereign laws:

> Certainly the Government of England cannot be thought to stand upon a slight Foundation, that has stood so long upon the single Basis of her own being reduc'd into one Body, were under the execution and care of one Universal Monarch. Nor could the Breach of Norman Conquest hinder the chasm of long enjoy'd Liberty from uniting again, and closing it self more firmly with the Cement of its former Constitutions; calculated by so many Kings of this Island for the Meridian of English Freedom. [133]

Despite the fact that great differences separated the Gothicists and the Levellers, attacks on the Gothic arguments by such men as Nalson after the Commonwealth experiment had ended make it clear that in Royalist quarters Gothicism had become identified with the more extreme democratic theories of the New Model Army. In point of fact, there was less real opposition between Nalson's faith and the Gothic faith in the sovereign law than Nalson was able to see. Had he read with greater care in the Gothic tracts of a moderate Gothicist like Twysden, for example, Nalson might not have dismissed the Gothic theories so lightly.

John Wilson's *Discourse of Monarchy* (1684) concedes the point that the Saxons had a witenagemot, but he denies that the common people had any representation therein:

[132] *Ibid.,* pp. 60-61.
[133] *Ibid.,* pp. 74-75.

That Great Councils of Kings, their Nobles, Wise men, and Chief Officers, were frequently held, of Ancient time, there is hardly any thing more obvious; but, whether the Commonalty, scarce yet civiliz'd, or if so, for the most part, if not wholly, without Literature, were any essential or constituent part, of those great Councils, and Government, might be a question at this day, if there were any sufficient grounds on which to raise it... What was our Saxon Witenage Mote, Micel Synods, Micel Gemotes, or Great Councels, but so many Assemblies of the Wise Men; concerning whom, it is not to be presumed, but that they were of the first rate; the lump of the People, (as I so lately toucht it) being for so many Ages, before, and after, not bred to Letters, and consequently, more apt for Blows, than Arguments, and readier to cut the knot in two, with their Tongues: and in all the Saxon Annals we find the principal or chief Wites, or Wise men of the Nation, the Assembly of Gods Servants (the Clergy, then so called) Aldermen (or Earls) great men, Chiefest men, Noblemen, the constituent parts of those great Councils, but no Commons to be found, or any represented them. [134]

Wilson's point that the common people were lacking in culture and were "more apt for Blows, than Arguments," is a poignant reminder of the despondency which overcame Milton as he came to see that while the Goths (and English) were valorous and ready to fight for liberty, they lacked in the end the wisdom, discipline, and prudential management of their valor which alone would capture and hold in safety the prize of liberty. Wilson reflects Royalism at its best. He shows that not only the Gothicists but the Royalists, too, had tradition on their side, a tradition of cultural enlightenment which preserved the best in the arts and sciences, a tradition of aristocratic superiority stressed not for the purpose of showing one's superiority over the commoners but as a social duty towards them, a theory of *noblesse oblige* at its very best. In most accounts of Milton's political development, his despair of the masses is explained by the influence over him of

[134] *Discourse of Monarchy* (London, 1684), pp. 153, 155.

Puritan ideas. Milton, that is to say, made a distinction between saints and sinners, the elect and the reprobate, on the basis of a Puritan belief that only the godly have the right to govern and that the reprobates must submit to be governed from above. It seems desirable, however, to bring Milton into alignment also with such a Royalist as Wilson, who on the basis of aristocratic tradition also distinguished between the elect who must govern and the uncultured who must submit to be governed. The common faith of the two men in cultural enlightenment should not blur, however, the real difference between them. Their differing attitudes toward Gothicism makes this clear. Wilson never believed that the people had the mental qualities to take part in public deliberations. He had, that is, no illusions to lose. But to Milton, the picture of the "wise-men" sitting in the witenagemot bolstered his hope of England's great destiny if Englishmen would govern themselves as wisely as they had in the past. But the recent events of the Civil War made only too clear that wisdom had departed from English public councils. Milton's Gothic knowledge constantly sharpened his perceptions of the problem as we have already seen, and as we can see, for example, in such an embittered passage as the one in which he complains that Englishmen had become "bastardized from the ancient nobleness of their ancestors." [135] The remainder of the passage makes it certain that Milton had in mind the general Gothic ideas, since he contrasts those who have become "bastardized" with those "who yet retain in them the old English fortitude and love of Freedom."

Robert Brady, personal physician to Charles II and James II was, during a part of his career, keeper of the records in the Tower, and he could not have lacked, therefore, material on England's past history. John Oldmixon, however, said of Dr. Brady that "he read the Records, as Witches say their

[135] *Eikonoklastes,* in Columbia *Milton,* V, 69.

Prayers, Backwards. That he makes them speak the quite contrary to what was intended." [136] Oldmixon may have in mind Dr. Brady's treatment of Saxon history. In the preface to his *Complete History of England* (1685) Brady says:

Concerning the Saxons there is not, that I can find, much more to be written of their Laws, Customs, and Usages, than what hath been said in the First part of that History [he means his *History*, Part I]; Yet seeing all men of the long Robe, that do industriously write of, or incidently meet with them, when they write of other Things, and in their Comments upon Magna Charta, and some other old Statutes, do magnifie and cry up the Liberties and Freedom of the Ordinary People under the Saxon Kings, to such a Degree, as makes them all Petty Princes, or at least Sharers in the Government, and that the Common Historians do report the same things of them. [137]

The year previous to the publication of his *Complete History* Brady had written a reply to William Petyt's Gothic arguments. Commenting on Petyt's analysis, Brady says:

From the Britains, he proceeds to the Saxons, who he says when they made themselves Master of the British Nation, brought their Country Laws with them; of which there can be no doubt (as I shall make it clear upon another occasion but not their popular Government) and brings the authority of Tacitus to prove that the Commons were an Essential and Constituent part of their Common-Council: De minoribus rebus Principes consultant, de majoribus omnes, ita tamen ut ea quoque quorum penes plebem arbitrium est, apud Principes pertractentur. Of lesser matters the chief of the People consult, of the greater All; yet so as those things of which the lowest part of the People are Judges, are first treated of by the better sort; and these were the Councils of the German People in general, not of the Saxons which name is not to be found in all Tacitus; but what if it be granted, that those people which were afterwards called Saxons were Governed by such Councils? was not their Government a Democracy? and the People so far from not having their Votes and Shares in these Councils as only they

---

[136] *Critical History*, p. 28.
[137] *Complete History of England* (London, 1685), p. vi.

had Voices in them, and if any had more power here than others, they were the Priests, who were a sort of Chairman in them. [138]

Brady attempts to demolish with heavy-handed sarcasm Petyt's claim that William accepted Saxon law: "I will examine the easiness and Kindness of William in denying the length of his Sword." [139] Brady concludes with the charge that Petyt "hath endeavour'd to impose upon our Historical Faith, and propagate to posterity many palpable and gross Errors, from whence great and unkind clashings, and diversities of Opinions amongst men may have their source and spring, nay even between Prince and People." [140]

Nathaniel Johnston's *Excellency of Monarchical Government* (1686) represents, like Goddard's attack on Neville's Gothicism, an oblique and not a direct attack. Johnston grants all the Gothic arguments and cites with approval the key passages from Tacitus. But he considers the Germanic deliberative assemblies to be purely military councils which never debated civic affairs. Consequently, he would destroy the Gothic claim that the English people once had been free in their parliaments. His twenty-third chapter discusses. "Of the German Government, and Laws of Several Countries; After breaking of the Roman Empire. and an Introduction to understand the Saxon Law-makers." He says of the Saxons:

I come therefore to their Princely and Military Government. For in so warlike a Nation, it is described by Tacitus, as fittest for that Service. He saith they take their Kings by their noble Extraction, and their Captains or Leaders by their Vertue or Prowess, nor is the Power of their Kings free and absolute; and their Captains by Example rather than Command, are obeyed. If they be ready handed, of a goodly Presence, and signalize their Prowess in the Head of their Armies, this gives them Com-

---

[138] *An Introduction To the Old English History, Comprehended in Three Several Tracts* (London, 1684), p. 3.

[139] *Ibid.,* p. 11.

[140] *Ibid.,* p. 111.

mand. Further he saith, The King or Prince is heard (that is valued, esteemed, and obeyed) according to his Age, his Nobility, his Warlike Atchievements or Eloquence, rather by the Authority of perswading, than by the power of Commanding. If the matter proposes displease, it is rejected with a fretting noise; if it please, they clash together their Spears; the honourablest kind of assent being to commend with their weapons. [141]

Johnston continues, describing the public assemblies:

As to their publick Consultantions, Tacitus observes further, That of lesser matters (such as I suppose concerned not the Private State of Affairs in War or Peace, but the particular ordering the matters of their private Jurisdictions) the Princes consult: about greater business all, yet so as those things, of which the lowest sort of the People are Judges, are first treated of by the Princes. By which I understand, Tacitus means by greater matters, the consultation about the defending themselves against their Enemies, especially against the Romans, where the unanimous suffrage of the greatest multitude was requisite.

By all which, it is apparent that there were several Principalities in Germany, and that the Souldiery made up a great part of the People: and where we read of the Suffrages, it is to be understood of theirs; and whatever freedom of Votes, etc. we read of, was principally in debating Military Affairs. [142]

It is apparent that Johnston in treating the Gothic argument seriously is employing a tactic which evades the Gothic democratic issue by the pretense that all which Tacitus says applies strictly to military affairs. It must be admitted that there was a good deal of shrewdness in Johnston's approach to the problem.

Peter Allix, a Frenchman who was compelled to leave France as a result of the revocation of the Edict of Nantes, set up a church for Protestant refugees in London. His fame as a scholar grew after his residence in England; when he was invited back to France he refused. His interest in the

---

[141] *Excellency of Monarchial Government* (London, 1686), p. 177.
[142] *Ibid.*, p. 179.

history of the land which harbored him is shown in his Gothic tract entitled *Reflections Upon the Opinions of Some Modern Divines Concerning the Nature of Government in General and That of England in Particular* (1689). Allix shows that he is vigorously pro-Gothic:

Though the People of the West allow'd their Princes the Title of King, yet it may be averr'd, that the most part of those Kingdoms, which had their Rise from the Ruins of the Roman Empire, never owned this Royal Law. The Power of their Kings was originally limited, as Caesar witnesseth in his Commentaries concerning the German Kings, which were, to speak properly, only Commanders or Generals. I make particular mention of the Germans, because, for the most part, they were the Founders of the Northern and Western Kingdoms; Germany, having been, as it were, the Nursery, from whence have proceeded most of those Nations, who at this Day have any name in Europe. See what Tacitus asserts concerning the German Kings; Nec Germanorum Regibus infinita aut libera potestas est; de minoribus rebus Principes consultant, de majoribus omnes. Rex aut Princeps auditur Authoritate suadendi, magis quam Jubendi potestate; si displicuit sententia, fremitu asperiantur. Neither is the Power of the German Kings altogether free or unbounded. Matters of lesser Moment are left to the Advice of the Princes, but those of greater Concern are debated by the whole Society; they hear the King as one having Authority to persuade, rather than any Power to command them; and if his Sentiments displease them, they are rejected with boldness. [143]

Allix calls upon the authority of Horn for his Gothicism:

If we consider the most remote times that History gives us any account of, we shall find that the Saxons, as to the Power of their Kings, followed the Example of the Ancient Germans, whose Authority, if we may believe Caesar and Tacitus, was altogether limited and restrain'd. We find in the *Mirror of Justices,* cap. 1, 2. that the first Saxons created their Kings, that they made them take an Oath, and that they put them in mind that they were liable to be judged as well as their meanest subjects. [144]

[143] *Reflections* (London, 1689), p. 56.
[144] *Ibid.,* p. 79.

Furthermore, Allix adds, "After that the Right of Succession was received in England, yet it never deprived the English People of the Right of choosing their Kings." [145]

Algernon Sidney's *Discourses Concerning Government,* although first published posthumously in 1698, were written some years before. He calls upon Tacitus for information of what he calls "the Gothic polity":

The great matters among the Germans were transacted 'omnium consensu. De minoribus rebus consultant principes; de majoribus omnes.' The "michelgemote" among the Saxons was an assembly by the whole people: the "baronagium" is truly said to be the same, in as much as it comprehended all the freemen, that is, all the people; for the difference between "civis" and "servus" is irreconcilable; and no man, whilst he is a servant, can be a member of a commonwealth; for he that is not in his own power, cannot have a part in the government of others... [146] All the northern nations, which upon the dissolution of the Roman empire, possessed the best provinces that had composed it, were under that form which is usually called the Gothic polity. They had king, lords, commons, dyets, assemblies of states, cortez, and parliaments, in which the sovereign powers of those nations did reside, and by which they were exercised... [147] The supreme magistrate, under what name soever he was known, whether king, emperor, asymnetes, suffetes, consul, dictator, or archon, has usually a part assigned to him in the administration of justice, and making war; but that he may know it to be assigned and not inherent, and so assigned as to be employed it is circumscribed by such rules as he cannot safely transgress. This is above all seen in the German nations, from whom we draw our original and government, and is so well described by Tacitus in his treatise of their customs and manners, that I shall content myself to refer to it, and to what I have cited from him in the former part of this work. The Saxons, coming into our country, retained to themselves the same rights. They had no kings but such as were set up by themselves, and they abrogated their power when they

---

[145] *Ibid.,* p. 80.
[146] *Discourses Concerning Government* (London, 1713), p. 79.
[147] *Ibid.,* p. 131.

pleased. [148] We have already mentioned the histories of the Saxons, Danes, and Normans, from which Nations, together with the Britaines, we are descended, and, finding that they were severe assertors of their liberties, acknowledged no human laws but their own, received no kings, but such as swore to observe them, and deposed those who did not well perform their oaths and duty, it is evident that their kings were made by the people according to the law, and that the law, by which they became what they were, could not be from themselves... [149] The Britons and Saxons lay so long hid in the obscurity that accompanies barbarism, that it is in vain to seek what was done by either in any writers more antient than Caesar and Tacitus. The first describes the Britons to have been a fierce people, zealous for liberty, and so obstinately valiant in the defense of it, that tho' they wanted skill, and were overpowered by the Romans, their country could not otherwise be subdued, than by the slaughter of all the inhabitants that were able to bear arms. He calls them a free people, inasmuch as they were not like the Gauls, governed by laws made by great men, but by the people... The Saxons, from whom we chiefly derive our original and manners, were no less lovers of liberty, and better understood the ways of defending it... Whoever would know the opinion of that wise author [i.e. Tacitus] concerning the German liberty, may read his excellent treatise concerning their manners and customs... [150] But we know of no time in which the Britons had not their great councel to determine their most important affairs: and the Saxons in their own country had their councils, where all were present, and in which Tacitus assures us they dispatched their greatest business. These were the same with micklegemots which they afterwards held here, and might have been called by the same name, if Tacitus had spoken Dutch... [151] If we look into our own original, without troubling ourselves with the senseless stories of Samothes, the son of Japhet, and his magicians, or the giants begotten by spirits upon the thirty daughters of Danais sent from Phenicia in a boat without sail, oars, or rudder, we shall find, that when the Romans abandoned this island, the inhabitants were left to a full liberty of providing

[148] *Ibid.,* p. 296.
[149] *Ibid.,* p. 363.
[150] *Ibid.,* pp. 380-381.
[151] *Ibid.,* p. 382.

for themselves: and whether we deduce our original from them, or the Saxons, or from both, our ancestors were perfectly free. [152]

John Dryden's opera, *King Arthur* (1691), presents an interesting problem in Restoration politics and in the Gothic tradition. According to Miss Brinkley, who has studied the political significance of seventeenth century Arthurian literature, Dryden's play is politically neutral. She takes seriously, that is, Dryden's own avowal (in his preface) that he had altered his play in order not to offend the government. [153] But no reference to Saxon polity could possibly be neutral, and if Dryden is indeed seeking not to offend, then he is managing more skillfully than Miss Brinkley supposes in balancing Saxon democracy and royalism. As Arthur defeats

[152] *Ibid.,* p. 408, Sydney's full display of Gothic ideas raises an interesting bibliographical problem in connection with a tract which first appeared in 1714 bearing the title *Of the Antiquity, Power and Decay of Parliaments* and authored, according to the title-page, by Thomas Rymer. The same tract was published, however, in 1744 in a two-volume work bearing the title *Of the Use and Abuse of Parliaments.* The essay covers 78 pages of volume I and bears the separate title "A General View of Government in Europe," section 1, "Of the Origin, Power, and Antiquity of Parliaments." An advertisement facing the title-page attributes the essay to Sidney. In 1763 the identical essay appeared in a volume entitled *Sydney on Government.* The editor of the 1772 edition of Sidney's writings, under the title *The Works of Algernon Sydney, A New Edition,* discusses the problem and says that "by the style in which it is written, the author's manner of reasoning, and the books which are cited in it," he is convinced that it is the production of a different hand. The editor of the *Works* was unaware, apparently of the 1714 edition of the tract bearing Rymer's name as author. The tract *is* Sidney's, but, on the other hand, the explanation is lacking why it should have been attributed to Rymer. The liberal sentiments of this Gothic tract seem hardly appropriate to what we know of Thomas Rymer and far more appropriate to Sidney, the Republican martyr.

[153] R. F. Brinkley, *Arthurian Legend in the Seventeenth Century* (Baltimore, 1932), p. 146; she follows Scott and Saintsbury in this interpretation.

Oswald, his Saxon enemy, in personal combat, he generously offers Oswald complete freedom:

*Arthur:* Thy life, Life, thy Liberty, thy Honour safe,
Lead back thy Saxons to their Ancient Elbe:
I wou'd restore thee fruitful Kent, the Gift
Of Vortigern for Hengist's ill-brought aid,
But that my Britains brook no foreign Power,
To Lord it in a Land, Sacred to Freedom;
And of its Rights Tenacious to the Last.

*Oswald:* No more than thou hast offer'd wou'd I take.
I wou'd Refuse all Britain, held in Homage;
And own no other Masters but the Gods. [154]

Dryden had evidently absorbed the ideas of Saxon liberty and invincibility as well as the ideas of Germanic enlightenment. Merlin, however, sums up the political significance of the play when he prophesies a combined British and Saxon future; that is, Dryden merges the ideas of Saxon democracy and of the Royalist conceptions which Miss Brinkley demonstrates were attached to the Arthurian tradition:

*Oswald:* Nor thou, brave Saxon Prince, disdain our Triumphs;
Britains and Saxons shall be one People;
One Common Tongue, one Common Faith shall bind
Our Jarring Bands, in a perpetual Peace. [155]

Dryden, in fact, seems to be determined to placate the Saxon democrats, for Conon has previously said of Oswald that "Arthur is all that's Excellent in Oswald; / And Void of all his Faults." [156] Dryden's previous play, *Albion and Albianum* (performed 1685), makes no such generous concessions to the democratic cause; in the earlier play, Democracy plots with Pluto in Hell to destroy Albion, the King. Dryden is probably paying sincere homage to the tradition of Saxon constitutionalism. Democracy in *Albion and Albianus* in his zeal "to make everyman a king," while he may be a travesty

[154] *King Arthur,* act V, sc. i; Scott-Saintsbury ed., VIII, 192.
[155] *Ibid.,* p. 193.
[156] *Ibid.,* p. 142.

of what Leveller doctrine of the Commonwealth period actually was, would also be repudiated by the Gothicists.

Because of his involvement in practical politics and the earnestness of his quest for a guiding philosophy, Sir William Temple's interest in the Gothic lore is of special importance. Tacitus is the source of Temple's knowledge of the Gothic polity:

The Principle of politick or civil Government in these Northern Nations seems derived from that which was Military among them. When a new Swarm was upon the Wing, they chose a Leader or General for the Expedition, and at the same time the chief officers to command the several Divisions of their Troops; these were a Council of War to the General, with whom they advised in the whole Progress of their Enterprise; but upon great Occasions, as a pitch't Battle, any military Exploit if great Difficulty and Danger, the choice of a Country to fix their Seat, or the Conditions of Peace that were proposed, they assembled their whole Troops, and consulted with all the Soldiers or People they commanded. This Tacitus observes to have been in use among the German Princes in his Time, to consult of smaller Affairs with the chief officers, but De majoribus omnes. [157]

A philological discussion which traces the etymology of *Baro* and *Feudum* (namely Spelman's *Glossarium* to Gothic sources, introduces the theme of the cradle of liberty and provides Temple with the opportunity to declare his admiration of Gothic democracy:

From the divisions, forms, and institutions already deduced, will naturally arise and plainly appear the frame and constitution of the Gothic government, which was peculiar to them, and different from all before known or observed in story; but so universal among these Northern Nations, that it was under the names of King, or Prince, or Duke, and his estates, established in all parts of Europe, from the north-east of Poland and Hungary, to the south-west of Spain and Portugal, though these vast countries have been subdued by so many several expedi-

[157] "Of Heroick Virtue," in *Works,* I, 218.

tions of these Northern people, at such diverse times, and under so different appelations, and it seems to have been invented by the sages of the Goths, as a government of freemen, which was the spirit or character of the Northwest nations, distinguishing them from those of the South and East, and gave the name of the Francs among them. I need say nothing of this our constitution, which is so well known in our island [but he goes on to tell for a full page]...However, it be this constitution has been so celebrated, or framed with great wisdom and equity, and as the truest and justest temper that has been ever found out between dominion and liberty; and it seems to be a strain of what Heraclitus said was the only skill or knowledge of any value in politics, which was the secret of governing all by all. This seems to have been intended by these Gothic institutions, and by the election and representation of all that possessed lands. [158]

Temple's *Introduction to the History of England* also identifies the Saxons as a Gothic people:

"The Saxons were one Branch of those Gothick nations, which swarming from the northern hive, had, under the conduct of Odin, possessed themselves anciently of all those mighty tracts of land that surround the Baltick Sea." There were two branches of Goths. The first, "those towards the south-East of Germany were called Franks, from their great love of liberty, and their valour in preserving it, and never submitting to the Roman Subjection;" the second branch was composed of "these fierce People called Saxons from a Weapon generally used among them, and more like a Scythe with the Edge reversed, which in their Language were termed Seaxes." [159]

The account continues, telling of Vortigern's misguided offer to ally with the Saxons, a description of the landing of Hengist and Horsa "of the Race of Odin," and concludes: "So as we may justly date the Original of all those amongst us, as well as our Nation it self, from these our Saxon ancestors. Britain which was before a Roman Province, was now grown

---

[158] *Works,* I, 218-219, 220. Miss Clara Marburg, in *Sir William Temple* (New Haven, 1932), thinks this discussion "proves nothing at all"; she also has the mistaken idea that Temple was "among the earliest" to turn attention to the Goths (pp. 39-40).
[159] *Works,* II, 537.

a Saxon Kingdom." [160] Two other brief statements in the
essay "Of Poetry" also identify the Goths as the progenitors
of the English people; Temple speaks of "those Northern
Kingdoms, the Seat of our Ancestors in all the Western parts
of Europe," and a second time he refers to "the ancient Western Goths, our Ancestors." [161] Thus there is ample evidence
of Temple's Gothic erudition and there can be no question of
the profound sympathy between his liberal conservatism and
the account he drew from the Gothic literature of Gothic
democracy.

A staunch admirer of Algernon Sidney, Robert Molesworth,
while serving as England's envoy to Denmark, ran afoul of
a Royalist clique in Stockholm and was recalled. Molesworth
gave vent to his indignation in a satire on Danish affairs
which makes effective use of the Gothic ideas. Molesworth's
attacks on his enemies at the Danish court appeared anonymously in 1694 under the title *An Account of Denmark as it
was in the Year 1692*. To call attention to the corrupt monarchical clique, Molesworth pointed out that anciently Denmark was free: "The ancient Form of Government here was
the same which the Goths and Vandals established in most if
not all Parts of Europe, whither they carried their Conquests,
and which in England is retained to this day for the most
part." [162] Parliaments were the gift of the Goths to the world:

Tis said of the Romans that those Provinces which they
conquered were amply recompensed for the loss of their Liberty,
by being reduced from their barbarity to civility; by the Introduction of Arts, Learning, Commerce, and Politeness. I know
not whether this manner of Arguing have not more of Pomp
than Truth in it; but with much greater reason may it be said
that all Europe was beholding to these People for introducing
or restoring a Constitution of Government for excelling all
others that we know of in the World. Tis to the ancient inhabit-

160 *Ibid.*, 540.
161 In Springarn, *Critical Essays*, III, 80, 86.
162 *An Account of Denmark* (London, 1694), p. 42.

ants of these Countries, with other Neighboring Provinces, that we owe the Original of Parliaments, formerly so common but lost within this last Age in all Kingdoms but those of Poland, Great Britain, and Ireland. [163]

Molesworth attributes the loss of Gothic liberty in Denmark to the intrigues of a French circle at the court. But he concludes hopefully that the spirit of liberty will revive, so strong is the Gothic love of liberty:

Many reasons might perswade one to think that the Government upon the bottom it stands cannot last long. As in the first place, that natural Love of Liberty which resided formerly in the Northern Nations more eminently than in other Parts of the World. What can be expected less from the Descendants of the ancient Goths and Vandals who propagated and established Liberty in so many other Countries than to shake a heavy Yoak of themselves, which their Fore-fathers were not able to bear? [164]

Molesworth has additional importance in the Gothic movement as the translator of François Hotman's *Francogallia,* the greatest document in a similar revival of interest in France in Germanic antiquities. [165]

In France, as in England, an antiquarian movement sprang up which sought in the same way for historical justification of the demands of Parliament to enjoy its full rights and privileges. The racial question, especially, was intensified in France since the crucial issue there was whether the Frenchmen were Franks or Gauls. The answer depended on the viewpoint which the historian took, aristocratic or democratic. From the aristocratic and Royalist point of view, it was declared that the Franks furnished the nobility of the nation and the Gauls the serfs who had been conquered by the Franks. In this way an attempt was made to link the power

---

[163] *Ibid.,* p. 42.
[164] *Ibid.,* p. 264.
[165] See Barzun, *French Race,* an admirable study of racial and nationalistic theories as they were affecting French historiography.

of the kings and nobles to a Frankish autocratic tradition. But from the alternative democratic point of view, if it could be shown that the Frankish conquerors were themselves scions of a Germanic stock and the Frankish state was therefore democratic, there seemed no reason why the common people should not force the King to revive the parliaments which had been their hereditary privilege. The greatest French lawyer of his time, François Hotman, wrote his famous treatise *Franco-gallia* (1573) in defense of democratic liberalism in an effort to show, as the title itself indicates, that there was no cleavage in the nation between Franks and Gauls. His thesis was that both the Franks and Gauls were ultimately German in origin, and the royal claim of a Frankish autocratic tradition was therefore historically false.

The subtitle which Molesworth appended to Hotman's original showed that his humiliation, engineered by the French clique in Denmark, was still rankling. Molesworth's title reads: *Franco-Gallia, or An Account of the Ancient Free State of France and Most Other Parts of Europe Before the Loss of Their Liberties.* [166] Molesworth's preface also reminded his English readers how fortunate they were in preserving the same Germanic liberties which the French had lost:

Therefore since a sincere Desire of Instructing the only Possessors of True Liberty in the World, what Right they have to that Liberty, of how great a Value it is, what Misery follows the loss of it, and how easily, if Care be taken in time, it may be preserved, has induced me to translate and send abroad this small Treatise. [167]

The burden of Hotman's argument is that both Franks and Gauls were originally Germans and they share, therefore, the same predilection for liberty and tribal assemblies. Hotman levies on the identical passages in Tacitus as the English Gothicists:

[166] *Franco-Gallia* (London, 1711).
[167] *Ibid.,* p. ii.

These things being thus briefly premised, we think it proper now to set forth in what manner the Kingdom of Francogallia was constituted. And we have already made it plain that the People reserv'd to themselves all the Power, not only of Creating but also of Abdicating their Kings. Which form of government, 'tis manifest our Ancestours had, before they were brought under the Romans. Altho 'tis probable the Franks did not derive this Constitution of their Commonwealth from the Gauls; but from their Countrymen, the Germans; of whom Tacitus, lib. de mor. Germ. says, 'Regibus non est infinita aut libera Potestas.' [168]

What is important in such foreign texts as these is their promotion of the idea of universal liberty, found wherever the German anciently established a home, in England, in France, and elsewhere. The corollary idea was the conception of a world rejuvenation brought about by this gift of liberty bestowed upon the world by the Goths.

A curious feature of the Whig defense of William of Orange is its revival of the Royalist theory of the 1640's which held that the King has absolute right by title of conquest. The argument was caustically attacked by Samuel Johnson, who pointed out to the overzealous Whigs that royal privilege, as preserved in the ancient witenagemot, ought to be sufficient even for a Whig. The attempt to endow King William with absolute right was subversive, Johnson declares, of the ancient tradition:

At last I am come to search after the Head of the Nile and the true old Landmark of the English Constitution. How Parliaments stood in the British times I am not so certain; but that there were Parliaments then, I am certain. I have it from the wise Gildas, that Vortigern and his foolish thaynes sent to the Saxons for help against the Picts and Scots, and took into their Bosoms a warlike and fierce Nation, whom at a distance they were afraid of. And they indeed of course beat those that infested Severus' Wall, but they made mine Hosts that invite them in, Hewers of Wood, and Drawers of water. And those of the Briains that opposed them, the Saxons drove out of their Coun-

[168] *Ibid.,* p. 63.

try, whereby as Gildas says all their records were lost. But out of that venerable Author, we plainly see that the Lamentable Letter which was sent some few years before to the Senate of Rome, was written by a British Parliament. [169]

Turning to the Saxons, Johnson sees a slight difference in the witenagemot from the British Parliament:

But after these Early Times, we have somewhat in King Edward the Confessor's Laws, which all succeeding Kings have been Sworn to, which I will try what to make of. It is an yearly Folkmote upon the Kalends of May. I do not know readily what a yearly Folkmote is, because those Laws of Edward the Confessor say that King Arthur invented it: Quod Arthurus Rex inclytus Britonum invenit. Then I am sure the Original Name of it was not Folkmote. Then we will mind the Name no more, but come to the thing.

Sir Henry Spelman in the Learnedest Glossary that ever was Writ, I will not except Mr. Sommer's, says thus under the word *Gemotum*: 'Wittenagemot idem apud Anglosaxones quod apud nos hodie Parliamntum, parumq. a Folcmoto differebat, nisi quod Hoc Annuum effet & e certis plerumq; Causis, illud ex Arduis Contingentibus & Legum condendarum gratia, ad arbitrium Principis indictum.' A Wittenagemot was the same thing amongst the English Saxons as now this Day a Parliament is amongst us; and a wittenagemot differed little from a Folkmote only that the last was Annual and chiefly sat about the Standing affairs of the Nation. The other was called at the King's Pleasure upon Emergencies of State and for the sake of making Laws. [170]

Johnson's *History and Defence of Magna Charta* similarly describes the witenagemot, the laws which are "the same which were brought from the northern parts of Germany by the Saxon invaders, the *dux bellorum,* the failure of the Norman Conqueror to destroy the older law, and so on. [171]

[169] *An Essay Concerning Parliaments at a Certainty* (3d ed.; London, 1694), pp. 22-23.
[170] *Ibid.,* pp. 23-24.
[171] "Introductory Discourse," *A History and Defence of Magna Charta* (Dublin, 1709), p. ii.

*Civil Polity* (1703), a tract which shows the influence of Harrington's economic theory, describes tribal assemblies among the northern people: "That the whole Community were assembled, and Consulted in Matters of Moment by the Northern nations, amongst which the Saxons are to be numbred, I think is without Controversie." [172] Doubtless the question was beyond controversy, so widely had the Gothic propaganda been disseminated.

Michael Geddes gives an account of the Germanic public assembly, blending in one narrative citations from Tacitus, Verstegen, and Jordanes: "Tacitus in his Book *De Moribus Germanorum* gives the following Account of the German form of Government... About lesser matters their Princes consult together, but about the greater they all do but so that the things of which the People have the Decision, must not be handled by the Princes." [173] Both republicanism and royal absolutism, therefore, are unthinkable in England:

For in England and Scotland that German Form of Government remains to this day... Now this being considered, is it not a great piece of Confidence in any that are for bringing England under a Commonwealth Form of Government if there be any among us so mad as to think of it, to assume to themselves the Honourable Title of True Englishmen; and have they, who would make our Princes arbitrary and Absolute, any better right to that Title: since it is plain, that the Angli were perfect Strangers to both these two Forms of Government. [174]

A tract entitled *Vox Populi, Vox Dei* (1709) has the distinction of passing through ten editions in one century and of being published in America on the eve of the revolution. As the title indicates, all of the power of government is lodged in the people as their Saxon birthright:

[172] Anonymous, *Civil Polity. A Treatise Concerning the Nature of Government* (London, 1703), p. 299.
[173] *Miscellaneous Tracts* (London, 1714; 1st ed., 1702-1706), III, 18.
[174] *Ibid.*, III, 20-21.

The Saxons, or Angli, were no less Lovers of Liberty and understood the Ways of defending it: They were certainly the most powerful and ancient Britains and Saxons had no Monarchs; and that our Ancestors had their Councils and Magistrates, as well here as in Germany; that as soon as the Saxons came into this country, they had their Miclegemots, which were generall Assemblies of the Noble and the Noble and Freemen who had in themselves the Power of the Nation. [175]

The Norman Conquest caused no alterations in the people's rights: "William the First (who is unjustly stiled the Conquerer, having subdued none but Harold, and those that abetted him) did obtain the Crown by a free choice and Submission of the Peers and the body of the People." [176]

Rapin describes the Saxon witenagemot:

To preserve a perfect union between the king and people, it was necessary to establish a way of communication between them. This was done by means of a Wittena-gemot, an assembly of wise men who represented the whole nation. This method the Saxons brought with them from Germany, where all public affairs were decided in such an assembly of which their generals, chosen in time of war, were presidents. [177]

John Oldmixon's *Critical History of England* (1724) similarly describes the Saxon council and, like Rapin, describes the English constitution specifically as Gothic:

Tacitus gives us some Light as to the Nature of the Saxon Government, speaking thus of the Germans, of whom the Saxons were a Part. De minoribus rebus Principes consultant, de majoribus omnes; ita tamen ut ea quoque quorum penes plebem arbitrium est apud Principes praetractentur. Res minores exponunt causas privatas & ad forum pertinentes, majores publicas. In celebrandis bisce Concilis, etc. Tacitus names the very

---

[175] The 10th edition, under the title *The Judgment of Whole Kingdoms and Nations, Concerning the Rights, Power and Prerogatives of Kings, and the Right, Privileges, and Properties of the People* (London, 1771), pp. 41-42; the tract is attributed to Defoe or Lord Somers.

[176] *Ibid.,* p. 58.

[177] *Historical Dissertation upon Whig and Tory,* I, xiii.

term Councils, as the Saxon writers do; which the Normans chang'd for a term of their own, that of Parliament. [178]

The sum of Oldmixon's discussion is a statement that "no Nation has preserv'd their Gothick Constitution better than the English." [179] That is to say, all of the non-Roman world benefited by the Gothic hegemony but England preserved most of its legacy of Gothic freedom: "Indeed it cannot be deny'd but the Gothick Governments were all free, and that their Kings were bound to govern according to their Laws. Most of the European nations, as well as the French, were once Masters of the same Freedom we enjoy." [180]

A *Freeholder* essay by Addison introduces the expression "Gothic balance" in a discussion which makes the point that faction and party bickering is creating too much unrest: "I have heard of a Senior Alderman in Buckinghamshire, who, at all publick Meetings, grows drunk in praise of Aristocracy, and is as often encountered by an old Justice of Peace who lives in the Neighborhood, and will talk you from Morning till Night on the Gothic Balance." [181] The Justice of the Peace would seem to be arguing that in the Gothic system of government the aristocracy are balanced by the common people; together, presumably, they compose the legislative power. The essay, at any rate, indicates the expression "Gothic balance" as existing in established usage. The expression is of considerable interest chiefly because of its continued use by Swift.

Earlier, Harrington had employed the term; the fact that both Harrington and Swift believed, whatever their differences otherwise, in a "poyse of orders" or collaboration among the various interests in the state, each interest with its respective

---

[178] *Critical History*, p. 21.
[179] *Ibid.*, p. 25.
[180] *Ibid.*, p. 24.
[181] *Freeholder,* no. 53, Friday, January 22, 1716.

rights, suggests the direct influence of Harrington both as regards the term and what it described.

Swift had made his debut in 1701 in the field of political pamphleteering with a plea for collaboration between the separate interests of the nation. He senses that the people make too much of their "natural genius" for liberty and, as a result, his skepticism is an excellent indication of the wide discussion of the theory of Gothic racial characteristics:

> They have it ready in their Mouths, that the People of England are of a Genius and Temper, never to admit Slavery among them; and they are furnished with a great many Commonplaces upon that Subject. But it seems to me, that such Discourses do reason upon short Views, and a very moderate Compass of thought. For, I think it is a great Error to count upon the Genius of a Nation as a standing Argument in all Ages; since there is hardly a Spot of Ground in Europe, where the Inhabitants have not frequently and entirely changed their Temper and Genius. Neither can I see any Reason, why the Genius of a Nation should be more fixed in the point of Government, than in their Morals, their Learning, their Religion, their Common Humour and Conservation, their Diet and their Complexion; which do all notoriously vary, almost in every age; and may every one of them have great Effects upon Men's Notions of Government. [182]

If we recall that Harrington interpreted the "Gothic balance" as a disruptive force in modern governments, Swift's independent treatment of the "Gothic balance" will be the more significant. Swift, unlike Harrington, admires the "Gothic balance" but writing under the influence of Sir William Temple's essay, "Origin and Nature of Government," in which Temple repudiates the climate theory, Swift also is dubious. While he admires the principles of Gothic government, Swift thinks it better to ground it in "reason and

---

[182] *A Discourse of the Contests and Dissensions Between the Nobles and Commons in Athens and Rome,* edited by H. Davis (Oxford, 1939), pp. 229-230.

nature" than in any conception of fixed racial psychology:

> That a mixt Government partaking of the known Forms received in the Schools, is, by no Means, of Gothick Invention, but hath Place in Nature and Reason, seems very well to agree with the Sentiments of most Legislators, and to have been followed in most States, whether they have appeared under the Name of Monarchies, Aristocracies, or Democracies. For, not to mention the several Republicks of this Composition in Gaul and Germany, described by Caesar and Tacitus. Polybius tells us, the best Government may be fairly translated, the Kings, Lords, and Commons. [183]

Swift, it is clear, sees Gothicism as a system of checks and balances in any kind of nominal government.

The specific term "Gothic balance" appears in Swift's essay, *Enquiry into the Behavior of the Queen's Last Ministry* (1715). His concern is still with balancing the interests in the nation, but the time has come, he thinks, to redress the balance so that the government will be a truly "mixt" one. It is unfortunately true, he believes, that once one of the interests gains undue power the people soften in moral fiber and rest supinely under tyranny; in this way, the prize of the "Gothic balance" has been lost:

> For whoever considers the course of the Roman empire after Caesar's usurpation, the long continuance of the Turkish government, or the destruction of the Gothic balance in most kingdoms, will see how controllable that maxim is, that *res volunt diu malè administrari:* Because as corruptions are more natural to mankind than perfections, so they are more likely to have a longer continuance. [184]

Swift's "Abstract of the History of England" (1719) contains his most extended remarks on parliaments and England's Gothic political inheritances. He dates the rise of parliaments from the reign of Henry II:

> As the institution of Parliaments in England is agreed by

[183] *Ibid.,* pp. 199-200.
[184] In *Prose Works* (Bohn ed.), V, 476.

several writers to be owing to this King, so the date of the first
hath been assigned by some to the fifteenth year of his reign;
which however is not to be affirmed with any certainty: for
great councils were convoked not only in the two preceding
reigns, but for time immemorial by the Saxon princes who first
introduced them into this island, from the same original with the
other Gothic forms of government in most parts of Europe. [185]

Swift continues, describing the Gothic balance as a gradual
evolution from essentially military beginnings, but his object
again is to show the wisdom of collaboration among the interests of the nation in a mixed government:

The institution of a state or commonwealth out of a mixture
of the three forms of government received in the schools,
however it be derided as a solecism and absurdity by some late
writers on politics, hath been very ancient in the world, and is
celebrated by the gravest authors of antiquity. For although the
supreme power cannot be said to be divided, yet it may be so
placed in the several hands, as each to be a check upon the
other; or formed into a balance, which is held by him that has
the executive power with the nobility and people in counterprise
in each scale. Thus the kingdom of Medea is represented by
Xenophon before the reign of Cyrus; so Polybius tells us, the
best government is a mixture of the three forms, regno, optima-
tum, et populi imperio: the same was that of Sparta in its primitive institution by Lycurgus made up of reges, seniores, et
populos; the like may be asserted of Rome, Carthage, and other
states: and the Germans of old fell upon the same model, from
whence the Goths their neighbours, with the rest of the Northern
people, did honour it. But an assembly of the three estates is
not properly of Gothic institution: for these fierce people, when
upon the decline of the Roman Empire, they first invaded
Europe, and settled so many kingdoms in Italy, Spain, and other
parts, were all Heathens; and when a body of them had fixed
themselves in a tract of land left desolate by the flight or
destruction of the natives, their military government by time
became civil; the general was king, his great officers were his
nobles and ministers of state, and the common soldiers the body
of the people; but these were freemen and had smaller portions

[185] *Ibid.*, X, 225.

of land assigned to them. The remaining natives were all slaves; the nobles were a standing council; and upon affairs of great importance, the freemen were likewise called by their representatives to give their advice. By which it appears, that the Gothic frame of government consisted at first but of two states or assemblies, under the administration of a single person. [186]

Whatever Swift's views were of Gothic government in its beginnings, there can be no question of his high regard for the Gothic system as it matured. In a letter to Pope, written January 10, 1721, Swift enthusiastically declares: "As to Parliaments, I adored the wisdom of that Gothic institution." [187] Thus the evidence is clear about the extent to which Swift's political thinking was fertilized by the ideas in the Gothic tradition. His remarkable independence in denying the validity of racial theories places him in the same category with Milton. For differing reasons, the tradition of English political inheritances was paramount in the minds of these two great men: Milton's philosophy of "liberty rightly used" hampered his acceptance or reliance on the racial theory; Swift's demand for grounding his theory of mixed government in "reason" led him to discount racism as irrational, although, at the same time, he was able to salvage out of the Gothic propaganda the "wisdom" of free parliaments.

The stream of Gothic ideas flowed on unimpeded, and swelled by the eighteenth century poetic effusions celebrating the Gothic liberty. The survey of Gothic tracts and histories can be indefinitely prolonged; one may conclude by noting the streams of history and poetry converging in Mrs. Catharine Macaulay's *History of England* (1763). Her text described the primitive folkmoot, the gradual evolution of parliaments, the retention of Anglo-Saxon liberties despite the Norman conquest, and so on. The title-page, on the other

---

[186] *Ibid.*, pp. 226-227.

[187] *Correspondence of Jonathan Swift,* edited by F. Elrington Ball (London, 1910-1914), III, 121.

hand, quoting lines from Thomson's poem, *Liberty*, crests the wave of Gothic ideas embodied in the prose of the text. We may conclude that Englishmen gave to the Gothic faith the assent of all their faculties, imaginative and logical.

The Gothic ideas were excogitated in a mood of national piety. Faith, however can be misplaced, and the greatest testimony to the nobility of the Gothic faith is its readjustment to the Leveller demands for "natural" rights and to the criticisms of Sir Roger Twysden and Jonathan Swift, the latter being especially notable as persevering in the Gothic faith where Milton faltered and finally failed.

From our survey of the part that the doctrine of Gothic liberty played in the seventeenth-century strife between King and Parliament, we learn that Gothicism was a basic concept, developing in the fiber of the nation. There were, to be sure, other arguments for democracy, but to the extent that the example of the past was an element in the democratic protests the Gothic propaganda forced the pace of seventeenth century political thought. If this claim errs on the side of exaggeration (as I do not think it does), the conclusions previously held on the subject are totally untenable. H. J. Ford says: "The great intellectual occupation of the age was examination of the source and nature of authority, and if there had been extant any tradition of the primitive Teutonic community, as the original sovereign, it would have been brought into notice, but such a thing was never mentioned." [188] Neither are the conclusions of Mary F. Tenney tenable. She says: "It is rare in England to find Tacitus brought to bear on political theory." [189] The evidence gathered in this study has shown that it is rare *not* to find Tacitus employed in the parliamentary struggle. By devoting himself exclusively to *literary* interest

[188] *Representative Government* (New York, 1924), p. 11.
[189] Quotation from her typescript, unpublished dissertation, p. 206; see also her "Tacitus through the Centuries to the Age of Printing," *University of Colorado Studies*, XXII (1935), 341-364.

in northern antiquities, Farley has missed the larger area of political discussion: "Opportunities were at hand, and fairly acessible, for the scholar who wished to make a special study of these "Gothic" matters, but the great mass of the English people knew little and cared little about them." [190]

The Gothic propaganda touched the lives of England's greatest and humblest citizens; all Englishmen knew—there were ample Gothic tracts—and they cared greatly. They sought for their liberty but found themselves a nation. This happened because men who express a desire to meet in public assembly to seek counsel of each other, to elucidate the truth progressively by free and tolerant discussion, have in the desire indicated their sense of the collective moral being which alone deserves the name of "nation." [191]

[190] *Scandinavian Influences,* p. 27.
[191] The logic of English nationalism going hand in hand with democracy has been brilliantly explained by Ernest Barker, *National Character and the Factors in its Formation* (New York and London, 1927).

# CHAPTER THREE
# GOTHIC ROMANCE

This section is devoted to showing that Tacitus and Jordanes supplied the framework of discussion of eighteenth-century theories of fiction, erected on a three-fold foundation: 1) the domiciliation of the Goths in the Orient; a rabbinical tradition, synchronizing German and Jewish history, supported this Asiatic version of the Gothic legend; 2) the description of jousting, trial by ordeal, heraldry, dubbing of the knight, and so on, as Gothic practices; 3) the attribution to the Goths of femininism; the Goths were assumed to be the first people in history to venerate women, to institute monogamous marriage, to adhere to the sanctity of the marriage vow, and to undertake perilous adventure in behalf of womankind.

Thus every aspect of the chivalric romance was accounted for, and it seemed entirely appropriate that the romances be called "Gothic" in two senses, specific and general: specifically, because the romances enshrined Gothic feminism and knight-errantry; the third element, dragons, sorcerers, elves, fairies, was held accountable on the basis of a new set of climate postulates introduced by the Oriental version of the Gothic story; generally, because the romances stood outside of the stream of classical culture; in other words, the romances were medieval, Germanic, non-Roman in their display of those qualities opposite to Roman torpor and depravity: the Gothic qualities were love of adventure, faith, manliness, honor, and piety.

## THE ORIENTAL THEORY: *EX ORIENTE LUX*

By bringing the Goths from Scandza across Europe and into Asia, Jordanes supplied the basis for an Oriental version of the Gothic legend. Later history postulated a second wave of migration westward and northward, repopulating the North, and in this sense it was still possible to describe Gothic democracy as a northern institution. Actually it made little difference, for political purposes, which version, the Oriental or Septentrional, was followed; all that was necessary was to show that the Goths were free: "I hold it both needless and fruitless to enter into the lists, concerning the original of the Saxons; whether they were Natives from the Northern parts of Germany, or the Reliques of the Macedonian Army under Alexander... The people were a free people." [1] "Whether we deduce our original from them [Asiatic people] or the Saxons, or from both, our ancestors were perfectly free." [2]

To theorists of the origin of fiction, however, some explanation was required to account for the fantastic and imaginative elements in storytelling; Gothic dueling and Gothic feminism did not take in the element of fantasy. The climate theory supplied the answer. The same North-South dichotomy which explained northern bodily vigor and southern torpor also explained the mental differences. Northerners were dull of imagination, southerners were highly imaginative. Dryden's well-known couplet is only one expression among many:

> True wit in Northern climates will not grow
> Except like orange trees, 'tis housed from snow. [3]

Milton's remark in the ninth book of *Paradise Post* that "an age too late or cold climate" might "damp his intended wing" in poetic flight is another expression of the theory that the northern climate is unfavorable to the imagination. In the *Spectator* papers, numbers 160, 339, and 405, Addison describes the Oriental exuberant fancy. John Husbands was of the

---

[1] N. Bacon, *Laws and Government*, p. 9.
[2] A. Sidney, *Discourses*, p. 408.
[3] "Prologue," *Aureng-Zebe,* in Scott-Saintsbury ed. V, 201.

opinion that "the genius of the East soars upon stronger Wings and takes a loftier flight, than the Muse of Greece, or Rome." [4] The preface to William Collins' *Persian Eclogues* (1742) informs the reader: "the stile of my Countrymen is as naturally Strong and Nervous, as that of an Arabian or Persian is rich and figurative. There is an Elegancy and Wildness of Thought which recommends all their Compositions; and our Genius's are as much too cold for the Entertainment of such Sentiments, as our Climate is for their Fruits and Spices." [5] Robert Lowth declared: "In the East, the beauty of climate, the richness of the soil, the abundance of Vegetation, laid open many sources of imagery to which we are strangers; and when any one point of resemblance presented itself to the flowing imagination of the Oriental poet he seized upon it with avidity." [6]

In addition to Jordanes' Scandza theory, the Odin myth also located the Goths in an Asiatic home. The Odin story is an invention of monkish chroniclers, a web of myth and real history which goes back to the Homeric and Virgilian accounts of the fall of Troy. If we begin with the *Heimskringla* and the *Prose Edda,* we have reduced to its barest essence the following story. The *Heimskringla* tells of a river, Tanaksvisl, which, emptying into the Black Sea, separates Asia from Europe. East of the Tanaksvisl, Tanais, the present Dnieper River, is Asia, chief city of which is Asgard and ruled over by Odin. Because of his magical power to see into the future, Odin knew that his people were destined to achieve a glorious destiny in the northern part of the world. Leaving his kingdom to his brothers, Odin led the Goths to Scythia. The story in the *Prose Edda* begins with the tower of Babel.

---

[4] Preface, *A Miscellany of Poems by Several hands* (Oxford, 1731).
[5] *Poems of William Collins,* edited by C. Stone (London, 1907), p. 5.
[6] *De sacra poesie Hebraeorum,* translated by G. Gregory as *Lectures on the Sacred Poetry of the Hebrews* (Oxford, 1753), p. 22.

Chief engineer of the project was Zoroaster but God confounded the plan. Zoroaster ruled over many Assyrian nations but the one tribe that retained the original tongue of Hebrew, despite Babel's fall, lived independently in Crete under their chief Saturnus. Saturnus had three sons: Jupiter, Neptune, and Pluto. Jupiter made war against his father, who had to flee and hide out in Italy under the alias of Njord. Jupiter's descendant in the fifth generation was Priam of Troy. Priam's daughter bore a son called Thor, and it is from this Thor that Odin descended in the twentieth generation. Pompey, at the head of victorious armies, threatened Odin's empire. Having learned through his magical powers of the glorious fortune awaiting his people in the North, Odin fled and brought his people to the North. [7]

The Odin story spread over all Europe. In the Saxon version by Widukind the Saxons are of Macedonian descent, a remnant of Alexander's Macedonian army (the Macedonians were regarded as Trojans). Fredegar makes Priam a Frank. Following Troy's fall, the Frankish party divided in two, one settling in Macedonia, the other in Asia. The latter group divided again, and under Franco, their eponymous hero, one party left for Europe. Dudo of St. Quentin offered the Norman version: the Normans are Danai, Hellenized Trojans. The English version is well known; [8] it is exceptional not to find Odin in the genealogy of English kings in chronicles written throughout the medieval period.

Aylett Sammes's *Britannia antiqua illustrata: Or the Antiquities of Ancient Britain, Derived from the Phoenicians* (1676), is the kind of compendium of sources which popularized the Odin myth. In Sammes's view, "Woden" led the

[7] A still useful account is by the Swedish anthropologist, Victor Rydberg, in the first eighty pages of his *Teutonic Mythology*, translated from the Swedish by R. B. Anderson (London, 1891).

[8] Farley, *Scandinavian Influences,* pp. 190-203; for the English version of the Trojan myth, see Brinkley, *Arthurian Legend.*

Goths on their migrations. He concludes his argument: "It is sufficient that out of these forementioned Records and Authors (to all which Wormius, Stephanius, Arngrimas Jonas, Messerius, Loccenius, and other Northern Writers give great credit as authentick for most part) we learn the Procession of our Ancestors from Asia under Woden." [9]

James Tyrrell also connects Odin with the Goths: "These Getae or Goths multiplying more than these Countries would well bear, in the time of Filemar the 5th King after Berig, great multitudes of them under his Conduct removed their Dwellings into the Asiatic Scythia, called Oudin in their Language." [10]

There can be no doubt that Sir William Temple had absorbed a large part of this lore. In the essay "Of Heroic Virtue" he writes:

It seems agreed by the curious inquirers into the antiquities of the Runic language and learning, that Odin or Woden or Goden (according to the different northern dialects) was the first and great hero of the western Scythian. That he led a mighty swarm of the Getes under the name of Goths, from the Asiatic Scythia unto the farthest north-west parts of Europe, that he seated and spread his kingdom round the whole Baltick sea, and over all the islands in it and extended it westward to the ocean, and southward to the Elve (which was anciently esteemed the bound between the Scythians and the Germans). That this vast country was in the ancient Gothic term called Biarmia, and is by some authors termed officina gentium, having furnished all those swarms of Goths, Vandals, Saxons, Angles, Jutes, Danes, and Normans, which so often infected, and at length subdued all the western provinces of Europe. [11]

Thomas Gray's prolonged studies in preparation for writing a history of English poetry brought the Odin legend within

[9] *Britannia antiqua illustrata,* p. 435.
[10] *General History of England,* p. 121. The sentence is badly written, and it evidently means that Oudin was the name for Filemar and not for Asiatic Scythia.
[11] In *Works,* I, 276-277.

his range. In his note book, under the heading "Goti," he tells :of the Scythian "Asers" who "coming from the remotest parts of the East, did at last settle themselves in the countries bordering on the Baltick." [12]

John Richardson, compiler of a huge Persian and Arabic dictonary, turns a cold eye on the Odin story. He acidly points out that if Odin and his army fled from Pompey's Roman forces, Odin must have led an army of weaklings. He asks how this army of weaklings could withstand the rigors of zero weather in Scandinavia, particularly after their long sojourn in the warm South. Richardson, nevertheless, upholds the Asiatic concept since he argues that "Tartary" is the "cradle of nations," and, offering a hint of the manner in which the tradition of Gothic liberty and enlightenment inter-twines with the theory of fiction, asserts that the Tartars have all of the virility, and so on, of the Gothic people: "Every observation, indeed, on the habits of those roving, daring people strikingly displays their love of liberty, and their simili-tude of character with the old Gothic nations." [13] Richardson goes on, as we shall see, to draw all romantic fiction from the Tartar-Persian fountainhead, emphasizing first the Oriental renown in fabulous tales of magic, elves, giants, and genie, and, second, Oriental jousting and trial by arms.

There was, in fact, no limit to the speculation about an Oriental "cradle of nations," situated in the vast recesses of Asiatic "Scythia." John Pinkerton's *Dissertation,* we have already seen, draws the Goths from Scythia; Pinkerton's bibliography is a comprehensive roster of authorities, ancient

---

[12] *Works of Thomas Gray,* edited by T. J. Mathias (London, 1814), II, 104ff. For Gray's antiquarian interests, see Roger Martin, *Essai sur Gray* (London and Paris, 1934), and William P. Jones, *Thomas Gray, Scholar* (Cambridge, 1937).

[13] *A Dissertation on the Languages, Literature and Manners of Eastern Nations* (Oxford, 1788); the dissertation was originally writ-ten as a preface to the Persian dictionary.

and modern, on the Asiatic version of the Gothic legend. Milton's idea that the Saxons derive their name from the Asiatic Sacae is strangely echoed in the eighteenth century in a theory that the Japanese are Sacae, as evidenced in the place- name Nagasaki: "Les Japonais gardent encore les nom des Sacques, dans celui de Sakae, l'une de leurs principales villes. Nangasaki, Amangasaki marquent la Nang & l'Amang des Saques." [14] Abbé Pezron's *Antiquity of Nations* (translated in 1706) presents the even more striking idea that the Germanic races arose in the East, since Teutons and Titans are etymologically the same! The Greek Titans, he says, "were either the same Titans, which to me seems probable enough, or at least their descendants, that also settled Colonies all Germany over; I mean amongst that Brave Nations, that was so renowned of Old, and much spoken of at this day, I mean those ancient and Valiant People called Teutons." [15] Pezron takes exception to Tacitus, who claimed that the Germans were indigenous:

Tacitus, in speaking of these People, whom he calls Germans, and whose Customs and Manners, he has so well described, shews us plainly, that he is inclined to believe they were Indigenes, that is, born in the Country from all Antiquity, without any Transmigrations at all, or a mixture with Foreigners. Ipsos Germanos Indigenes Crediderim, minimeq; aliarum Gentium Adventibus, hospitiis mixtos. Tacitus, tho' otherwise a very exact and judicious Author, in writing at this Rate, is strangely mistaken; for this is no other than to make the Germans spring up of the Earth like Pumpkins. [16]

---

[14] Pierre François Hugues [called d'Hancarvil:e], *Recherches sur l'origine, l'esprit et les progress des arts de la Grèce* (London, 1785), I, 153-154. For Milton, see *History of Britain,* bk. III: "They [Saxons] were a people thought by good writers to be descended from the Sacae, a kind of Scythian in the North of Asia."

[15] *The Antiquity of Nations,* translated by David Jones (London, 1809), p. x.

[16] *Ibid.,* p. 207.

For the same reasons, Tacitus was mistaken in believing Germany to have been the cradle of races: "The Prerogative belongs only to the East, so that it may be said that Asia was the cradle of the humane Race, and their Original Country: It was from thence those Swarms came, which filled Germany and the other Western and Northern countries." [17]

The translator's preface of *A General History of the Turks, Moguls, and Tatars* (1730) assumes that every one knows that the English are a Tartar people:

> Our contempt for the Tatars would still lessen perhaps, did we consider how nearly we stand related to Them; that our Ancestors came originally from the North of Asia, and that our Customs, Laws, and way of Living were formerly the same with theirs: In short, that we are no other than a Colony of Tatars... And what were the Goths, Huns, Alans, Swedes, Vandals, Franks, and other Tribes of People who many ages after descending southward overthrew the Roman Empire, but swarms from the same Hive?... As for the Saxons, Danes, and Normans, who in the latter Times made successive Conquests of England, every one knows, or at least believes, they came originally from Tatary. [18]

These various Asiatic speculations succeeded, as Grimm and his generation of philologists would have said, in Indo-Germanizing Europe. Modern philologists, free of the Aryan dogmas of the earlier school, have no such assurance that the Semitic branch stands outside of the Indo-European family. The point has special interest because a tradition preserved in rabbinical commentary, by synchronizing German and Jewish history, brought a Semitic element into the Germanic complex. In other words, the Biblical-rabbinical tradition also located the pristine home of the Germans in the East. [19]

---

[17] *Ibid.*, p. 208.
[18] Anonymous, *General History of the Turks, Moguls, and Tatars* (London, 1730), I, iii.
[19] See Appendix C: "The Rabbinical Tradition."

## GOTHIC TRIAL BY ARMS

References to Gothic dueling in eighteenth-century literature frequently are made in the transferred sense of "barbarous." On the other hand, Warton, Hurd, Mallet, Blair, and
Percy clearly seek to demonstrate that romances originated
among the Goths and reflect the Gothic institution of dueling:
in this regard, the epithet "Gothic" is ethnic and the source
is Tacitus: "Having taken by whatever means a prisoner from
the tribe with whom they are at war, they pit him against a
picked man of their own tribe, each combatant using the
weapons of his own country. The victory of the one or another
is accepted an indication of the issue." [20] (Tacitus is striking
at Roman decadence by extolling the Germanic love of fair
play and their wish to prevent needless slaughter.) Again, the
references to Danish and Burgundian dueling probably find
their source in the *Leges Burgundionum,* the laws of Gundo-
bald (d. 516) who legalized judicial combat; in this sense,
also, dueling was "Gothic." [21]

William Segar attributes trial by arms to the Lombards,
and refers to Lombard laws governing the institution: "These
particular fights were first used among the people called
Lombardes, as appeareth by the lawes written by Aliprandus
one of the kings that governed that Nation." [22] Sir Robert
Cotton's "Of the Antiquity, Use, and Ceremony of Lawfull
Combats in England" describes trial by arms as Gothic and
Lombardian. According to Cotton, dueling existed before the
laws were written, "untill the Gottish and Lombard kings,

[20] "Germania" X in *Complete Works,* p. 714.

[21] See Norman A. Bennetton, *Social Significance of the Duel in
Seventeenth Century French Drama,* Johns Hopkins University Studies
in Romance Literature and Language (Baltimore, 1938), p. 13.

[22] *The Book of Honor and Arms* (London, 1590), p. 2. Christine de
Pisan, *Fayttes of Armes* (Printed by Caxton, 1489), calls the duel a
product of "lombardyshe lawe," Early English Text Society, CLXXXIX
(London, 1932), 261.

seeing their subjects more addressed to martial discipline then to civil government, reduced those tryalls to forme and rule." [23] An essay by "Mr. Davies" in the same collection with Cotton, entitled, "Of the Same," calls dueling Gothic and Vandalic: "For it first tooke beginning among the Gothes and Vandalls; from them it was derived to the Saxons and other people of High Almaine, from them to the Normans; and from the Normans to us." [24] Thomas Comber's *Discourse of Duels* (1687), traces the institution to the Goths:

> I would not look for their Original among so civilized a people as the Heathen Romans, but judge it more probable that they were derived from the Manners of the rude and uncultivated Northern Nations, who afterwards overspread the Roman Empire, and brought in this as well as many other Pagan customs among the Western People, where they planted themselves. [25]

Comber's view is at the opposite pole from that of the eighteenth-century writers on Gothic fiction who picture Gothic dueling not only as the highest expression of chivalry but inspired by Christian ideals. Temple, in "Of Heroic Virtus," anticipates the eighteenth century panegyrics:

> Their decisions of Right and Just were by Arms, and mortal Combats allowed by Laws, approved by Princes, assisted by formal Judges, and determined by Death or Victory. From hence came all those Jousts, and Tiltings and Tournaments, so long in use, and so much debated in these parts of the World; their Marriage-feasts were solemnized by Lances and Swords, by Blows, by Wounds, and sometimes by Death, till that Custom was disgraced by the deplorable end of Henry the Second of France, and the fatal Launce of Montgomery... 'Tis known in Story how long and how frequent this was in use among all the Gothick Races, and in the several Kingdoms or Principalities

---

[23] In Hearne's *Curious Discourses*, II, 173, printed from Cotton's manuscript lecture read to the Society of Antiquaries.

[24] *Ibid.*, II, 181.

[25] *Discourse of Duels* (London, 1687), p. 3.

erected by them, even after the Proof of Christianity among them. [26]

The *World,* which enlisted in the eighteenth-century campaign to abolish dueling, remarks ironically: "This delicacy of sentiment, this refinement of manners, was reserved for the politer Goths, Visigoths, Ostrogoths, Vandals, etc., to introduce, cultivate, and establish..." [27] The list of tracts on Gothic dueling could be easily extended. We may conclude with a Cambridge prize poem of 1775:

> and from the hives
> And regions of the North o'er happier climes
> Pour forth their countless swarms of various name,
> Lombards, and Vandals, Heruli, and Goths:
> These, unaccustomed to that milder law,
> Which regulates the strife of polish'd realms,
>
> By ignorance and superstition led,
> To Heav'n's tribunal made their bold appeal,
> And from the fortune of the fight decreed.
> Clad in bright arms behold the champions stand,
> And like two coursers eager for the race...

The poem continues, describing a trial by arms. [28]

## GOTHIC FEMINISM

The alleged Gothic idealization of women is the third component in eighteenth-century theories of fiction. Tacitus' *Germania* again initiated the discussion, and he appears to have had in mind two ideas: a gynecocracy in which women were prized for their wisdom in counsel, and a conception of Germanic moral purity as evidenced by their strict moral code:

VIII:   Tradition says that armies already wavering and giving way have been rallied by women who with earnest entreaties and bosoms laid bare, have vividly represented

---

[26] In *Works,* I, 217.

[27] *World,* no. 113, February 27, 1755.

[28] Peter Layard, "Duelling," *Cambridge Prize Poems,* edited by Rev. T. Seaton (Cambridge, 1817), p. 272.

the horrors of captivity which the Germans fear with such extreme dread on behalf of their women that the strongest tie by which a state can be bound is to give among the number of hostages maidens of noble birth. They even believe that the sex has a certain sanctity and prescience and they do not despise their counsels or make light of their answers.

XVIII: Their marriage code is strict and indeed no part of their manners is more praiseworthy. Almost alone among barbarians they are content with one wife, except a very few among them, and these not from sensuality, but because their noble birth procures for them many offers of alliance.

XIX: Very rare for so numerous a population is adultery, the punishment for which is prompt.

In *Beowulf* we find "freoðu-webbe," a woman described as a "weaver of peace." Adam of Bremen's "terra feminarum" to describe the land occupied by the tribe of Kwains or Quinni is due to his misunderstanding of the tribal name for *cwen,* a woman, and probably reflects a conception of gynecocratic government among the Amazons. [29] The gynecocratic idea is reflected in Pierre d'Avity: "We also find in writing, that the Germans (being in a manner defeated) have often repulsed their enemies by the encouragement of their wives to whose spirits they did attribute a certain foresight and holynesse, by reason whereof they did not reject their counsell, nor contemne their advice in their assemblies." [30] Richard Whitlock also records the Germanic practice of consulting women: "The Celtae falling into Civill broyles were (when no other means could) by their Wives Arbitration reconciled." [31] In Thomas Carte's *General History of England,* we also find a discussion

[29] See *The Whole Works of King Alfred the Great,* J. A. Giles, general editor (Jubilee ed.; London, 1858), II, 38, refers to Adam of Bremen.

[30] *Estates, Empires, and Principalities,* p. 559.

[31] *Zootomia* (London, 1654), p. 325.

of Celtic gynarchy: "But it was peculiar to the Celtic nations not to march, or fight, without the advice of women to constitute them judges of the contraventions of public treaties and the laws of nations; to admit them to their councils of war, and to consult them on the most important occasions of public concern." [32] An Oxford prize poem of 1791 by George Richards tells of the "illustrious Fair ones, wont to brave Helvellinus' storms," and in a note quotes and glosses the line: "What is said of the ancient German women is applied by Mr. Mason and our early historians, to our country-women of earlier ages. The important offices which they filled in the government, so unusual in the Savage State, fully justify this application." [33]

Possibly the gynecocratic idea would tend to hamper the conception of helpless womanhood, pining to be rescued by Gothic knights-errant, but, in any case, it was part of the picture of Germanic feminine idealism which the theorists of fiction were drawing. There is no dearth of material extolling the Germanic veneration of women. Verstegen, especially, disseminated the idea:

Tacitus showing their great continency saith, that Matrimony is severely observed among them, and that of all barbarous people, they only did content themselves one man with one woman, except some very few which not for unruly lust, but for their Nobility sake were sued unto, for sundry marriages. Adultery is seldome committed in so populous a Nation, and the punishment for it incontinently inflected at the best liking of the husband. [34]

The historians repeat Verstegen's remarks, and the picture of Germanic feminism became a constituent element in the theories of fiction propounded in the eighteenth century. Sociological speculation of the period is concerned with Germanic

[32] *General History of England* (London, 1747-1755), I, 72-73.
[33] *The Aboriginal Britons* (Oxford, 1791), p. 8.
[34] *Restitution of Decayed Intelligence*, p. 49.

feminism. William Hayley, author of *A Philosophical, Historical, and Moral Essay on Old Maids* (1785) says:

Of all people on the globe, those to whom the sisterhood of
Old Maids have been most indebted, are undoubtedly our brave
progenitors of the North, The manly and generous Goths have
acquired a degree of glory, 'above all Greek, above all Roman
fame,' by paying the most tender deference to the fair sex and
by setting the highest value on the virtue of chastity. [35]

The forests of the North were the "nurseries of chivalry"
according to the writer who styles himself "Adam":

It is to the barbarians, who spread conflagration and ruin,
who trampled on the monuments of art, and spurned the append-
ages of elegance and pleasure, that we owe the bewitching
spirit of gallantry which in the ages of refinement, reigns in
the courts of Europe. That system, which has made it a principle of honor among us to consider the women as sovereigns;
which has partly formed our customs, our manners, and our
policy; which has exalted the human character by softening the
empire of force; which mingles politeness with the use of the
sword; which delights in protecting the weak, and in conferring
that importance which nature or fortune have denied—that
system was brought hither from the frozen shores of the Baltic,
and from the savage forests of the North. The northern nations,
in general, paid a great respect to women. Continually employed
in hunting or in war, they condescended only to soften their
ferocity in the presence of the fair. Their forests were the nurseries of chivalry. [36]

## GOTHIC ROMANCES

Three hypotheses were suggested in the eighteenth century
for the purpose of explaining the origin of romances. 1) the
Oriental theory of Huet and Temple: the Crusaders, upon
their return to Europe, introduced the Saracen tales which are
the source of all romances; 2) the northern Scaldic theory of

[35] *A Philosophical, Historical, and Moral Essay on Old Maids* (London, 1785), III, 111.

[36] *Woman. Sketches of the History, Genius, Disposition, Accom-
plishments, Employments, Customs, and Importance of the Fair Sex*
(London, 1790), pp. 62-63.

Mallet and Percy: knight-errantry, feminine idealism, jousting, existed long before the feudal system; the northern Scalds introduced into Normandy their chivalric fables when they accompanied Rollo's army on its invasion; from France, the romances spread to England; 3) the combined northern and Oriental theory of Warton: "And wonders wild of Arabesque combine / With Gothic imagery of darker shade." Warton's theory came to predominate, although Ritson, for example, disclaimed all three theories on the assumption that the instinct for storytelling is universal and requires, therefore, no cultural hypotheses. [37]

It is evident that the first two theories are essentially the same with only slight differences. The climate postulate regarding the "naturally" exuberant Oriental imagination is countered simply in the Mallet-Percy theory by the assertion that, the climate conception notwithstanding, the northern fables also had witches, dragons, and enchantments; the Germanic women enjoyed the same adulation as the Oriental odalisque; Gothic knights and Oriental warriors were both sworn to aid ladies in distress. The only difference is in the direction of flow of influence: either the northern Goths transported their chivalry southward to the Orient or, approaching the problem from the other end, chivalry was transported northward from an Oriental home. In either case, the romances were "Gothic" either on the basis of the Scandza theory, the Odin legend, or the Biblical Japhet-Tuisco genealogy. Warton's strategy, then, is that of a mediator. He grants both the Scaldic and Oriental theories and proceeds to show that the romances actually preserve the folk-memory of the Gothic habitats both in the North and in the Orient.

[37] See John C. Dunlop, *The History of Prose Fiction*, (London, 1888) which is still useful, largely because Dun'op wrote in 1812 when the Gothic legend was still rife; his bibliography preceding the text is a summary of what the eighteenth century read on the subject of fiction.

Bishop Huet's *Treatise of Romances and Their Originals* (1671; translated 1672 and 1715) considers the Oriental theory and concludes that "their invention is due to the Orientals, I mean to the Egyptians, Arabians, Persians, and Syrians." [38] Huet ends, however, by contradicting his original thesis that the Orient was the fountain of fiction. In his conclusion, he reasons that if fiction is a product of ignorance and ignorance is universal, then fiction can arise everywhere: "'There is then no reason to contend but that French, German, and English Romances, and all the Fables of the North are of the Countrey's growth, born upon the place, and not imported from elsewhere." [39]

Huet's notion relating fiction to ignorance confuses the Oriental issue, but in Temple we find a more logical relationship established. Temple's basic assumption is that poetry has always preceded prose in literary history—he is among the earliest of English writers to establish a primitivistic origin of poetry. [40] These primitivistic poetic effusions lacked art, but for the same reason they were replete with enchantments, elves, and the like. With the few bits of Norse poetry in mind which the pioneers in Gothic antiquities had dug up, Temple traces the overflow of the Gothic "dithyrambick" imagination into romances composed in Spain during the Gothic conquest. His essay On Poetry first established the primitivistic origin of poetry:

Instead of Critick or Rules concerning Poetry, I shall rather turn my Thoughts to the History of it, and observe the Antiquity, the Uses, the Changes, the Decays, that have attended this great Empire of Wit.

It is, I think, generally agreed to have been the first sort of

[38] *Treatise of Romances* (London, 1672), p. 10, translator unknown.
[39] *Ibid.*, p. 98.
[40] Lois Whitney, "Studies in Eighteenth Century Primitivistic Theories of Epic Origins" (University of Chicago, unpublished dissertation, 1921).

Writing that has been used in the World, and in several Nations to have preceded the very Invention or Usage of Letters. The last is certain in America, where the first Spaniards met with many strains of Poetry, and left several of them Translated into their Language, which seemed to have flowed from a true Poetick Vein before any Letters were known in those Regions. The same is probable of the Scythians, the Grecians, and the Germans. Aristotle says the Agathyrsi had their Laws all in Verse; and Tacitus, that the Germans had no Annals nor Records but what were so.

He concludes: "It appears that Poetry was the first sort of Writing known and used in the several Nations of the World." [41]

Temple calls Norse poetry "Gothic runes":

The common vein of the Gothick Runes was what is Termed Dithyrambick, and was of a raving or rambling sort of Wit or Invention, loose and flowing, with little Art or Confinement to any certain Measures or Rules; yet some of it wanted not the true Spirit of Poetry in some Degree, or that natural Inspiration which has been said to arise from some Spark of Poetical Fire wherewith particular Men are born...

But as the true Flame of Poetry was rare among them, and the rest was but Wild Fire that Sparkled or rather Crackled a while, and soon went out with little Pleasure or Gazing of the Beholders, Those Runers who could not raise Admiration by the Spirit of their Poetry endeavoured to do it by another, which was that of Enchantments: This came in to supply the Defect of that sublime and Marvellous, which has been found both in Poetry and Prose among the Learned Antients. The Gothick Runers, to Gain and Establish the Credit and Admiration of their Rhymes, turned the use of them very much to Incantations and Charms, pretending by them to raise Storms, to Calm the Seas, to cause Terror in their Enemies, to Transport themselves in the Air, to Conjure Spirits, to Cure Diseases, and Stanch Bleeding Wounds, to make Women kind or easy, and Men hard or invulnerable, as one of Atchievments, by Force of these Magical Arms. The Men or Women who were thought to perform such Wonders or Enchantments, were, from Vüses, or Wises, the

[41] In Spingarn, *Critical Essays,* III, 85, 88.

Name of those Verses wherein their charms were conceived, called Wizards or Witches.

Out of this Quarry seem to have been raised all those Trophees of Enchantment that appear in the whole Fabrick of the old Spanish Romances, which were the Productions of the Gothick Wit among them during their Reign; and after the Conquests of Spain by the Saracens they were applied to the long Wars between them and the Christians. From the same perhaps may be derived all the visionary Tribe of Faries, Elves, and Goblins, of Sprites and of Bul-beggars, that serve not only to fright children into whatever their Nurses please, but sometimes, by lasting Impressions, to disquiet the sleeps and the very Lives of Men and Women, till they grow to Years and Discretion; and that, God knows, is a Period of time which some People Arrive to but very late, and perhaps others never. At least, this belief prevailed so far among the Goths and their Races, that all sorts of Charms were not only attributed to their Runes or Verses, but to their very Characters; so that, about the Eleventh Century, they were forbidden and abolished in Sweden, as they had been before in Spain, by Civil and Ecclesiastical Commands or Constitutions. 42

The main point of Bishop Richard Hurd's *Letters on Chivalry and Romance* (1762) in their conception of the origins of fiction grants that the Crusades may have opened a new vein of literary composition. Hurd urges, however, that the Crusade theory begs the question, since the Crusades themselves were but the product of the previously existing Gothic gallantry expressed in the Gothic romances. In other words, there would have been Gothic romances without the Crusades:

That unless the seeds of that spirit, which appeared in the Crusades, had been plentifully sown and indeed grown up into some maturity in the feudal times, preceding that event, I see not how it could have been possible for the western princes to give that politic diversion to their turbulent vassals which the new hypothesis supposes.

In short, there are two distinct periods to be carefully observed, in a deduction of the rise and progress of Chivalry.

42 *Ibid.,* III, 95-97.

The first is that in which the empire was overturned, and the feudal governments were everywhere introduced on its ruins, by the northern nations. In this area, that new policy settled itself in the west, and operated so powerfully as to lay the first foundations, and to furnish the remote causes, of what we know by the name of chivalry.

The other period is, when these causes had taken a fuller effect, and shewed themselves in that signal enterprize of the Crusades. [43]

Gothic chivalry, trial by arms, feminine idealism, provide the substance of the Gothic romances, Hurd says; but in another respect Hurd stands quite outside of the North-South controversy. Far more than Mallet, Percy, and Warton, Hurd has a greater political sophistication, which he shows in two ways. First the *Letters on Chivalry* constantly stress the political conditions created by feudalism as engendering Gothic chivalry: "But Chivalry, properly so called...seems to have sprung immediately out of the Feudal Constitution." [44] Second, his grasp of political and constitutional problems is revealed in his Dialogues V and VI "On the Constitution of the English Government." Hurd, like Swift, has a keen evolutionary insight in the growth and modification of political institutions. Thus, like Swift, he approves of Gothic liberty, but he sees the feudal constitution as the perfect instrument, evolved out of the tribal council; beyond this perfect legal instrument, the cry for Gothic liberty is a delusion, "so that I cannot by any means commend the zeal which some have shewn in seeking the origin of this house [Commons] in the British or even Saxon annals. Their aim was to serve the cause of liberty, but, it must be owned at the expence of truth, and, as we now perceive, without the least necessity." [45]

[43] In *Moral and Political Dialogues* (3d ed.; London, 1765), III, 218-219.

[44] *Ibid.*, III, 198-199.

[45] *Ibid.*, II, 168. Hurd refers (p. 115) to Nathaniel Bacon's *Discourses* and summarizes (p. 118): "You see then how fully the spirit

Other than this political perception of the root of the problem, Hurd narrates the ideas, by this time conventional, of Gothic chivalry:

The old inhabitants of these Northwest parts of Europe were extremely given to the love and exercise of arms.

Not but the foundation of this refined gallantry was laid in the antient manners of the German nations ... their consideration of the sex was prodigious, as we see in the history of their irruptions into the Empire; where, among all their ravages and devastations of other sorts, we find they generally abstained from offering any violence to the honour of the women. [46]

The Crusades, Hurd goes on to explain, merely offered the best opportunity for the expression of Gothic arms—daring in hazardous enterprise, adventure to relieve the oppressed, and so on. [47] In these senses, the romances are "Gothic." The remainder of the *Letters on Chivalry* presents the well-known appreciations of Spenser, Milton, and Shakespeare as supreme "Gothic" poets. [48]

Bishop Thomas Percy is the chief English proponent of the northern theory of the origin of romances. In his "Essay on the Ancient Metrical Romances" (1765), he states his thesis:

of liberty possessed the very language of our Saxon forefathers. And it might well do so; for it was of the essence of the German constitutions." See also (p. 129) a description of feudal tenures as "essential to all the Gothic or Germanic constitutions."

[46] *Ibid.,* III, 198, 209.

[47] *Ibid.,* III, 212-213.

[48] Warburton held to the Crusade theory in explanation of the spread of the romances; in all likelihood, Hurd is criticizing Warburton's essay which was written (unsigned) to serve as a preface to Charles Jarvis' translation of *Don Quixote* (London, 1742). Warburton finds dueling, feminism, and magic prevalent among the northern nations (pp. viii. xiii, xv). The call to the Crusade imbued northern chivalry with high idealism: "During the prevalence of these barbarous customs, St. Peter's successors took the opportunity of fishing some utility out of them, by inciting the princes of Christendom to undertake to recover the holy sepulchre from the hands of the Saracens" (p. xv).

"That our old romances of chivalry may be derived in a lineal descent from the ancient historical songs of the Gothic bards and scalds, will be shown below." [49] The Arabic theory is controverted: "As Odin and his followers are said to have come precisely from those parts of Asia, we can readily account for the prevalence of fictions of this sort among the Gothic nations of the North, without fetching them from the Moors in Spain." [50] Gothic trial by arms, and feminism, existing long before feudalism, sufficiently explain the subject matter of the romances:

'Chivalry as a distinct military order, conferred in the way of investiture and accompanied with the solemnity of an oath, and other ceremonies' was of later date, and sprung out of the feudal constitution, as an elegant writer has clearly shown. [He cites Ste. Palaye, *Mémoires de chevalerie*, for which see Warton, below.] But the ideas of chivalry prevailed long before in all the Gothic nations, and may be discovered as in embryo in the customs, manners, and opinions of every branch of that people. That fondness of going in quest of adventures, that spirit of challenging to single combat, and that respectful complaisance shown to the fair sex (so different from the manners of the Greeks and Romans) all are of Gothic origin, and may be traced up to the earliest times among all the Northern nations. [51]

Percy's main source of Gothic ideas is Paul Henri Mallet's *Northern Antiquities* which he translated in 1774. This influence, however, can be easily exaggerated, since there was available to Mallet and Percy both a common store of considerable knowledge of Gothic moral purity, manliness, and so on. Mallet, in any case, is not concerned with the origins of fiction although his descriptions of Gothic gallantry would lead to the northern conception. Percy's preface, however, to his translation of Mallet contemplates the problem of fic-

[49] *Reliques of Ancient English Poetry* (London, 1839), III, 3.
[50] *Ibid.,* III, 8.
[51] *Ibid.,* III, 4.

tion: "From a very few rude and simple tenets, these wild
fablers had, in the course of eight or nine centuries, invented
and raised an amazing superstructure of fiction." [52]

Mallet's chapter twelve describes Gothic gallantry: "We
even owe to them that spirit of gallantry which was so little
known to the Greeks and Romans, how polite soever in other
respects." [53] "But this is not all," Mallet continues,

at a time when piracy and fondness for seeking adventures
exposed weakness to continual and unexpected attacks, the
women, especially those of celebrated beauty, stood in want
sometimes of deliverers, and almost always of defenders. Every
young warrior, eager after glory (and this was often the character of whole nations) must have been glad then to take upon
him an office, which promised such just returns of fame, which
flattered the most agreeable of all passions, and at the same
time gratified another almost as strong, that for a wandering
and rambling life. [54]

Mallet concludes by telling affectingly the stories of Regner
Lodbrog and Harold Harfagre as typifying northern gallantry, chivalry, manliness, and so forth. He accounts for the
strained imagery, hyperboles, and "allegories" of northern
romance, not by the Oriental climate postulate, but by northern fierceness of courage which expresses itself "naturally,"
he thinks, in exuberant language. [55]

Thomas Warton's essay "Of the Origin of Romantic Fiction in Europe" appeared in 1774 as one of the three "Dissertations" prefixed to his *History of English Poetry*. Warton's work is that of a mediator between the northern and
Oriental theories. He grants the point that the Crusades
spread fabling over Europe, but he pushes the Arabic influence further back to the Arabic settlers in Spain during
the eighth century; from Spain, through commercial channels,

[52] *Northern Antiquities* (London, 1774), I, xviii.
[53] *Ibid.*, I, 315.
[54] *Ibid.*, III, 318-319.
[55] *Ibid.*, III, 393.

the romances spread to France (entering the ports of Toulon
and Marseille), and from France to England. On the other
hand, he also grants the northern Scaldic theory. In the latter
connection, Warton's main point is that the Scaldic theory
must nevertheless be referred to Asiatic regions, since Odin
led an Asiatic band to Scandinavia when Pompey's defeat of
Mithridates made life untenable in Asia. Warton alone appears to have a chronological sense of the centuries between
Odin's *northward* migration and the return *southward* of the
Goths in their historic defeat of Rome.

Actually, as we have seen, the two conflicting theories had
been mediated before in the demonstration that, the Oriental
climate postulate notwithstanding, the northern tales also
have their quota of elves and incantations. Warton's efforts,
however, to reconcile the two theories brings to light a new
aspect of romance literature. Warton shows that the folk-
memory of the Gothic home in the North accounts for the
gloomy forests, ice, and precipices; the fantasy and strained
metaphorical language preserves the folk-memory of the
Gothic habitat in the warm regions of Asia. Thus Warton's
theory explained, for example, the Ossianic poems both in
the Biblical intensity of their expression and the gloom and
ice. Warton's theory remained the influential one, since it
appeared to account for all the facts by excluding none which
was relevant.

It is not without importance to determine, if possible, the
sources of Warton's ideas. Blair, Drake, Richardson, Moore,
Clara Reeves, all express, like Warton, indebtedness to
Sainte-Palaye. As a matter of fact, these followers of Warton refer to Sainte-Palaye only because Warton does. Warton's source, as far as it can be accurately determined, is
not Sainte-Palaye, whose treatise merely connects romances
with feudalism. Warton's real source is Abbé Millot, editor
from Sainte-Palaye's manuscripts of the *Histoire litteraire*

*des troubadours* (Paris, 1774). The *Histoire* is prefaced by a "Discours préliminaire," unsigned, but the Censor Royal on page 470 says he has read the *Histoire* "composée d'après les manuscripts de M. De Sainte-Palaye." M. l'Abbé Millot is referred to as "le savant Académicien et l'habile Rédacteur." Warton's explicit references make clear that he has read the 1774 edition of Sainte-Palaye prepared by Millot, and there can hardly be a question of Warton's borrowings from Millot's "Discours," not only for the dissertation on fiction but for the *History of English Poetry*. The discussion of German feminism, beginning on page thirty-two of the "Discours," is especially apropos to the question of Warton's source.

Warton's "Dissertation" begins:

That peculiar and arbitrary species of fiction which we commonly call Romantic, was entirely unknown to the writers of Greece and Rome. It appears to have been imported into Europe by a people, whose modes of thinking, and habits of invention, are not natural to that country. It is generally supposed to have been borrowed from the Arabians. But this origin has not been hitherto perhaps examined or ascertained with a sufficient degree of accuracy. It is my present design, by a more distinct and extended inquiry than has yet been applied to the subject, to trace the manner and the period of its introduction into the popular belief, the oral poetry, and the literature of the Europeans. [56]

Arabic fiction was introduced into Europe earlier than the Crusades: "But it is evident ... that these fancies were introduced at a much earlier period. The Saracens, or Arabians, having been for some time seated on the northern coasts of Africa, entered Spain about the beginning of the eighth century." [57] Warton then begins the attack on the Mallet-Percy northern theory:

[56] "Of the Origin of Romantic Fiction in Europe," in *History of English Poetry*, edited by Richard Price (London, 1840), I, i.
[57] *Ibid.*, I, ii.

Hitherto I have considered the Saracens, either at their im-
migrations into Spain at about the ninth century, or at the
time of the crusades, as the first authors of romantic fabling
among the Europeans. But a late ingenious critic has advanced
an hypothesis, which assigns a new source, and a much earlier
date, to these fictions. I will cite his opinion of this matter in
his own words. [Warton quotes Percy, and the footnote reads:
Percy on Ancient. Metr. Rom. i. p. 3,4, edit. 1767. Monsieur
Mallet, a very able man and a very elegant inquirer into the
genius and antiquities of the northern nation, maintains the
same doctrine.] [58]

"I do not mean," adds Warton, "to reject this hypothesis; but
this I will endeavor to show how far I think it is true, and
in what manner or degree it may be reconciled with the
system delivered above." [59] The Odin story is offered as the
means of reconciling the two versions of the Gothic legend,
and Warton points to the chronological gap separating the
Scandza migration and the Odin flight. [60] The chronology
makes both theories a priori possible.

A comparison of northern and Persian (he calls them
Georgian—compare with Collins' *Persian Eclogues*) institutions, religon, and beliefs leads to the observation on the
dual northern and southern characteristics of romances:

Their poetry ... was filled with those fictions which the most
exaggerated pagan superstition would naturally implant in the
wild imaginings of an Asiatic people. And from this principle
alone, I mean of their Asiatic origin, some critics would at
once account for a certain capricious spirit of extravagance,
and those bold eccentric conceptions, which so strongly distinguish the old northern poetry. [61]

Granting the Asiatic theory and the long retention of psych-

---

[58] *Ibid.,* I, xviii.
[59] *Ibid.,* I, xx.
[60] *Ibid.,* I, xxiii; the same point is made in Warton's *Observations
on the "Fairly Queen" of Spenser* (London, 1807), I, 88-89.
[61] *Ibid.,* I, xxiv.

ological patterns of behavior, it is still true that in their new northern home new imagery enters into the romances:

Yet ideas and sentiments of this sort, once imbibed, are long remembered and retained, in savage life... In the mean time, we may suppose, that the new situation of these people, in Scandinavia might have added a darker shade and a more savage complexion to their former fictions and superstitions; and that the formidable objects of nature to which they had become familiarized in those northern solitudes, the piny precipices, the frozen mountains, and the gloomy forests, acted on their imaginations, and gave a tincture of horror to their imagery. [62]

John Richardson, James Beattie, Clara Reeve, and John Moore are interesting as theorists of the origin of fiction, but they merely reproduce and combine in varying proportions the Arabian theory, the northern theory, the effects of the Crusades and feudalism, the picture of Gothic veneration of woman, Gothic trial by arms, and so on; Warton, Hurd, Mallet, Percy, and Sainte-Palaye are given as sources. [63] Dr. Nathan Drake's discourse on fiction, however, invites special consideration. Drake, like Warton, seeks to reconcile the northern and Asiatic theories. The result is in Drake a new terminology based on a distinction between two kinds of Gothic: the "terrible" and the "sportive."

Of the various kinds of superstition which have in any age influenced the human mind, none appears to have operated with so much effect as what has been termed the Gothic. Even in the present polished period of society, there are thousands who are yet alive to all the horrors of witchcraft, to all the solemn and terrible graces of the appalling spectre. The most

[62] *Ibid.*, I, xxv.

[63] Richardson, *Dissertation*; Beattie, "On Fable and Romance," in *Dissertations*, II, 233-320; Reeve, *Progress of Romance* (1785; Facsimile Text Society ed.; New York, 1930); Moore, "A View of the Commencement and Progress of Romance," prefixed to *Miscellaneous Works of Tobias Smollett* (London, 1797).

enlightened mind, the mind free from all taint of superstition, involuntarily acknowledges the power of Gothic fancy; and the last favourable reception which two or three publications in this style have met with is a convincing proof of this assertion. The enchanted forest of Tasso, the spectre of Camoens, and the apparitions of Shakespeare, are to this day highly pleasing, striking, and sublime features in these delightful compositions.

And although this kind of superstition be able to arrest every faculty of the human mind, and to shake, as it were, all nature with horror, yet does it also delight in the most sportive and elegant imagery. The traditional tales of elves and fairies still convey to warm imagination an inexhausted source of invention, supplying all those wild, romantic and varied ideas with which a wayward fancy loves to sport. The Provencal bards, and the neglected Chaucer and Spenser, are the originals from whence this exquisite species of fabling has been drawn, improved, and applied with so much inventive elegance by Shakespeare...

The vulgar Gothic therefore, an epithet here adopted to distinguish it from the regular mythology of the Edda, turns chiefly on the ministration of the Spectre, or the innocent grambols of the Fairy, the former, perhaps, partly derived from the Platonic Christianity, the latter from the fictions of the East, as imported into Europe during the period of the Crusades. [64]

The Gothic "novel of terror" has not been our concern; the gradual establishment in the period of a new category of aesthetic beauty—the sublime—explains the *schauerroman*. Filaments extend, however, between the novel of terror and the chivalric romance. It is significant that Drake in his concern with the "terrible" Gothic has blurred the distinction between the two types. The trend is observable in James Beattie, whose care over the details of Gothic dueling and Gothic feminism shows that his primary, and indeed only,

[64] Drake's remarks originally appeared in the form of a preface to his novel, *Henry Fitzower;* they were reprinted in his *Literary Hours; Or Sketches Critical, Narrative, and Poetical* (3d. ed.; London, 1804), I, 137-138, 139.

concern is with the romance of chivalry. Yet, even Beattie, in his description of the conditions of actual feudal life as a factor in the growth of romance, also describes precisely those features of "terror" embodied in the *schauerroman*:

The castles of the greater barons, reared in a rule but grand style of architecture; full of dark and winding passages, of secret apartments, of long uninhabited galleries, and of chambers supposed to be haunted with spirits; and undermined by subterranean labyrinths as places of retreat in extreme danger; the howling of winds through the crevices of old Walls, and other dreary vacuities; the grating of heavy doors on rusty hinges of iron; the shrieking of bats, and the screaming of owls, and other creatures, that resort to desolate or half-inhabited buildings... [65]

Drake goes on not only to discuss the distinctions between the "terrible" and "sportive" Gothic, but to present a poem and a tale embodying the distinction. The examples are a blur of romance and terror. Drake says, in introducing them,

Although so great a disparity evidently obtains between the two species of Gothic superstition, the terrible and the sportive, yet no author, that I am acquainted with, has, for narrative machinery, availed himself of this circumstance, and thrown them into immediate contrast. In a beautiful fragment lately published by Mrs. Barbauld under the title of Sir Bertrand, the transition is immediately from the deep Gothic to the Arabic or Saracenic superstition; which although calculated to surprise, would have given more pleasure, perhaps, and would have rendered the preceding scenes of horror more striking, had it been of a light and contrasted kind. Struck, from such an opposition to imagery, I have determined to devote a few papers to this design, and in the following Ode and Tale, which are solely amenable to the tribunal of fancy, much of both species of the vulgar gothic superstition is introduced. [66]

The "Ode to Superstition" follows. The first picture is of hags in a caverned cell, drinking warm blood, then dancing in

[65] *Dissertations,* II, 278.
[66] *Literary Hours,* I, 147

the moonlight around a blasted oak. The poet bids Superstition to flee and the picture changes as elves and sprites
come "light-sporting o'er the trembling green." Drake's notes
at the end explain: "The two species of Gothic superstition,
the gloomy and the sportive, are, in this Ode, represented as
the offspring of different parents; the former being produced
by Fear and Midnight, the latter by Hesper and the Moon." [67]
The tale, *Henry Fitzower,* is told in three parts, the first two
of which are "terrible," the last, "sportive." The story is of
Henry's love for Adeline; Walleram, the villain captures her;
there are Gothic dungeons, witches, creaking doors. Henry
kills the villain and departs with his lady-love. This introduces
the "sportive" sequence: music instead of shrieks, fairies
dancing, and so on.

Essays fifty-three to fifty-five, "On Scandinavian mythology," in Drake's *Literary Hours,* discussing Gothic chivalry
and trial by arms, and the like, but more interestingly, again
attempt to explain the two types of Gothic on the basis of the
two climates, northern and Asiatic:

Odin, indeed, when he conducted his colony from the Caspian
to the shores of the Baltic, placed himself at the head of a
nation, already addicted to the charms of poetry, and even
familiar, perhaps with the rich landscape of Georgia; but in the
wilds of Scandinavia, where Nature assumes a more terrific
shape, where all is savage, gigantic and sublime, imagination
is soon become more powerfully affected and forcibly combined
with the martial mythology of their leader, in imparting a ster-
ner tone to the buses, and air of loftier enthusiasm. [68]

The Gothic legend was a treasure house to which England's
literary critics also brought a contribution. Their contributions
run in unbroken sequence with those of the historians, scholars, parliamentarians, and poets we have met in our study.
Subtly overlaying and underlaying the faith in Gothic liberty

[67] *Ibid.,* I, 150-154.
[68] *Ibid.,* III. 350.

and enlightenment, the critical appraisals of the so-called Gothic romances created the same image of the gallant, humane, pious, energetic, and adventurous Goth.

Perhaps it is true that the Gothic ideal in England remained no more than an ideal. Perhaps it is true that the Gothic romances did not really reflect English life. These things one can admit without, at the same time, diminishing the significance of the Gothic legend. The truth is that if literature does not reflect life, it reflects the best of life. In other words, it does make a difference what kind of ideal one seeks to grasp. The truth becomes overwhelming when viewed in the lurid light of recent events in Germany where the Gothic faith ended neither in virtue, humanity, nor honor.

# APPENDIX A
## CLIMATE AND LIBERTY

The conception of Germanic virility received powerful support from a theory of environmental conditioning. The frigid temperature of the Gothic habitat in the northern region of Scandza was held to be, according to a prevalent climate theory, the physiological factor explaining Germanic vigor and zeal for liberty. Per contra, the southern peoples were invertebrate and docile toward tyrants as a result of life in hot, enervating climates. Thus, the Nordic-Latin contrast appears under a fresh, quasi-scientific perspective.

Theories of the influence of climate on character are as old as Aristotle. It was Paul the Deacon, historian of the Longobards, however, who brought the climate theory to bear on Gothic history. We recall that Jordanes called Scandza a hive of races (*officina gentium*) and a womb of nations (*vagina gentium*). Jordanes makes no attempt to explain why the Goths left their *urheim* but Paul the Deacon finds in the climate theory an anterior explanation of the Gothic migrations. The effect of the cold, according to Paul, was fecundity; consequently, because of overpopulation, the Goths were compelled to migrate. Paul says nothing of liberty, but centuries later his climate theory was invoked to explain the Germanic "natural" zeal for liberty. Thus "nature" seemed to vindicate the Germanic destiny to bring about either through sheer populousness or through their splendid manly qualities, induced by the cold climate, a rejuvenation of the world. The South was ordained by "nature" to decay.

"The region of the north," Paul begins his work,

in proportion as it is removed from the heat of the sun and is chilled with snow and frost, is so much the more healthful to the

16

bodies of men and fitted in the propagation of nations, just as, on the other hand, every southern region, the nearer it is to the heat of the sun, the more it abounds in diseases and is less fitted for the bringing up of the human race. From this it happens that such great multitudes of peoples spring up in the north. [1]

Pierre Charron's text on the skeptical philosophy, *De La Sagesse,* was frequently published in translation during the seventeenth century. Charron connects the Germanic love of liberty, their manly qualities, with the effect of cold:

The cause of all these corporal and spiritual differences, is the inequality and difference of the inward heat, which is in those countries and people, that is to say, strong and vehement in the Northerns by reason of the great outward cold, which incloseth and drieth [driveth?] the heat into the inward parts... Weak and feeble in the Southerns, the inward heat being dispersed and drawn into the outward parts, by the vehemency of the outward heat... The other distinction more particular, may be referred to this general of North, and South: for we may refer to the conditions of the Northern, those of the West, and that live in the mountains, warriours, fierce people, desirous of liberty, by the reason of the cold which is in the mountains... By reason of their war-like fierceness, they will not endure to be commanded by authority, they love their liberty, at leastwise elective commanders. [2]

[1] *History of the Longobards* (c. 720), translated by W. D. Foulke (New York, 1907), p. 3. See "Appendix II, Roman Sources" (p. 306) for Paul's knowledge of Jordanes. A new etymology of *Germania* enters. Paul's derivation of Germania from *Germinare* Foulke shows to be based on Isidor of Seville; the etymon would explain German fecundity; see Isidor, *Etymologiarum,* bk. xiv, ch. 4, edited by W. M. Lindsay (Oxford, 1911). For the same derivation, see William of Malmesbury: "quia tantum virorum germinat," in *Rerum Anglicarum Scriptores Post Bedam Praecipui...* edited by Sir Henry Savile (London, 1596), p. 3. See also Robert Manning of Brunne, *The Story of England,* edited by Frederick J. Furnivall, Rolls series, LXXXVII (1) (London, 1887), 257; Robert Fabyan, *The New Chronicles of England and France,* edited by Henry Ellis (London, 1811), pp. 59-69; Richard Grafton, *Chronicle,* I, 75-81.

[2] *Of Wisdome,* translated by S. Lennard (London, 1670), pp. 156-157.

Cardinal Bentivolgio (cited later by Roger Twysden, one of the foremost Gothicists), also stresses the impatience of northern people with authority:

Non può negarsi che nelle parti Settentrionalli d'Europa non restino tuttavia forme di governi più liberi, non potendo far molte cose il Re d'Inghilterra senza il consentimento delle provincie soggete. Piu limitata ancora nel Re di Danimarca e l'autorita, piu limitata nel Re di Polonia; e molto ristrelta apparisce ancora ne Principe di Germania. Ma e necessario di confessare all' incontro ch' e stato sempre, e che si conserva tottavia molto grande l'autorita del supremo capo in tutti questi governi. [3]

Francis Bacon, disregarding the Mongolian invasions, has the curious idea that invasions historically have always been from the North because of the northern martial spirit:

It hath seldom or never been seen that the far southern people have invaded the northern, but contrariwise. Whereby it is manifest that the northern tract of the world is in nature the more martial region: be it in respect of the stars of that hemisphere; or of the great continents that are upon the north, whereas the south part, for aught that is known, is almost all sea; or (which is most apparent) of the cold of the northern parts, which is that which, without aid of discipline, doth make the bodies hardest, and the courages warmest. [4]

In his discussion of the climate theory, Giovanni Botero assembles the prime authorities, Paul the Deacon, Jordanes, and Olaus Magnus, one of the modern Uppsala scholars:

[3] "Della relazione delle provincie unite di Fiandra," in *Opere Storiche* (Milano, 1805), I, 121: "It cannot be denied that in the northern part of Europe there does not now remain forms of Government more free, more powerless to do many things, than the king of England, without the consent of the subject province. More limited still is the authority vested in the king of Denmark and even more limited in the king of Poland, and it appears still more restricted in the Prince of Germany. But it is necessary to confess, on the other hand, that such has always been the case and this authority of the supreme head in all these governments is still preserved very great."

[4] "Of Vicissitudes of Things," in *Works* (Riverside ed.; New York, 1878), II 273.

And as the Northerne-man by nature is hot and moist (the Elements of faecunditie) so there is no question, but that of all people they are, and have bin, the most populous. For from the Goths, Scythians, the German, and the Scandians, not only vast deserts, and goodly cities have been founded, and inhabited, but from their loynes also have Colonies beene derived throughout all Europe. Well therefore might Methodius and P. Diaconus resemble their Armies to swarmes of Bees. And most true it is, that Iordanes and Olaus terme the North, the Store-house of Mankind. [5]

There follows for seventeen pages an elaborate analysis of the differences, as a result of climatic conditioning, between northern and southern peoples. Northerners are courageous, prone to action; conversely, southerners are weak and contemplative.

Jean Bodin, like Aristotle, divides the world into three regions: North, South, and Temperate. Inhabitants of the temperate zone have in combination the northern characteristic of vigor and the southern characteristic of wit; hence, the stable governments are found established in the temperate zone. Because of their vigor, northerners are too prone toward liberty: "For the people of the North, and those that live upon mountaines, being fierce and warlike, trusting in their force and strength, desire Popular estates, or at least elective Monarchies; neither can they easily endure to be commanded impereiously. So all their kings are elective, whome they expell if they insult or tyrannize." [6] Bodin, as a matter of fact, carefully qualifies his position on the climate theory since elsewhere he points out that the influence of climate can be overcome by the help of God and the disciplined will. [7]

William Slatyer's verse *History of Great Britainie* (1621)

[5] *Relations of the Most Famous Kingdoms and Commonwealths Through the World* (London, 1616), pp. 5-6.
[6] *The Six Bookes of a Commonweale* (London, 1606), p. 563.
[7] *Methodus ad facilem cognitionem historiarum* (Paris, 1572), p. 118.

discourses on the climate theory, emphasizing northern "firie spirits":

> How for their worth can I set forth
> Those farrest people of the North
> Whose minds as free as bodies faire,
> Though bred ith' cold and frozen aire,
> To ride, to run, to plead, or fight,
> Their laurell Crownes, and martiall might
> Were such, all Nations farre and neere,
> Have seene or felt, or sore did feare.
>
> Those hotter clymes yield frozen blouds,
> When North of Tanais frozen flouds,
> Beene firie spirits, warlike brutes,
> The Massagett's and painted Iutes;
> Numberlesse as Hybla's swarmes, the Scythes,
> Danes, Suevians, Norwayes, Moscovites,
> Gaules, Germans, and the folke that held
> The North and Brittish Iles of eld:
> Who th' off springs justly can despize,
> That from the Northern clymes did rise?

Slatyer has an interesting margin note to the second line, "Those farrest people of the North":

> All Naturalists affirming, the more Southerne peoples to be subtill, politique, and ingenious: neither can they, if they would, deny, but that al our part of the North, being but the Temperate Zone, affordeth peoples ingenious, bold & warlike and for outward lineaments of body, strong, goodly, and beautifull; that no Nation can deservedly have greater prayses, then they have at all times purchased: and however the Proverb *stupidus thrax,* may intimate very farre North, more dull of apprehension, it hath beene ever seene that these have beene in divers gifts admirably excelling. [8]

Milton's important role as a proponent of parliamentary Gothicism has been discussed, but the question of his access

---

[8] *History of Great Britainie,* ode I, "Of Samothes," canzo iii "European Nationes, and Especially the Britons Originall, with all Deserved Praise in their Honor," p 9.

to the unit-ideas in the Gothic agglomerate such as the climate theory raises his name at this point, particularly since it corresponds with the publication of Joshua Sylvester's translation in 1633 of Du Bartas' *Divine Weeks,* thought to be Milton's prime source of the climate theory. Attention, therefore, is called to the study by Professor George C. Taylor of Du Bartas' influence on Milton. Professor Taylor is wary of "the fallacy of the unique source" and has devised, therefore, a simple test which he believes would distinguish ideas which were widespread and available to both Milton and Du Bartas, from a common source, from those ideas which by exclusion derive uniquely from Du Bartas. When he applies this test to Milton's passages on northern antiquities he concludes that if his methodology is sound, the ideas stem solely from Du Bartas. The fact of the case, however, as must already be amply clear, is that there was a broad stream of Gothic ideas flowing through English and foreign literatures. Milton *may* have found the climate theory in Du Bartas, but on the other hand he and Du Bartas could easily have had any number of common sources. [9]

In Du Bartas' account of the colonization of the world following the fall of Babel, Japheth proceeded northwards. The North became in this way the home of the Goths:

> Such was the Goth, who whilom issuing forth
> From the cold, frozen Ilands of the North,
> Incampt by Vistula.

The North became more populous than the South:

> Frō thence indeed, Huns, Herules, Franks, Bulgarians,
> Circassyans, Sueves, Burgognians, Turks, Tartarians,
> Dutch, Cimbers, Normans, Alains, Ostrogothes
> Tigurines, Lombards, Vandals, Visigothes,
> Have swarmed (like Locusts) round about this Ball,

[9] G. C. Taylor, *Milton's Use of Du Bartas* (Cambridge, Mass., 1934).

And spoyl'd the fairest Provinces of all:
While barren South had much a-doo to assemble
(In all) two hoasts; that made the North to tremble: [10]

These passages may have been (but not necessarily) the
source of Milton's lines:

A multitude like which the populous North
Poured never from her frozen loins, to pass
Rhene or the Danaw, when her barbarous sons
Came like a deluge on the South... [11]

The North and South, in Du Bartas' account of the world,
differ in other ways:

O! see how full Wonders strange is Nature:
Sith in each climat, not alone in stature,
Strength, hair and colour, that men differ doo,
But in their humours and their maners too...
The Northern man is fair, the southern foul
That's white, this black; that sfiles, this doth scoul:
Th' one's blithe & frolike, th' other dul & froward;
Th' one's full of courage, th' other fearful coward. [12]

The praise of northern courage is the closest Du Bartas comes
to the democratic implications of the Gothic ideas. Largely
for this reason, the influence of Du Bartas on Milton will
hardly suffice to explain Milton's interests in northern antiquities. Professor Taylor, for example, omits entirely consideration of the propaganda for Parliament's rights in Milton's
*Pro populo defensio Anglicano*; he does not, indeed, recognize that the plea for democracy is as essentially a part of
the Gothic core of ideas as the climate theory, and he therefore omits Milton's prose from his survey.

[10] *Divine Weeks and Works,* translated by J. Sylvester (London,
1633), "The Colonies," third part, second day, second week, pp.
129, 132.
[11] *Paradise Lost,* bk. I, ll. 351ff.
[12] *Divine Weeks,* p. 132.

James Howell also associates valor with northern psychology:

For my part, as a Great Philosopher holds it for a maxime, that Mountaignous people, are the most pious; so they are observed to be the hardiest, as also the barrener a Country is the more Masculine and Warlike the spirits of the Inhabitants are, having as it were more of men in them; Witnesse The Scythian and Goth, and other rough-hewen hungry Nations which so often over-runne Itally, for all her Policy and Learning. [13]

Percy Enderbie also treats northern psychology from the viewpoint of geographical determinism:

Among all the Germans there was at that time no one Nation which for great adventures both by Sea and Land was more renowned than the Saxons. For touching qualities of the minde, they were bold, hardy, and vainglorious, patiently enduring labour, hunger, and cold, whereunto by the constitution of their bodies, and temperance of the Climate, they seem to be framed, as being very strong, and yet not unwieldy, tall of stature but not uncomely or out of due proportion. For the North Region by reason of the coldnesse of the air, which driveth the naturall heat inward, bringeth forth men commonly of greater courage and ability of body, than those countreys that lye nearer the sun. [14]

The scientific coloration which the climate theory gave to the Gothic propaganda for free parliaments aided in the acceptance of the Gothic ideas. It is an interesting reflection, therefore, on what passed in the period for science, that the physiological theory competed with a theory of stellar influence. William Camden, for example, attributes the northern love of liberty to the influence of Mars:

But overpassing their naturall inclination by heavenly influence answerable to the disposition of Aries, Leo, and Sagittary; and Jupiter with Mars dominators for this North west part of the world, which maketh them impatient of servitude, lovers

[13] *Instructions for Forreine Travell* (London, 1642), p. 62.
[14] *Cambria triumphans* (London, 1661), pp. 177-178.

of liberty, martiall and couragious; I will onely in particular note somewhat and that summarily of the Britains, Scottish, and English, the tree principall Inhabitants. [15]

With Trajano Boccalini's *Ragguagli di Parnasso,* in its English translation, we come upon the most charming expression, certainly, of the idea that the German people have an instinct for liberty. [16]

The humor of the *Ragguagli,* or *Centuries of Advices from Parnassus* as the work was entitled in English, was entirely on the surface, for underneath there was a biting satire on the Spanish domination of Italy and the Papal active alliance with the Spanish side. It is little wonder that Boccalini had such a great vogue in England, for as his translator said in his preface, "There is one thing which shou'd particularly recommend our Author to Englishmen, and that is his zeal for Liberty, and his generous abhorrence of those wicked Politicks which have so much disturb'd the Peace of the World and the Happiness of Nations."

The *Ragguagli* is a fantasy in which Apollo reigns over Parnassus, and summons before him poets, writers, and politicians of all countries. Tacitus is one of the writers. The entire book glows with a reverence for Tacitus, although in the satire Tacitus is made to appear as a proponent of tyranny.

In the "Second Century, Advice 28," the theme of the Germanic instinctive love of liberty is treated with delicious humor. The theme is worked out in such a way as to connect the German love of liberty with their notorious love for alcoholic drink. In this sequence of the fantasy, Giovanni della Casa has come forward to present his courtesy-book, the

---

[15] *Remaines,* p. 9.

[16] Henry Carey, 2d Earl of Monmouth, translated the *Ragguagli* in 1657. There were other editions in 1669, 1674, and in 1706 revised by John Hughes. See E. G. Gardner, "Traiano Boccalini," *Dublin Review,* CLIIIX (1926), 236-255.

famed *Galateo*. The German contingent present in Apollo's court take offense at the *Galateo's* warning against heavy drinking:

But the Germans storm'd like mad men, and not only refused to be stinted in their Cups, according to the Rules of Italian Sobriety, but obstinately insisted to have it declared in Galateo, that their everlasting Drunkenness was a principal Virtue, and one of the most requisite Qualifications that the German Princes and Republics cou'd desire in their People, for the security of the Government. But this Request was rejected by all the Literati as impertinent, and directly tending to incourage Debauchery: and as to the particular of Sobriety and Moderation in drinking, the Germans were earnestly exhorted to submit to Galateo's Precepts, since they were pointed at for Sots by all the Nations of Europe.

The Germans resolutely reply'd, that those sober Nations ought to be call'd Sots, who living under Arbitrary Powers suffer'd themselves to be oppress'd by the extravagant Humors and brutal Cruelty of one Man; but the Drunken Germans ought to be esteem'd very sober, who having had Wit enough to procure their Liberty, wanted not their Senses to preserve it. That every Man who is not a Blockhead must believe, that the Drunkenness of the Germans had been the Foundation of the many famous Republicks among 'em. For the safety of a State, and the universal Peace depending only on the fidelity of the Ministers of Princes and Republicks, and on the Candor and Sincerity of every Man's Soul, what more desirable than to see the Germans by their excessive drinking continually vomit up their closest Secrets, and most hidden thoughts? They added, that by long Experience they had found, those were the best Counsellors of their Country, who having drown'd all their private Interests in the Juice of the Grape, and wash'd off that base Varnish of dissimulation, which is the offspring of Sobriety, spoke from their Hearts like Germans, not from the Mouth only, like the Italians and other sober Nations. And further, the Germans are known to value themselves upon the glorious Name of a Martial People, Therefore they cou'd not with patience hearken to the dull phlegmatick Debates of sober Men, which for the most part are full of Cowardice and Circumspection even to a fault, tho they cover it with the Cloke of Prudence. But because they delight in bold and generous Resolutions, they never allow any Man to give State-Advice fasting; but let him first take a hearty Dose of Wine to fire him with Generosity, and then he may be heard: it being the peculiar Virtue of that wondrous Liquor rather to drive away Fear from the Heart, than Judgment from the Head. The Germans therefore as Tacitus says (de mor. Ger.) De reconcilandis invicem, inimicis, et Jungendis Affinitatibus, et adsciscendis Principibus de pace denique ac bello, plerumque in conviviis consultant; tanquam Nullo magis tempore ad simplices cogitationes poteat animus, aut ad magnis incalescat. They debate of the reconciling Enemys, the making Alliances and Leagues, and in short all the business of Peace and War, generally over their Cups. [17]

Boccalini has made clever use of the current notion that the Germans are topers in order to castigate the lethargic Italians into action against their Spanish oppressors. The contrast of the German martial spirit and love of liberty with Italian slothfulness is very effective.

"Century 2, Advice 6," discusses the problem: "All the Monarchys of the Universe, being jealous of the great Power and Prosperity of the German Commonwealths, take measures in a General Diet to secure themselves from being overrun by em." The Lord High Chancellor in a long speech brings out that the Germans are chiefly responsible for the decline of monarchies, for the reason that "the Germans, those unparallel'd Artists in the Mysterys of making Clocks, and forming Commonwealths, have invented those schemes of perpetual Liberty, which for so many Ages, the wisdom of Philosophers sought after in vain; and which seem to threaten Monarchys with certain Extirpation." [18] Monmouth's explanation in the preface that the book recommended itself particularly to Englishmen because of the author's "zeal for liberty" indicates

[17] *Centuries of Advices,* Hughes revision (London, 1706), pp. 241-242.
[18] *Ibid.,* pp. 191-192.

the book's importance and its place in the revival of interest in Tacitus.

The climate theory and the conception of the freedom-loving, manly, energetic German appear frequently in combination, but this was by no means necessary. Without the sanction of the pseudo-scientific environmental theory—or when it is explicitly repudiated (as by Swift and Temple) or radically modified (as by Milton)—the notion of the free, manly German was passing into the Gothic lore. Those who repudiate or modify the climate theory hold a special interest, since they anticipate a modern idea, which regretfully still needs defending, that even if there is a climatic influence, psychic or mental effects do not necessarily follow.

# THE LEVELLERS: CLIMAX AND CRISIS IN THE GOTHIC TRADITION

If we avoid with the utmost care the idea that all those favoring the retention of parliamentary prerogative were Gothicists and that wherever we have a hint of democracy we have a Gothic influence, we shall be able better to locate the exact front on which the Gothic and Leveller ideas met and clashed. History was to the Gothicists *fundamentum doctrinae*. The Gothicists were better equipped than all other seventeenth-century revolutionaries to comprehend the problem of "anti-Normanism," precisely because their eyes were steadfastly fixed on pre-Conquest Saxon freedom which they insisted had never been abrogated, the Norman Conquest nothwithstanding. Contrariwise, the Levellers believed that parliamentary anti-Normanism was itself the most insidious form of Normanism because it subtly robbed the people of their rights, using the appeal of tradition and history, where the king's Normanism was so grossly obvious. The issue, then, between Levellers and Gothicists was joined on anti-Normanism. The otherwise penetrating study of Leveller doctrine by T. C. Pease is deficient on this score. Since Pease omits the tradition of Saxon liberties, he fails to bring into juxtaposition with Leveller doctrine the exact forces which attempted to hold the ground for traditional constitutionalism against Leveller "natural law." [1]

[1] Pease, *The Leveller Movement* (Washington, D. C., 1916). See an important review of Pease by Sir Charles H. Firth, *English Historical Review,* XXIII (1918), 136-137, which although admiring, also points out Pease's neglect to consider anti-Normanism.

The Cromwellian interregnum seethed with novel political theories. Properly to see the implications of the Leveller attack for the success or failure of that variety of traditional democracy which we have called Gothicism, it will be well to go back to Nathaniel Bacon. Bacon's tract, as we have seen, is a milepost in the seventeenth century Gothic tradition. As a milepost, it looks backward to the ground covered since Verstegen, but as a milepost, it also looks forward to a new development: the idea of parliamentary sovereignty. Although at a rapid glance the idea of parliamentary sovereignty would seem to represent a climax to all for which the Gothicists fought, a closer study will reveal that it represents a distortion of Gothicism. The Leveller attack resulted. A comparison of Bacon's *Historical Discourse* with David Jenkins' *Lookingglasse* of the same year will make this development clear.

In Judge David Jenkins' restrained defense of the King we find for the first time an effort on the part of a Royalist to elevate his thinking to the level of political strategy achieved by the Gothicists. He repudiates, not less vigorously than any Royalist pamphleteer who bawled for the King's title by conquest, the Gothic thesis that English monarchs have always been elective, but his premises belong to another realm of discourse altogether:

The government of Kings in this Isle of Britain, hath been very ancient, even as ancient as History itself; for those who deny the story of Brutus to be true, doe finde out a more ancient plantation here under Kings, namely under Samothes grandchilde to Japhet son of Noach, from whom the ancient Britaines that inhabited this Land, are according to their conceits descended: Kings or Monarchs of great Britaine had and did exercise far more large and ample power, and did claime greater Prerogatives over the people under their government and jurisdiction, then the Kings of England have done since the Norman Conquest, as it is to be seen at large both in the Brittish Chronicles and records of these times, and in our English histories, and may also be gathered out of the writings of the Romans who invaded this Island and lived here upon the place: and I doe not finde that even the people put them out at pleasure, but that the Kingly government and right of the Crowne, descended alwayes by hereditary descent and application. 2

Jenkins was known to his contemporaries as "the heart of oak" because of his settled determination during his tenure on the bench to administer the law honestly and without favor. Although an avowed Royalist, he opposed the King's selfish use of monopolies as detrimental to the best interests of the nation, nor did he flinch from condemning the King's attempt in the ship-money case to extort taxes illegally. In the face of these facts, we might well expect from "the heart of oak" more enlightened views on Parliament. Actually, he does view Parliament's privileges with far more insight into the historical development of English institutions than his denial of the Gothic elective monarch would appear to indicate. He states his view of parliament in the opening sentence of the *Looking-glasse*: "I must confess to you, that I doe apprehend that there is a Legislative Power in the Parliament, but I take it to be in *sensu conjuncto,* not in *sensu diviso,* in a sense when the King is joyned to both Houses of Parliament, not when he is divided from them either in his Will or Person." 3

On this level of argumentation, once we determine precisely what Jenkins meant in describing Parliament's legislative capacity as held in *sensu conjuncto,* we shall recognize that Royalist political theory had raised itself to the level of political science and had paid its respects to tradition and history. We shall not be disappointed in our expectation that the honest "oak's" legal integrity remained unimpaired although he was writing at a time when he was under constant surveillance and harassment by Parliament's agents.

2 *A Looking-glasse for the Parliament...* (Printed in the Eighth yeer of the Parliaments Tyranny and Oppression 1648), p. 24.
3 *Ibid.,* p. 2.

The phrase "in sensu conjuncto" was no mere political sophistry. It was a political norm set by tradition and prescription during centuries of English life. What the phrase meant was that Parliament and King were indivisibly, organically united. Parliament and King, in this conception, are the two indispensable elements of a valid parliament. Outside of Parliament the King had merely the dignity of his royal person, only in the council did he have his *imperium*. The sacral character of the old Teutonic leader presiding over the deliberative assembly had imbedded itself so firmly in English political thinking that a seventeenth-century writer like Jenkins could still be stirred by the old *Königzauberei,* the mystical, almost poetical, conception of the "King in Parliament."

When feudalism enveloped the old Teutonic conception of an organic council, it left its characteristic impress upon it. The service of feudalism to later centuries was to fix the doctrine of the "King in Parliament" in the common law of the land. The common law was looked upon as sovereign, immutable, completely binding upon both King and Parliament, and prescribing the limits of their respective privileges. Hence, under the common law, it was inconceivable that the prerogatives respectively of King and Parliament would ever enter into conflict with one another. Prerogatives are casually defined as privileges, but no feudal political theorist ever conceived of privileges or rights without their reciprocal duties or obligations. Prerogatives are in reality the bounds set to liberty, and in practice they meant that the King could not extend his prerogatives without destroying the liberties granted to him reciprocally by the people. This is precisely what Pym meant when he declared at the trial of Strafford: "Take away the King's protection from the people, and you take away the peoples allegiance to the King. Prerogative is the bounds of liberty, and (my Lords) they must not contest one with another." [4] Nor was Pym the only one to recognize the problem, for an obscure Mr. Smith (who surely deserves a better fate than obscurity) also pleaded:

Prerogative and liberty are both necessary to this kingdom; and like the sun and moon, give a lustre to this benighted nation, so long as they walk at their equall distances; but when one of them shall venture into the other's orb, like those planets in conjunction, they then cause a deeper eclipse. What shall be the compass then, by which these two must steer. Why nothing but the same by which they are, the law. [5]

If we bear in mind that Jenkins is arguing in essence for the principle of the sovereignty of law embodied in an organic Parliament, we perceive the consistency of his condemnation of the King's irresponsibility in the ship-money case. He condemned the King's efforts to extort taxes illegally in the form of ship-money, not because he wished to destroy the King's prerogative, but only to recall it to its lawful limits which did not include taxing powers. On the other hand, he did not tie Parliament's legislative power to the King's conjunction in their deliberations in order to diminish Parliament's prerogatives, but in order to restate precisely what the bounds of Parliament's liberties under the sovereign law were. In the *Looking-glasse*, his polemic is directed mainly at a restatement of the bounds of Parliament's liberties because he had become convinced that Parliament had become a worse aggressor than the King had been. The *Looking-glasse*, therefore, is Royalist theory on the defensive. Jenkins was endeavouring to show that the royal party abides by the sovereign law; the Royalists stand for the old organic Parliament where harmony resulted from the balance kept between prerogative and liberty.

[4] *Mr. Pymmes Speech to the Lords in Parliament, Sitting in Westminster Hall, on the tryall of Thomas Earle of Strafford on the twelfth of Aprill* (London, 1641), p. 2.
[5] *An Honourable Speech spoken in Parliament, Oct. 28, 1641,* in *Harleian Miscellany,* V, 11.

Jenkins' arguments display the characteristic strength and weakness of the lawyer's approach to constitutional theory. The constitution, after all, lives outside of the law courts, and as tension mounted between the King and the Parliamentary party it was perhaps inevitable that a solution would be found outside of the old constitution. Jenkins' eagle-eye perceived the danger, and he is meticulously correct in dating its upsurge from eight years previous to 1648. (Note the imprint on the title-page of his tract: "Printed in the Eighth yeer of the Parliaments Tyranny and Oppression, 1648.") In 1640, for the first time in English history, Parliament had broken decisively with the doctrine of sovereign law by claiming sovereignty for itself above the fundamental law. It was quite beside the point that Parliament was asking for the same absolute powers which it denied to the King. Under the actual circumstances, Parliament could and did make the claim to supreme power, even above the fundamental law, hallowed as it was by tradition and prescription. [6]

[6] The shift from sovereign law to sovereign parliament has been described by Professor Charles H. McIlwain in *The High Court of Parliament* (New Haven, 1910). The immediate background of the doctrine of parliamentary supremacy has been described by one of Prof. McIlwain's students: Margaret Atwood Judson, "Henry Parker and the Theory of Parliamentary Sovereignty," pp. 138-167 in *Essays in History and Political Theory in Honor of Charles Howard McIlwain* (Cambridge, Mass., 1936). In *The Case of Shipmoney Briefly Discoursed* (published November 3, 1640), Parker like Jenkins attacked the king's illegal taxing policy. Like Jenkins, he is guided in this tract by the conception of an organic parliament with its balance of prerogative and liberty. He defines prerogative as not dangerous but "a harmonious composure of policy, scarce to be paralleled in all the world, it is neither so boundlesse as to apprise the people in unjust things, nor so strait as to disable the King in just things; by the true fundamental constitutions of England, the beame hangs even between the King and the subject" (p. 7). By the next year, in the *True Grounds,* Parker was already urging that the supreme power must be undivided. In 1642 his tracts spoke unequivocally for parliamentary supremacy over the law.

How loath seventeenth-century men, even of non-Gothic persuasion, were to break with the past is shown in Jenkins' appeal to the centuries-old tradition of an organic Parliament. His unwillingness, however, to follow the Gothicists into the Saxon past and grant that the Saxon ruler was elective affords us an unexpected insight into a new development in the Gothic movement which we should otherwise miss. If we recall that such a typical Gothicist as Nathaniel Bacon, for example, also contended for the principle of sovereign law binding the King and Parliament "in sensu conjuncto," the real contrast between Gothic and Royalist theory in the 1640's is brought out for the first time. [7] Bacon's attack, therefore, on the King's absolutism was, like Jenkins' attack on royal greed in the ship-money case, not intended to destroy the King's lawful prerogative but to confine it within its lawful limits; conversely, his Gothic defense of Parliament was not intended to proclaim the sovereignty of Parliament over the law but to reestablish Parliament's prerogative as just and lawful. This leaves the sole remaining issue between Jenkins and the Gothicists to be the question whether the monarch was elective or hereditary. Interestingly enough, this exposes the flaw in the reasoning of both Jenkins and the Gothicists. For if we pause to think of the matter, it becomes obvious that the question whether the ruler was elective or hereditary is utterly irrelevant and misleading. What is of vital importance is whether the King, whatever his origins, would be content to rule under the sovereign law.

It was impossible for Jenkins to concede that the monarch was elective, for the grant of elective rights to the people also bestowed on them correlative rights to depose the King. Even

---

[7] N. Bacon: "The law is the sole umpire between the King and people, and unto which not only the people, but also the King must submit"; see above p. 137 ff. for a discussion of Bacon's *Historical and Political Discourse.*

a legal tyro could see that in this event Parliament would be acting as judge and accuser in its own cause. [8] At the very bottom, therefore, the real source of the difficulty between the Gothic defenders of Parliament and the Royalists was not differences as to what the supreme law was—in point of fact we have seen both Jenkins and Bacon in agreement on the fundamental law—the real source of the difficulty was the question to whom the right to interpret the law should be entrusted. Cromwell's son-in-law, Ireton, placed the entire controversy in the proverbial nutshell when he declared: "That which hath occasioned the war in this nation is not the knowing what the limitations of that power e.g. the king's power are, or of what nature is the supreme trust, but only that we have not known in what persons, or what parties, or what council, the trust have lain." [9]

Historical precedent absolutely forbade that the trust be placed entirely in the hands of Parliament, for a parliament which excluded a king was invalid. By indirect reasoning, however, historical precedent as expounded by the Gothicists could well apply. Despite Bacon's agreement with Jenkins on the point of preserving the King and Parliament "in sensu conjuncto," the historical precedent of the Saxon elective

[8] Much earlier, King James had foreseen the direction democratic thought was taking. James pointed out that even if there were a contract which freed the people when the king broke the contract, still if the people were to be the judges whether the contract was broken or not, then they will be both judge and plaintiff in the trial, "except that first a lawful trial and cognition be had of the ordinary Judge of the breakers thereof, or else every man may be both party and Judge in his own cause," *Trew Law of Free Monarchies* (1598), in *Political Works of James I*, edited by C. H. McIlwain (Cambridge, Mass., 1918), p. 68.

[9] Colonel Ireton speaking in the Whitehall debates, in *Puritanism and Liberty*, edited by A. S. P. Woodhouse (London, 1938), p. 131. Woodhouse's volume is a collection of the Putney and Whitehall debates, with additional pamphlet material of the time further illustrating the points made in the debates.

monarch was reinterpreted and made to yield the idea that those who made the King were ultimately greater than the King. It was all very well to say that a supreme law existed, but in the end there had to be a body to interpret the law. John Bradshaw, president of the trial of Charles I, gave the complete answer to Ireton's query about where the trust of the law must lie: "There is something superior to law, the parent or author of the law, and that is, the people of England." [10] Another spokesman for the Parliamentary Party declared: "The Law is more powerful then the King, as being Governor and Moderator of his lusts and actions: But the whole Body of the people are more powerful then the Law, as being the parent of it. For the People make the Law, and have power when they see cause, to abrogate or abolish it." [11]

Attention is called to the fact that Bradshaw and the anonymous author of *The Peoples Right* evidently use "people" and "parliament" as equivalent terms. It is quite difficult, indeed, to distinguish between the two, since the distinction is constantly breaking down. A loose definition, therefore, as in Sir Thomas Smith's *De republica Anglorum,* usually suffices to explain away whatever difficulty appeared: Parliament

representeth and hath the power of the whole realme both the head and the bodie. For everie Englishman is intended to bee there present, either in person or by procuration and attornies, of what preheminence state, dignitie, or qualities soever he be, from the Prince (be he King or Queene) to the lowest person of Englande. And the consent of Parliament is taken to be everie man's consent. [12]

The two terms are exactly equivalent only in a New England

[10] *State Trials,* edited by H. L. Stephen (London and New York, 1899-1902), IV, 1, 116.
[11] Anonymous, *The Peoples Right Briefly Asserted* (London 1649), p. 5.
[12] *De republica Anglorum,* edited by L. Alston (Cambridge, 1906), p. 49.

town meeting, but in any larger community the distinction
between the people present and not present, in loose definition, disappears in the idea that all the people compose the
parliament in the sense that they are represented by "procuration and attornies."

The Putney debates, which are the record of the debates
held in the council of the Parliamentary "New Modell" Army,
assume importance as the occasion upon which the Levellers
voiced the idea, among other novel constitutional theories, that
the people and parliament are distinct.

One of the stipulations expressly made in the *Army Agreement of the People,* published October 28, 1647, was that
"since Parliament was only a minor, it should yield to the
people." [13] It now appeared that there were certain rights
which the people had reserved for themselves forever beyond
the reach of parliament. A higher law, the law of nature, protected the liberties of the people, and whenever the law of
nature came into conflict with constitutional law, the latter
was invalid. It was now no longer a question of the rights of
Englishmen but a question of the natural rights of man.
Magna Charta was reëxamined and found to be "but a mess
of pottage"; another writer asserted "it is ridiculous for private men to build hopes upon rotten titles of ages long passed,
upon weak maximes of law"; still another writer jibed at the
"dotards who seek to square all in antiquity." The question
was whether Gothicism had within itself the resources to meet
these derisive challenges to its ideals. The fountain of Saxon
liberties, according to the radicals in the army, was discovered
to be a poisoned well. Even the histories were found to be
infected subtly by the poisoned waters. The Levellers charged
that the very tradition of Saxon liberties was created in the
chronicles by the enemies of the people, with typical Norman

[13] *Agreement,* printed in S. R. Gardiner, *History of the Great Civil
War* (London, 1901-1904), III, 607-609.

cunning, as part of a plot to rob the people of their liberties while deluding them with the mere show of freedom. The reason why Magna Charta, heretofore considered to be the palladium of English liberties, received the brunt of the Leveller attack, may be traced directly to this embittered cynicism. Magna Charta now was looked upon either as a modification of "Normanism" so slight as to be ineffective, or else it was a deception designed to fool the people with the show of freedom while actually it left them less free than ever.

"Above all things you must not be Anti-parliamentary," pleaded one of the more moderate writers; but in view of Parliament's high-handed dealings with the nation, it was inevitable that the plea would fall on deaf ears. 14 In the first place, Parliament's claim to supremacy over the law or the right to judge the law as it saw fit, although countered ineffectively by the Royalist criticism that in that event Parliament was prejudging the law in its own favor, aroused a suspicion that the people had ejected the king and had found in Parliament a many-headed master. All too soon for the cause of peace, the suspicion was confirmed in Parliament's disregard of the fundamental civil liberties of freedom of speech and press. *Areopagitica* was one result; John Liburne's education as a Leveller began when he protested against the suppression of his pamphlets: "May it not be truly said, that we have fought ourselves into slavery & our Government turned into a Tyranny? it is a griefe to speak it, and for to bide it, it availeth not, being now come to the knowledge and sight of all men." 15 In the second place, the punitive measures

14 Marchmont Nedham, *The Case of the Kingdom Stated* (London, 1647), preface, leaf A2 recto.

15 *Liberty Vindicated Against Slavery* (London, 1646), p. 24. The very next sentence continues: "Our Ancestors of old lived in the highest pitch of perfect Liberty, and wee now in dejected servility are not used as free men, but as abjects, yea, as meere slaves." At this date, Lilburne was not yet a Leveller but a member of the moderate

taken by Parliament against the New Model Army, which had at very great risk fought the Royalists to a standstill, also aroused a distrust of parliaments. Parliament decreed in February and March of 1647 that the New Model disband except as a body to be reëmployed in a reconquest of Ireland. The soldiers were given only a small part of their pay in arrears, and the promise of indemnity given to them by Parliament for their action against the King's forces seemed to the men to be insecure and even suspicious. What was especially galling, however, was the inference behind Parliament's high-handed dealings that the soldiers were mere mercenaries. One can readily appreciate how exasperating this must have been to men who had risked life and fortune for a political ideal. [16] In the third place, the predominance of Presbyterianism in Parliament caused a connection to be made in the minds of the Puritan soldiers between religious and parliamentary oppression.

A nation's troubled conscience, not a partisan hunger for political power, demanded answers to the final questions: Where is the source of equitable government if parliaments fail? Is Freedom only a fiction? Are liberal laws the supremely

party, the Independents. He objects to parliament's tyranny, and he is holding parliament to the same principles by means of which the nation turned out the king. But he still holds to the mooring-post of Saxon liberty in the past. As a Leveller, later, however, he put the axe to the very root and declared that the Saxon liberties were a Chinese wall of legalism imprisoning the people and that the dead legalism must be brought to life with and infusion of natural law. Lilburne's transitional Independent position in this tract was generally the position adhered to by the officers in the Army Councils who tried to restrain the privates who had come under the influence of Leveller theory.

[16] See Anonymous, *The Army No Usurpers* (London, 1653), pp. 1-2, asserting the right of the army to resist a tyrannical parliament, since they are "gallant men (not souldiers of fortune and men of mercenary Principles) for the love of their Country, and hopes of great things promised, expose their lives to hazard."

clever contrivances of tyrants who give liberty with one hand but who draw back blood, pain, and oppression with two hands? The Levellers found an inclusive answer: the source of equitable government is in God. God's natural law had superior validity to all human, positive law; and if this seemed nebulous or vague, yet it did for a certainty make clear that any positive law which contravened natural law was invalid. Parliaments and positive laws are, therefore, merely creations of men, and men being but the frail vessels bearing God's will on earth it is not surprising that parliaments and laws will occasionally reflect the sinfulness in which they are humanly created.

The fiction of freedom and the duplicity which may underlie the grant of liberal laws were, thus, factors in England's history standing exposed in the cold light of "anti-Normanism." At one end of the scale, the Levellers saw "Norman" guile and duplicity—at the other end, the mere pragmatic sanctions of secular, parliamentary law which needed constantly to be brought into harmony with the superior sanction of divine, natural law. The Levellers, consequently, take their place in the history of democratic thought in England as the political theorists who turned secular, political thought back into the original channel-bed of religion. Religion never failed in English political life to guide and inspire political theory. Not the least interesting aspect of the clash between secular Gothicism and the divine, natural law, was the ultimate victory of secular Gothicism, greatly enriched by the religious element contributed by the Levellers even in defeat.

All the cherished political ideals of the Gothic cult fell under the Leveller blows. In 1645 William Walwyn, an outspoken Leveller, poured hot words of scorn on the past, which he declared to be irrelevant and worse; first, it was misleading because it offered neither light nor solace, and second, it was hypocritical, for although Englishmen were educated to think

of legislation of the past as noble achievements of the free
English spirit, closer scrutiny showed past parliaments to
have been engaged merely in providing bread and circuses:
"Magna Charta (you must observe) is but a part of the
people's rights and liberties, being no more but what with
much striving and fighting, was by the blood of our Ancestors,
wrestled out of the power of those Kings, who by force had
conquered the Nation, changed the lawes, and by strong hand
held them in bondage." Walwyn continues that parliaments
occupied themselves regulating petty trades, the order of
hunting ("who should keep Deere and who should not"),
and so on.

And when by any accident or intollerable oppression they
were roosed [roused] out of those waking dreames, then whats
the greatest thing they ayme at? Hough with one consent, they
cry out for Magna Charta (like great is Diana of the Ephesians)
calling that messe of pottage the birthright, the great inheritance
of the people, the great charter of England. 17

Walwyn is, in reality, preaching what the twentieth century
is likely to call "class-consciousness." He is saying that the
people must maintain a constant vigil lest government en-
croach upon their natural rights. There never was a free
grant of liberties to the people, and, even if there were, these
are still (as Walwyn says) "but a part of the people's rights
and liberties." The basic people's rights are natural, in-
defeasible rights, and they should be placed forever beyond
the reach of parliaments. Walwyn does not refer to "Norman"
tyranny, but other Levellers took up the theme and pointed
out that although parliamentarians had much to say about
the Norman Conqueror's false claim to title by conquest,
nevertheless they are, hypocritically, Normans themselves

17 *England's Lamentable Slavery* (1645), pp. 3-4, attributed to Walwyn; no title-page, no license, no date except at the end.

who oppress the people although pretending to be their liberators.

Lilburne, the probable author of *A Remonstrance of Many Thousand Citizens...Printed in the Yeer, 1646,* points out that parliaments have occasionally left the people less free than they found them. The remedy is to reduce all law to equity and natural law:

> Yee know, the Lawes of this Nation are unworthy a Free-People, and deserve from first to last, to be considered, and seriously debated, and reduced to an agreement with the common equity, and right reason, which ought to be the Forme and Life of every Government. Magna Charta itself being but a beggerly thing, containing many markes of intollerable bondage, & the Lawes that have been made since by Parliaments, have in very many particulars made our Government much more oppressive and intollerable. [18]

Sir John Wildman, who, as we shall see, figured importantly in the Putney debates as the defender of the Levellers, traces the false tradition of constitutional liberalism directly back to its sources in falsified chronicles:

> Our case is to bee consider'd thus, that wee have bin under slavery. That's acknowledged by all. Our very lawes were made by our Conquerors, and wheras itt's spoken much of Chronicles. I conceive there is noe credit to be given to any of them; and the reason is because those that were our Lords, and made us their vassalls, would suffer nothing else to be chronicled. [19]

Cowling also pointed out in the Putney debates that recourse to law for the preservation of liberties has always been unavailing; only the ceaseless vigil of the people won for them the few liberties they have: "Cowling," reports Major Clarke, the stenographer attending the Putney debates, "made a speech expressing that the sword was the only thing that

[18] *A Remonstrance,* p. 15.
[19] *"Clarke Papers"* in Woodhouse, *Puritanism and Liberty,* pp. 65-66. The *"Clarke Papers"* are the record of the Putney debates.

had from time to time recovered our rights, and which he ever read in the word of God had recovered the rights of the people; that our ancestors had still recovered from the Danes and Normans their liberties by the sword." [20]

John Warr has been passed over in histories of the Puritan rebellion, but he is distinguished among all the pamphleteers, and especially among the Levellers, for his insight into the dialectics of liberty. Freedom to John Warr appears to have been almost a cosmic principle imbedded in the orderly operation of the universe itself and partaking, consequently, of the eternal validity wholly comparable with that possessed by the divine law of nature. His dialectics necessarily recognize the fact of political oppression, but he is not inclined to consider oppression seriously except as it points to the ultimate triumph of Freedom. Warr's actual language recalls Shelley's aeolian spirit, a kind of apotheosis of the spirit of freedom breathing a message of liberty over the world. His concern with pre-Conquest history and the problem of historical continuity are prime instances of the influence exerted by the discussions of Gothicism on the Levellers in bringing to the fore the problem of "Normanism."

The motto on the title-page of his tract reveals Warr's anti-Norman bias: "The laws of England are full of tricks, and contrary to themselves; for they were invented and established by the Normans, which were of all nations the most quarrelsome, and most fallacious in contriving of controversies and suits." [21]

Like Wildman and Cowling, Warr believes that there is never an armistice between the "people" and government, for whatever liberties the people had were won by the sword:

Those Laws which do carry any thing of Freedom in their

[20] *Ibid.*, p. 96.
[21] *The Corruption and Deficiency of the Lawes of England* (London, 1649), conveniently found in *Harleian Miscellany*, VI, 212-225.

bowells, do owe their Originall to the Peoples choice; and
have been wrested from the Rulers and Princes of the world
by importunity of intreaty, or by force of Armes: For the great
men of the world being invested with the Power thereof, cannot
be imagined to eclipse themselves or their own Pomp, unlesse
by the violent interposition of the peoples spirits, who are most
sensible of their own burdens, and most forward in seeking
reliefe. So that Exorbitancie and Injustice on the part of the
Rulers was the rise of Laws in behalf of the People, which consideration will afford us this generall Maxime, that the pure
and genuine intent of Lawes was to bridle Princes, not the
People, and to keep Rulers within the bounds, of just and
righteous Government: from whence, as from a fountain, the
rivulet of subjection and obedience on the peoples part, did
reciprocally flow forth, partly to gratify, and partly to incourage
good and vertuous Governors. [22]

Warr continues:

From which Assertion we may deduce a twofold corollarie:
1. That at the Foundation of Governments, Justice was in
men, before it came to be in Laws; for the onely Rule of Government to good Princes, was their own wills; and people were
content to pay them their subjection upon the security of their
bare words: So here in England, in the daies of King Alfred,
the Administration of Justice was immediately in the Crown,
and required the personall attendance of the King.
2. But this course did soon bankerupt the world, and drive
men to a necessity of taking bond from their own Princes, and
setling limits to their Power; hence it came to passe that Justice
was transmitted from men to Laws, that both Prince and People
might read their duties, offences and punishment before them.
And yet such hath been the interest of Princes in the world
that the sting of the Law hath been plucked out as to them;
and the weight of it fallen upon the People, which hath been
more grievous, because out of its place, the Element of the
Law being beneficiall, not cumbersome within its own sphere.
Hence it is, that Laws (like swords) come to be used against
those which made them; and being put upon the rack of self
and wordly interest, are forced to speak what they never meant,

[22] *Harleian Miscellany,* VI 213, opening paragraph of the book.

and to accuse their best friends, the People. Thus the Law becomes any thing or nothing at the courtesie of great men, and is bended by them like a twig. [23]

It is the special quality of Warr's confidence that Freedom will wrest the world from the powers of oppression that makes it possible for him to turn from this embittered account of past history to an optimistic view of the future:

But yet the minds of men are the great wheeles of things; thence come changes and alterations in the world; teeming Freedom exerts and puts forth it self; the unjust world would suppresse its appearance, many fall in this conflict, but Freedom will at last prevaile, and give Law to all things.

So that here is the proper Fountain of good and righteous Laws, a spirit of understanding big with Freedom, and having a single respect to Peoples Rights, Judgement goes before to create a capacity and Freedom follows after to fill it up. And thus Law comes to be the bank of Freedom, which is not said to straighten, but to conduct the streame. A people thus watered are in a thriving posture; and the rather because the foundation is well laid, and the Law reduced to its originall state, which is the protection of the Poor against the Mighty. [24]

Turning more directly to English past history, Warr exposes the falseness of the tradition of liberalism:

The influence of force and power in the sanction of our English lawes, appears by this, That severall alternations have been made of our lawes, either in whole, or in part, upon every conquest. And if at any time the Conqueror hath continued any of the Ancient lawes, it hath been only to please and ingratiate himself unto the people, for so generous Thieves give back some part of their money to Travellers; to abate their zeal in pursuit.

Upon this ground I conceive it is, why Fortescue (and some others) do affirm: That notwithstanding the severall conquests of this Realm, yet the same lawes have still continued... Which opinion of his can be no otherwise explained (besides what

23 *Ibid.,* VI, 214.
24 *Ibid.,* VI, 214.

we have already said) then that those succeeding did still retain those parts of former Lawes, which made for their own interest; otherwise 'tis altogether inconsistent with reason, that the Saxons who banished the Inhabitants, and changed the Name, should yet retain the Lawes of this Island. Conquerors seldom submit to the law of the conquered (where Conquests are compleat as the Saxons was). [25]

Thus Warr reverses the role of the Saxons in English history and the issue is joined between Gothicism and Leveller doctrine. The Saxons are, in the sense which Warr conceives of Normanism as the eternal negation of liberty, as much Normans as the French conquerors under William of Normandy. Tradition and custom are, therefore, irrelevant:

By this it appears that the notion of fundamental law is no such Idoll as men make it: For what (I pray you) is fundamentall law but such customs as are of the eldest date, & longest continuance? Now Freedom being the proper rule of Custom, 'tis more fit that unjust customs should be reduced, that they may continue no longer, then that they should keep up their Arms, because they have continued so long. The more fundamentall a law is, the more difficult, not the less necessarie to be reformed. [26]

There are, then, two notes struck in Warr's writing. On the one hand, he condemns the past, specifically the Saxon past. He is caustic on the way in which the people have been gulled with only the appearance of freedom:

Grant, that the People seem to have had a Shadow of Freedom in chusing of Laws, as consenting to them by their Representatives, or Proxies (both before and since the Conquest) for even the Saxon Kings held their Conventions or Parliaments) yet whosoever shall consider how arbitrary such Meetings were...and withal how the Spirit of Freedom was observed and kept under...will easily conclude that there hath been a

[25] *Ibid.*, VI, 216; compare this with Hunton's account of the Saxon "expulsion," *supra* p. 130 ff.
[26] *Harleian Miscellany*, VI, 217.

Failure in our English Laws, as to the matter of Election or
Free Choice, there having been always a Rod over the Chusers,
and a Negative Voice, with a Power of Dissolution, having
always nipped Freedom in the Bud. [27]

Whatever liberties the people have were won by the sword:

> Yea, the laws of the Conqueror were so burthensome to the
> people, that succeeding Kings were forced to abate their price,
> and to give back some freedom to the people. Hence it came
> to pass, that Henry the First did mitigate the laws of his father
> the conqueror, and restored those of King Edward; hence like-
> wise came the confirmation of Magna Charta... These freedoms
> were granted to the people, not out of any love to them but
> extorted from princes by fury of war, or incessantness of
> address; and, in this case, princes making a vertue of necessity,
> have given away that which was none of their own, and they
> could not well keep, in hope to regain it at other times; so that
> of what freedom we have, by the law, is the price of much
> hazard and blood. [28]

Warr turns, nevertheless, from this depreciation of the past
to a profound faith in the eventual victory of the spirit of
liberty when "teeming Freedom exerts and puts forth it self...
Freedom will at last prevaile, and give to Law all things."
Freedom is the eternal affirmation of God's divine plan for
mankind in the same way that laws, especially supposedly
liberal laws when not subordinated to natural law (Lilburn
called it "right reason"), are the eternal negation of divine
law. The conflict between Freedom and Normanism is in-
eluctable, but it is a cosmic certainty that Freedom will ultimately conquer. If the question were asked: when or where,
as a matter of fact, have men ever been free? the answer is
found in the Biblical paradise, where men lived free as they
were created by God. Professor D. G. Ritchie quotes aptly
from Tom Paine, whose *Rights of Man,* deriving immediately

[27] *Ibid.,* VI, 219.
[28] *Ibid.,* VI, 219

from American and French revolutionary currents, actually
goes back to Leveller doctrines:

The error of those who reason by precedents drawn from
antiquity, respecting the rights of man, is that they do not go
far enough into antiquity... Portions of antiquity, by proving
everything, establish nothing. It is authority against authority
all the way, till we come to the divine origin of man at the
creation. Here our enquiries find a resting place and our reason
finds a home. [29]

George Walker, author of *Anglo-Tyrannus* (1650), is even
more scathing on the false tradition of ancient liberties, and
he pours his scorn on the "dotards who square all by antiquity." [30] He frankly recognizes that a revolutionary situation
exists; that is, a solution for England's troubles must be found
outside of the law: "If our present Governours had been bound
up to former rules, we never could have attained that estate
which now by Gods mercy and their prudence we enjoy." [31]

As Walker reads the history of past parliaments he finds
that kings have given to the people with one hand and have
taken back with two. They have called parliaments into
meeting with a great show of granting the people their liberties, but really for the purpose of obtaining subsidies for all
sorts of nefarious schemes and for lavish gifts to favorites:

In our chronicles, where though in the Theorie and System
the English Government hath been limited and bounded by
good, and distinguishing lawes, yet in the exercise and practical
part of every Kings raign, we shall find it deserve as bad a
name as others, who are called most absolute. The Poets fable
of Tantalus hath been verified in us, who though we have been
set up to the chinne in freedom, and have had liberty bobbing at
our lips, yet never could we get a drop to quench our thirsts,

[29] Ritchie, *Natural Rights* (London, 1894), p. 42.
[30] *Anglo-Tyrannus, or the Idea of a Norman Monarch, Represented
in the Parallel Reignes of Henrie the Third and Charles Kings of
England* (London, 1650), dedication to the reader, leaf A4, recto.
[31] *Ibid.*, leaf A4 verso.

or a snap to stay our stomacks, this being added to our sufferings to want in the midst of seeming abundance, and as the vulgar have it, to starve in a Cooks shop. [32]

Walker declares ironically, "O what a blessed thing is want of money and how bountifull are Kings when they are quite beggared!" [33] If Henry the Third had ample funds, he never would have confirmed Magna Charta. But requiring funds, he called a Parliament for the purpose, prepared to grant the representatives a pittance of freedom in exchange for subsidies:

A Parliament therefore is summoned to Westminster, and of them a relief demanded but no pennie, without a *Pater Noster,* no money unless their Liberties be confirmed, and now necessity which makes the Old Wife trot, persuades Henry to be so gracious to himselfe as to comply with them. Thus Magna Charta and Charta de Foresta were confirmed, which though purchased before, and then entred upon and possest by the people, yet have been paid for to some purpose if we consider the sums given since, and to little or none if we sum but up the profit our Landlords let us reap by them. [34]

Later Walker adds: "Observe here the happy estate of our Ancestors under Monarchy, who, if they gained but this advantage...of receiving a few good Grants, and enjoying a pittance of freedom... yet were sure to pay through the nose for it afterwards with double and treble interest for forbearance." [35]

Justifying the revolution, Walker concludes by proclaiming the triumph of freedom over the fraud and perjury perpetrated by the old law:

I appeal to the judgment of all rationall creatures, whether it be not so perspicuous that the dimmest eye, on this side of blindnesse, not winking out of design, must perceive. 1. That

[32] *Ibid.,* p. 2.
[33] *Ibid.,* p. 29.
[34] *Ibid.,* p. 7.
[35] *Ibid.,* p. 20.

continuall claim hath been made by the English to their rights and Liberties, so that in point of Law no pretended succession, continued by force, fraud, and perjury, can be a just plea to barre us of our inheritance, our Native Freedome, which we have now gained possession of, the most high and just judge having given sentence for us upon our appeal, and of his free grace enabled us to enter in despight of those who so long have kept possession against our Ancestors. [36]

William Cole, author of *A Rod for Lawyers* (1659) is similarly disillusioned with the liberal tradition:

It is the usual cry amongst the Masters of Oppression the Lawyers, and ignorant people that know no better, that the Laws of England, as also the ways of executing them, are the safest and best in the World, and whosoever shall alter the said laws, or ways of executing them, will unavoidably introduce a mischief instead of a benefit. But to these it is answered, that the major part of the Laws made in this nation, are founded on principles of tyranny, fallacy, and oppression for the profit and benefit of those that made them.

But some will say, that although we were conquered, yet your Noble Ancestors, by dint of sword in the Barons War, regained their freedom and influenced the King to condescend to that famous Law, called Magna Carta.

For answer, know this, that when the nobles in those days found the King altogether inclined to his minions, and Flatterers, and thereby made Laws to enslave the said nobles, as well as the commons worse than they had been before, They saw there was a necessity for them to stand up for their own priviledges, who being popular, what by fear and love, they engaged the commons with them in War, and took the King prisoner, forcing him to consent to all things that were necessary, to preserve themselves from the King's will, but never in the least acted from any love to the poor commons, but what they were absolutely necessitated, neither freed the said commons from the bondage they were in to themselves. [37]

---

[36] *Ibid.,* pp. 54-55.

[37] *A Rod for Lawyers* (London, 1659), p. 35; reprinted also in *Harleian Miscellany,* VII, 25-35. Arthur L. Cross has called attention to Cole but treats him as an isolated phenomenon, which, of course,

It is interesting to see that the communists of the period, the Diggers, also pointed out that past revolutions have always left the peoples less free. The upper classes, eager to seize power, enlist the aid of the commoners, but once having gained power begin to persecute the people. The Diggers argued that Parliament was illogical in turning out the King but retaining the Norman law which protected private property; Parliament, that is, was illogical, if it was not actually following a hypocritical design to seize Norman power for itself. Professor George Sabine has edited the works of the Digger leader, Gerrard Winstanley, and has done scholarship a great service in finding and printing a Digger song which actually makes this criticism of Parliament:

> When great Men disagree
> About Supremacy,
>
> Then doe they warn poor men
> To aid and assist them
>    In setting up their self-will power
>    And thus they doe the poor devour.
>     . . . . .
> Yet they cunningly pretend
> They have no other end
> But to set the poor Free
> From all their slavery:
>    And thus they do the poor deceive,
>    In making them such things believe. [38]

Any examination of the spiritual and intellectual credentials of the Levellers which fails to take in the Clarke Papers must be incomplete. The Clarke Papers are the written record set down by Major Clarke of the debates held in the army coun-

he is not: "An Unpopular Seventeenth-Century View of Magna Carta," *American Historical Review*, XXIX (1923), 74-76.

[38] "The Diggers Christmass-Carol" (1650), stanzas two and three, *The Works of Gerrard Winstanley*, edited by G. H. Sabine (Ithaca, 1941), p. 667.

cils at Putney in October of 1647. The New Model Army was by this date thoroughly exasperated with Parliament's poltroonery in its dealings with the nation. Since the officers appeared undecided and wavering, the privates were left to themselves. Led by the more articulate and determined Levellers, the soldiers met among themselves and set up agents called Agitators to represent them in the General Council of the Army. Thus the Putney debates were between the Agitators and the officers on the occasion of a meeting of the General Council. Colonel Ireton, Cromwell's son-in-law, spoke in the Council against the Levellers, and it is quite apparent from the record how difficult his position was. He had thrown his lot in with the army, since he knew very well how sorely the men had been tried by Parliament. But, on the other hand, the Leveller dominance over the soldiers aroused all his apprehensions. The Leveller repudiation of the tradition of parliamentary law raised the specter of anarchy before his eyes. Ireton did not doubt the integrity of the Levellers. He rather foresaw that their revolutionary ideal would have to effect a compromise with the demands of actual life, especially property rights. The necessity for the radicals to compromise thrust itself upon William Wildman and Thomas Rainborow, the Leveller spokesmen in the debates, at the very outset of the discussion.

Wildman begins by questioning whether an unjust parliament should be obeyed. (Woodhouse points out that Wildman is paraphrasing the *Representation of the Army* addressed on June 14th to Parliament; Wildman cites the same two examples of an unjust command as those in the *Representation*—a pilot who willfully runs his ship on the rocks, a general who turns the cannon around on his own troops—these are not to be obeyed, by the law of nature.) He says:

The other [thing I would mention] is a principle much spreading, and much to my trouble and that is this: that when persons once be engaged, though the engagement appear to be unjust, yet the person must sit down and suffer under it; and that therefore, in case a Parliament, as a true Parliament, doth anything unjustly, if we be engaged to submit to the laws that they shall make, though they make an unjust law, though they make an unrighteous law, yet we must swear obedience. I confess, to me the principle is very dangerous, and I speak it the rather because I see it spreading abroad in the Army again— whereas it is contrary to what the Army first declared: that they stood upon such principles of right and freedom, and the laws of Nature and Nations, whereby men were to preserve themselves though the persons to whom authority belong should fail in it. [39]

Wildman here is taking the Leveller position that the powers of Parliament as such are limited, but we recall that in common with Walwyn, Lilburne, Warr, and Cole, he was also of the opinion that in the past, parliaments had in fact failed to preserve the people's liberties and that only direct armed action won the people their liberties.

Ireton makes his reply to Wildman:

I am far from holding that if a man have engaged himself to a thing that is not just—to a thing that is evil, that is sin if he do it—that man is still bound to perform what he hath promised; I am far from apprehending that. But when we talk of just, it is not so much of what is sinful before God (which depends upon many circumstances of indignation to that man and the like), but it intends of that which is just according to the foundation of justice between man and man. And for my part I account that the great foundation of justice [that we should keep covenant one with another]; without which I know nothing of justice betwixt man and man—[in] particular matters I mean, nothing in particular things that can come under human engagement one way or another. There is no other foundation of right I know, of right to [any] one thing from another man, no foundation of that [particular] justice or that [particular] righteousness, but

[39] Woodhouse, *Puritanism and Liberty,* p. 24; the matter enclosed within square brackets are textual emendations or corrections of the original shorthand manuscript.

this general justice and this general ground of righteousness,
that we should keep covenant one with another. Covenants freely
made, freely entred into, must be kept one with another. Take
away that, I do not know what ground there is of anything you
can call any man's right. I would very fain know what you gentlemen, or any other, do account the right you have to anything
in England,—anything of estate, land or goods, what you have,
what ground, what right you have to it. What right hath any
man to anything else, than I have. I have as much right to take
hold of anything that is for my sustenance, [to] take hold of
anything that I have a desire to for my satisfaction, as you..
For matter of goods, that which does fence me from that [right]
which another man may claim by the Law of Nature, of taking
my goods, that which makes it mine really and civilly, is the
law. That which makes it unlawful originally and radically is
only this: because that man is in covenant with me to live
together in peace one with another, and not to meddle with that
which another is possessed of, but that each of us should enjoy,
and make use of, and dispose of, that which by the course of
law is in his possession, and [another] shall not by violence
take it away from him. This is the foundation of all the right
any man has to anything but to his own person. This is the
general thing: that we must keep covenant one with another
when we have contracted one with another. [40]

In sum, Ireton is granting the Leveller argument that a
natural right is a moral right, since to expect a man to commit
an immoral act is unnatural. But he is insisting that a natural
moral right is not a civic right. His charge against the Levellers is that among those individuals who claim their natural
rights there is not even the preliminary moral agreement, or
covenant, as he calls it, to respect one another's moral rights
or the moral agreement reached by the majority. Consequently, he stresses the sanctity of private property, which would
disappear if the civic covenant were abrogated. Cromwell
himself also pretended to see in natural rights a principle

[40] *Ibid.*, pp. 25-26.

subversive of private property: "Why may nott those men vote against all propertie?" [41]

The Leveller rebuttal to Ireton's charge that natural law is subversive of property-rights is most interesting, since it touches the political problem at the vital spot where political and economic rights meet and clash. The council has begun a discussion for the purpose of ratifying the Agreement of the People of November 3rd. The first clause is being debated, namely,

> That the people of England, being at this day very unequally distributed by counties, cities, and boroughs, for the election of their deputies in Parliament, ought to be more indifferently proportioned, according to the number of inhabitants; the circumstances whereof, for number, place, and manner, are to be set down before the end of this Parliament.

Ireton objects to extending the franchise:

> The exception that lies in it is this. It is said, they are to be distributed according to the number of the inhabitants: 'The people of England,' etc. And this doth make me think that the meaning is, that every man that is an inhabitant is to be equally considered, and to have an equal choice in the election of those representers, the persons that are for the general Representative; and if that be the meaning, then I have something to say against it. But if it be only that those people that by the civill constitution of the kingdom, which is original and fundamental, and beyond which I am sure no memory of record does go—
> [Cowling, interrupting]: Not before the Conquest.
> Ireton: But before the Conquest it was so. If it be intended that those that by that constitution that was before the Conquest, that hath been beyond memory, such persons that have been before [by] that constitution [the electors], should be [still] the electors, I have no more to say against it. [42]

Ireton is interested, as he presently makes clear, in restricting the franchise to those who meet the property qualification for

[41] *Ibid.,* p. 63.
[42] *Ibid.,* p. 52.

voting as prescribed by the fundamental law. Rainborow meets Ireton's argument with a remark which is the classic of Leveller doctrine:

> For really I think that the poorest he that is in England hath a life to live, as the greatest he; and therefore truly, sir, I think it's clear, that every man that is to live under a government ought first by his own consent to put himself under that government; and I do think that the poorest man in England is not at all bound in a strict sense to that government that he hath not had a voice to put himself under; and I am confident that, when I have heard the reasons against it, something will be said to answer those reasons, insomuch that I should doubt whether he was an Englishman or no, that should doubt of these things. [43]

Ireton replies:

> That's the meaning of this 'according to the number of inhabitants?' Give me leave to tell you, that if you make the rule I think you must fly for refuge, to an absolute natural right, and you must deny all civil right; and I am sure it will come to that in the consequence. I think that no person hath a right to an interest or share in the disposing of the affairs of the kingdom, and in determining or choosing those that shall determine what laws we shall be ruled by here—no person hath a right to this, that hath not a permanent fixed interest in this kingdom, and consequently are [also] to make up the representers of this kingdom, who taken together do comprehend whatsoever is of real or permanent interest in the kingdom.

He concludes: "And if we shall go to take away this, we shall plainly go to take away all property and interest that any man hath either in land by inheritance, or in estate by possession, or anything else—[I say], if you take away this fundamental part of the civil constitution." [44]

Finally, Ireton's flat statement that "All the main thing that I speak for, is because I would have an eye to property" [45]

[43] *Ibid.*, p. 53.
[44] *Ibid.*, pp. 53-54, 55.
[45] *Ibid.*, p. 57.

brings on a withering attack from the soldiers. Rainborow protests: "The chief end of this government is to preserve persons as well as estates, and if any law shall take hold of my person, it is more dear than my estate." [46] Edward Sexby reminds Ireton that they had fought in the army to recover their rights as Englishmen, and therefore they have a right to the vote even if propertyless, for, as he says: "If we had not a right to the kingdom, we were mere mercenary soldiers." [47] Clarke cleverly directs an oblique attack on Ireton's position by asserting that, as a matter of fact, natural law *does* sustain the sanctity of property: "Yet really properties are the foundations of constitutions [and not constitutions of property]. For if so be there were no constitution yet the Law of Nature does give a principle [for every man] to have a property of what he has, or may have, which is not another man's." [48]

Ireton, however, sticks to his guns: "For by the same reason that you will alter this constitution, merely that there's a greater [liberty] by nature [than this] constitution [gives]— by the same reason, by the Law of Nature, there is a greater liberty to the use of other men's goods, which that property bars you of." [49]

In point of fact, there was not a jot of evidence to prove that the Levellers were committed to a communistic program. The name "Levellers" was given to them by their enemies, and it is a fact that Lilburne, in his tract *The Legal and Fundamental Liberties,* repudiated Winstanley, leader of the Diggers, a genuinely communistic group. Winstanley took as the name of his followers, the "True Levellers," proving that both sides saw the contrast. [50]

[46] *Ibid.,* p. 67.
[47] *Ibid.,* p. 69.
[48] *Ibid.,* p. 75.                    [49] *Ibid.,* p. 79.
[50] See Sabine's introductory essay to his edition of Winstanley's tracts.

The extreme form in which the two opposing theories of government were cast exposed them to mutual misunderstanding. If time were not pressing and emotions not rising high, perhaps the Levellers would have seen that Ireton was not prepared to sacrifice every humane consideration to property rights; Ireton, on his part, would have seen that the Levellers were not proposing anarchy.

The extreme individualism of Leveller theory is only a surface manifestation, which can, it is true, be misleading. In the form in which the Levellers projected their theory of government under natural law, the stress fell on the individual's natural right to consider the the covenant between government and himself broken when the government failed to protect him. Although this individualistic bias would seem to produce only the grotesque idea that an individual fulfills his civic duty best when he refrains from civic duty, nevertheless, it is understandable how the particular circumstance of Parliament's claim to absolute power brought about the situation. But the real intent of the Levellers was not individualistic. At the bottom of this contradiction lay the Leveller assumption that the appeal to natural law was an appeal to right reason, and the second assumption, following upon the first, that right reason would always produce the same judgments in different minds. [51] Thus the Levellers were content that they were not a mere band of individualists determined to resist any form of government whatsoever. They were quite unaware themselves that their appeal to a universal, collective right reason was an appeal to the very convention which they were attacking in the first place as detrimental to the individual's natural birthrights. If Ireton were able at all to detect this logical inconsistency in Leveller theory, it would only have reinforced his belief that a covenant of civic rights and duties,

[51] See Ritchie, *Natural Rights,* p. 14, a brief but penetrating discussion of the logical basis of Leveller thought.

taken in terms of such a charter as Magna Charta, for example, was ample protection of the people's rights, and that, in fact, it was precisely what the Levellers were seeking. [52]

Ireton was deeply shaken, as we have seen, by the anarchic tendencies of his comrades-in-arms. He tried patiently to convince the soldiers, in the face of Parliament's perfidy, that there were ample liberties within the tradition of free parliaments, and that anarchy must result if English charters were abrogated: "When I do hear men speak of laying aside all engagements to consider only that wild or vast notion of what in every man's conception is just or unjust, I am afraid and do tremble at the boundless and endless consequences of it. If you do paramount to all constitutions hold up this law of nature, I would fain have any show me where you will end." [53]

Ireton stood for the social cohesion offered by the tradition of constitutional law. He stood, that is, for the experienced ideal of democracy which the Gothicists held forth as a mooring post to which the nation's development could be securely tied. To Ireton, as to the Gothicists, nationalism was not a primary concept but was subsidiary to a higher unity, democracy. He believed that a nation which had discovered its moral collective being (which he described as a moral covenant to abide by traditions and past custom) has in the very act discovered its capacities for self-government—for democracy, to state it in a word. Ireton, as he made it abundantly clear, had not a shadow of doubt concerning the moral integrity of the Levellers as individuals. He strove patiently to conciliate them, but he could not concede their civic moral

[52] See Bishop Bramhall in *Serpent-Salve* (1643), in *Works of...John Bramhall,* Library of Anglo-Catholic Theology (Oxford, 1844), III, 366: "We have a surer charter than that of nature to hold by, Magna Charta, the Englishmen's jewel and treasure, the fountain and foundation of our freedom, the walls and bulwarks, yea, the very life and soul of our security."

[53] Woodhouse, *Puritanism and Liberty,* p. 27.

integrity. The Levellers lacked, as he saw it in terms of the moral collective being which *precedes* the foundation of governments, just that moral agreement among themselves to respect the government after it was founded. [54]

The issue between Ireton and the Levellers may be restated as the question of reform versus revolution. Both sides were unquestionably committed to the democratic way of life, but there was a great difference between them. Ireton stood for the gains which *had* been made in the experienced ideal of democracy. The Levellers, on the other hand, stood for the gains which could be made in the future if natural law were made the paramount law. Thus the Levellers brought to light a weakness in the Gothic position when they showed that a reverence for tradition and custom can, at times, be reactionary. Rainborow's profoundly noble observation that "the poorest he in England hath a life to live as the greatest he" had value to Ireton as a reminder first, that property exists for men and not men for property; secondly, as a reminder that tradition and custom, while they may be excellent, are not enough. Rainborow was pointing out that political institutions, hallowed though they may be by time, often tend to become ends in themselves, and perennially we have to be reminded of the ends which political institutions are intended to serve, namely, the human ends implied in Rainborow's remark. In short, Rainborow was pointing out that the Gothicists might be having the history yet without having the life.

The Levellers, as a party, disintegrated, and rather ignominiously, there is some reason to believe, amidst intrigue to restore the king. But while the party disintegrated, the theory

---

[54] See a later attack on natural rights which summarizes Ireton's position: "All the Arguments for a Natural Democracy are built upon false Suppositions; and when ever the People have any part in the Sovereignty it is by *the After-Constitution, and not by Nature*" Anonymous, *The Opinion of Divers Learned and Leading Dissenters, Concerning the Original of Government* (London, 1680), p. 6.

of the rights of man remained, as the history of English political thought after Locke shows, the expression of Whiggism in England. If one views English political history in a large enough frame, the gradual extension of the franchise, the augmentation of the powers of Commons, the various acts of social legislation, are indications of how deeply the seeds of Leveller doctrine were sown. The Levellers are "the men on England's conscience," and all Americans who know Lincoln as "the man on America's conscience" will know instantly what this means. As a matter of fact, there is a real historical link between English Leveller theory and the American Bill of Rights which aimed to place certain rights forever beyond the reach of Congress. There have always been American presidents who believed as the Levellers did that men must live "per viam facti and not by Lawes." Lincoln was greatly impatient of constitutional restraints, and at times he frankly ignored them. Jefferson constantly wrangled with the Supreme Court, and Jackson bluntly told the Court to enforce their own decisions; Theodore Roosevelt's attempt to recall their decisions, and Franklin Delano Roosevelt's attacks on the "nine old men" were similarly waged in the name of the "natural" rights of man.

In England, men of Ireton's profound respect for constitutional tradition and Whigs with the Leveller noble social consciousness have together shown that tradition need not be impervious to progressive ideas, and, conversely, that progressive ideas need not be impervious to the accumulated wisdom of experience. This, perhaps, is another way of pointing to the English habit of effecting the most revolutionary changes in the mildest way possible. Actually, this is what occurred in the reinvigoration of the Gothic cult, after the Restoration, side by side with Whiggism.

Although Ireton upholds tradition without specifically invoking the Gothic version and Warr is the only radical who specifically denounces the Saxon past, our discussion has, nevertheless, made clear what the implications were for the future of the Gothic propaganda as a result of the revolutionary radicals. It is certain that the post-Leveller Gothic tracts are not the same as the pre-Leveller Gothic tracts, in the hands, that is, of thinkers of independent intelligence such as Sir Roger Twysden or Swift. Swift is ardent for Gothic constitutionalism, but he insists on testing it by what he himself calls "right reason." To a man of Swift's caliber, to judge whether tradition is ethically intolerable or tolerable, a man must act on the basis of his reason. To act otherwise is to argue that the highest duty of a citizen is to maintain tradition, without regard to the quality of tradition. To observe a contrast, there is Coke who stoutly defended the ancient tradition of parliamentary prerogative. Coke served Parliament ably and fearlessly. At another juncture of history, however, lacking Swift's "reason," Coke would have been an arch-reactionary, clamoring for tradition in a time when change would be necessary.

## APPENDIX C

# THE RABBINICAL TRADITION: JAPHET, GOMER, TUISCO

The "toledoth," or genealogies preserved in the ethnographic Genesis 10, provided the starting-point of a discussion which directed attention to an Asiatic origin of the Germanic peoples:

1. Now these are the generations of the sons of Noah, Shem, Ham, and Japheth: and unto them were sons born after the flood.
2. The sons of Japheth; Gomer, and Magog, and Madai, and Javan, and Tubal, and Mesech, and Tiras.
3. And the sons of Gomer; Ashkenaz, and Riphath, and Togarmah.
4. And the sons of Javan; Elishah, and Tarshish, Kittim, and Dodanim.
5. By these were the isles of the Gentiles divided in their lands; every one after his tongue, after their families, in their nations.

The genealogies follow after the prophecy made in Genesis 9 : 27 preceding, that "God shall enlarge Japheth." The passage contains a paronomasia on the name Japheth which probably means "enlarged" (from a root *Pathah,* to extend); that is, a prophecy is intended that the world will be divided among the sons of Noah but Japheth will receive the largest portion for his inheritance. [1]

In the commentaries heaped upon the name Japheth he is connected either with the hegemony of the northern portions of the world, or with the parentage of Tuisco, the eponymous

[1] See *The Book of Genesis,* edited by S. R. Driver (Westminster Commentaries; New York 1888), I, 81 ff., a clear-headed summary of the complex problem of the genealogies.

god of the Teutons, or with a conception of a family of fair-complexioned (blond) sons. Gomer and Magog, and the sons of Gomer—Ashkenaz and Togarmah—are in one way or another assimilated to German history, Magog specifically to Gothic history.

A Syriac commentary by Barhebraeus reflects the interpretation of Japheth which connects him with northern hegemony and a family of fair sons: "These are the families of the sons of Noah...and from them were the peoples differentiated after the Deluge, seventy-two tongues: fifteen of the fair sons of Japeth, who are in the north...and thirty of the blacks, the sons of Ham, who are in the south...and twenty-seven of the brown sons of Shem..." [2]

Philo Judaeus favors the etymology which supports the view of a massmigration led by Japheth to regions undesignated in Philo but in all other writers always to the North: "Why do the people of Aos, and of Rhodes, and the isles of the Gentiles, spring from Japhet? Since he has the name denoting breadth (namely Japhet), being expanded in his growth and increase..." [3]

The Old English commentary of Aelfric pictures a northern colonization by Japhet: "Of Cham, Noes sunna, com þæt Chananisce folc, of Iaphet, þam ginstan, þe wæs gebletsod þurh Noe, com þæt norðerne mennisc be þære Nortsæ, for þan þe ðri dælas sind gedælede þurh hig, Asia, on eastrice

---

[2] W. C. Graham and M. Sprengling, *Barkebraeus' Scholia on the Old Testament* (Chicago, 1931), p. 45, containing the Syrian text and the translation. Genesius and Knobel, modern authorities, derive Japeth from *Yaphah*, to be beautiful. The derivation of Japeth from *Yaphah*, to be beautiful, is also found in Saadia (tenth century) and is rejected by Abraham Ibn Ezra (twelfth century). It is also implied in a Talmudic comment on Genesis 9: 27 (Megillah 9b).

[3] Philo Judaeus, *Quaestiones et Solutiones in Genesin* ii, 80; English translation by C. D. Yonge, *The Works of Philo Judaeus* (London, 1854), IV, 404.

þam yldstan suna, Affrica on suðdæle þæs Chames Cynne, Europa on norðdæle Iapheþes of springe." [4]

In William L'Isle's translation of 1623 (*A Saxon Treatise*) this reads: "Of Cham Noes sonne are the Canaanites, & of Iapheth his youngest whom Noe blessed, came the Nations bordering on the North Sea. For they made three parts. Asia, the East countrey for the eldest sonne; Africa, the South countrey for Chams issue; and Europe toward the North, for the offspring of Iaphet." [5]

The medieval document known as the *Chartres Manuscript* lists in detail the Germanic tribal groups in the Japhet posterity:

Tres filii Noe diuiserunt orbem terre in tres partes post diluuium: Sem in Asia, Cham in Africa, Iafeth in Europha. Ad Europham de genere Iafeth Alanus cum tribus filiis suis quorum nomina sunt Hission, Armenon, Nengo. Hission habuit quator filius: Francus, Romanus, Almannus, Brito. Armenon autem V filios habuit: Gothus, Ualagothus, Cebustus, Burgundus, Longobardus; Nengo habuit III filios: Uandalis, Saxo, Bogarus, Ab Hisscioe autem quator gentes oret sunt, Franci, Latini, Almanni, Britones; ab Armenone autem Gothi, Ualagothi, Cebidi, Burgundi et Longobardi; a Nego autem Bogari, Uandali, Saxones, et Turingi. Iste autem gentes subdivisi s[unt] per totam Europam. [6]

Gomer, son of Japheth and grandson of Noah, comes in for more attention than Japhet and was more influential in establishing an eastern home for the Germans. From antiquity the name Gomer was conceived either as the origin of the tribal name Cimmeri, or, as in the rabbinical commentary, the origin of the tribal name Germani.

[4] *The Old English Version of the Heptateuch, Aelfric's Treatise on the Old and New Testament and his Preface to Genesis*, edited by S. J. Crawford (Early English Text Society, 160; 1922), p. 27.

[5] Translation supplied on same page (p. 27n) of Early English Text Society edition.

[6] *Chartres Ms.* edited by L. Duchesne, in *Revue Celtique*, XV (1894), 177.

Josephus (*Antiq.* i. 7) takes the name Gomer to refer to those whom the Greeks called Galatians, formerly called Gomarites (see also Isidore, *Etymol.* ix. 2,1). Therefore, Gomer is generally identified with the Celtic race called in Homer the Kimmeroi (*Odyssey* xi. 14) who are known as inhabiting the Chersonesus Taurica, still called to this day Crimea (see Herod. iv. 12). The Kimmeroi were confused with the Cimbri (Strabo vii. 2,2; Diod. Sic. v. 32). The name Cimbri is recognized again in the people who occupied the Cimbrian Chersonesus in Denmark in the north of Europe, and also in the Cymry of Wales. Gomer's progeny is recalled in the Assyrian inscriptions as the Gimirra. The Assyrian cuneiform records mention Esarhaddon (681-668 B.C.) as having defeated the Gimirrai. [7]

In the course of the eighth or seventh centuries the Kimmerians, pressed by the Scythians, crossed the Bosphorus into Asia Minor. They undoubtedly merged with the Scythians, and were called Scythians for this reason. Henry Rawlinson reports Achaemenian inscriptions of both Sacae and Scythians reappearing in Babylonian transcripts as Gimiri. [8]

The Hebrew *G* is regularly a substitute for Greek *K*: Hebrew *gamol* (a camel) for Greek *kamelos*. Gomer is characteristically Semitic tri-consonantal: GMR, hence Cimbri, by metathesis KRM, hence, Crimea, and as in the rabbinical exegesis, GRM, that is to say, Germani. In *Yoma* 10a Gomer is Germania; all the variants and their Talmudic sources, midrashim, targumim, may be consulted in Jacob Levy, *Wör-*

---

[7] See A. Dillmann, *Genesis* (Edinburgh, 1897), I, 326-327; A. Knobel, *Die Genesis* (Leipzig 1852), p. 100; Martin L. Rouse, "Bible Pedigree of the Nations of the World," *Transactions of the Victoria Institute,* XXXVIII (1906), 123-150; A. Neubauer, *La Geographie du Talmud* (Paris, 1868), "Appendice," pp. 421ff; Franz Julius Delitzsch, *New Commentary* (New York, 1889), I, 299ff; and the various Bible dictionaries *s.v.* "Gomer."

[8] T. R. Howlett, *Anglo-Israel* (London, 1892), p. 49.

*terbuch über die Talmudim und Midrashim,* volume I, page 361. [9] The combined classical and rabbinical discussions gradually sift downward to the historians.

Sir Walter Raleigh's *History of the World* places Gomer at the head of Cimbrian history:

Of Gomer the like may be said. First he seated himself with Togorma, not far from Magog and Tubal, in the borders of Syria and Cilicia. Afterward he proceeded further into Asia the less; and in long tract of time his valiant issue filled all Germany, rested long in France and Britain, and possessed the utmost Borders of the Erath, accomplishing (as Melancthon well notes) the signification of their Parents Name, which is utmost Bordering...they were called Cimbri. [10]

John Clapham shows that England was colonized by Gomer's progeny:

It is recorded by the most true, and antient of all Histories, that the Iles of the Gentiles, and north partes of the world, were first divided and inhabited, by the posteritie of Iaphet; from whose eldest sonne called Gomer, the Cimbrians (as Writers report) deriv'd their name and descent, imparting the same to the Gauls and Germans, and consequently to the Inhabitants of this Ile. [11]

Edward Ayscu's *Historie* (1606) tells the Gomer story: "The people now called Gaules (say they) were before that named Gomirries or Gomerites of Gomer. These were afterwards by the Latines called Cimbri. [12] Du Bartas includes the story in his hexameric scheme:

[9] Berlin und Wien, 1924. See also M. Jastrow, *A Dictionary of the Targum the Talmud Babli and Yerushalmi, and the Midrashic Literature* (London and New York, 1903) p. 270 b.

[10] London, 1687, p. 78, right column. Raleigh's reference to Melancthon is an indication of the contribution made by the German Hebraists, especially Münster and Melanchthon, to the discussion.

[11] *The Historie of Great Britaine* (London, 1606), p. 1.

[12] *A Historie Contayning the Warres, Treaties, Marriages, and Other Occurences Between England and Scotland* (London, 1607), p. 3.

Forth of his Gomer's loigns (they say) sprung all
The war-like Nations scattered over Gaul,
And Germans too (yerst called Gomerites). [13]

Milton's *History of Britain* records the origins of the Gomer
progeny: "After the Flood, and the dispersion of Nations, as
they journey'd leisurely from the East, Gomer the eldest son
of Japhet, and his Off-Spring, as by Authorities, Arguments,
and Affinity of divers Names is generally believ'd, were the
first that peopled all these West and Northern Climes." [14]
Matthew Poole's *Annotations Upon the Bible* (1688) is an
indication of the way in which the Gomer legend became a
part of standard Biblical commentary: "[Re: Gomer] Whose
posterity are reckoned among the Northern People Ezek. 38.6
and were seated in the Northern parts of the lesser Asia, and
afterwards about Thracia, and from him were called Gomari,
and by an easie change, Cimbri, or Cimmerii." [15] The list
could be made endlessly long. We may conclude with Sheringham's *De Anglorum cent origin disceptatio* (1670), since his
knowledge of Hebrew put him in touch directly with rabbinical
sources. [16]

Ashkenaz is also favored by Hebrew legend, again connecting the Germans with an Ask race; אילא appears in the
rabbinical literature for Askenaz. In Jeremiah 51: 27 the Ashkenaz are recorded as attacking Babylonia; they may be,
therefore, the tribe who in alliance with the Assyrians burst
into the Mesopotamian valley and are to be identified with
the Ash-ku-za of Assyrian inscriptions and known to Greeks
later as Scythians. [17]

[13] *Divine Weeks*, Sylvester translation, "The Colonies," third Part,
second Day, second week, p. 338.

[14] Bohn edition, I, p. 2.

[15] Volume I, *s.v.* "Genesis" X.

[16] Chapter xvi, pp. 399-448; Sheringham quotes from Targum Jerusalem and Targum Jonathan.

[17] *The Talmud Yerushalmi* (*Yer. Megillah* I, II. 71b) and *Targum
Yerushalmi* (on Gen. 10 : 3).

Rashi, the well-known commentator (1040-1105), refers to Germany as *eretz ashkenaz* (eretz means land) in his commentary on the Talmud (Hullin 93a). Knobel among modern scholars connects Ashkenaz with Asa, or Asiatics equals Ashgenos. The Askenians also suggest the Sacae race; Ammianus Marcellinus (xxiii. 60), refers to the Ascanimia Mountain as in the territory of the Sakai (Askenians equals Asake equals Sacae). One citation from an English writer will suffice perhaps to indicate the Renaissance knowledge of the Biblical genealogies, and, incidentally, will also indicate the jumble of variant interpretations floating about in the period: "Eusebius makes Ascanez the Father of the Goths. The Jews in their Targum make him the Root of the German nation... Melancthon being of the same opinion, that the Tuiscones were descended of the Ascanez (for Tuiscones, saith he, is as much to say, as of the Ascanez, praeposito articulo die Ascanez)..." [18]

Togarmah in the midrashim is also Germania. Poole's commentary will again reflect typical seventeenth-century exegesis: "[re: Togarmah] Whose posterity are joined with Gomers. See *Ezek.* 27: 14 and 38: 6, and were as some think, the Phrygians and Galatians, and of them the Gauls and the Germans: Or, as others, the Armenians and of them the Turks." [19]

Magog is clearly and unmistakably connected first with the Scythians and in the time of the Gothic invasions with the Goths. Josephus (*Antiq.* i. 6) says the Scythians are descendants of Magog. Isidore (*Etymol.* ix. 2,27) connects Magog with Scythians and Goths: "Magog a quo quidam arbitrantur Scythas et Gothos traxisse originem." Also in *Etymologiarum* (ix. 2,89): "Gothi a Magog filio Iaphet nominati putantur de similitudine ultimae syllabae, quos veteres

18 Raleigh, *History of the World*, p. 82, right column.
19 *Annotations*, I, *s.v.* "Genesis" X.

magis Getas quam Gothos vocaverunt." Jordanes, as we have seen, describes how the Goths came to Scythia under Berig after having left Scandza, and he says:

It is said than when half the army had been brought over, the bridge whereby they had crossed the river fell in utter ruin, nor could anyone thereafter pass to or fro. Even today one may hear in that neighborhood the lowing of cattle and may find traces of men, if we are to believe the stories of travellers, although we must grant that they hear these things from afar. [20]

This is the specific link between the Scythians, the giants Gog and Magog, and the Alexander legend of the lost tribes of Israel locked up behind the Caspian gates which we find spread over the entire medieval period. [21] Jerome identifies Magog with the Gothic invasions: "Scio quendam Gog et Magog...et Gotthorum nuper in terra nostra bac-

[20] Mierow translation, p. 57.

[21] In a forthcoming book on Renaissance giant-lore, I shall attempt to unravel this exceedingly involved story. In English history, the struggle between Brutus and the giants, Gog and Magog, is only one aspect of what I have discovered, as a by-product of my Gothic researches, that the term "giant" does not necessarily refer to a creature of huge size; the various assertions made by the seventeenth-century historians that the Jutes (the founding-fathers in the Gothic tradition!) were giants cannot possibly mean that they thought they were of huge size. The whole problem of Renaissance giant-lore has awaited a correct solution only for lack of sufficient knowledge of the rabbinical commentary on Genesis. The statement in the Hebrew of Genesis that there were "giants [nephilim] in the land" probably did not mean men of huge stature and only at times in later commentary is it taken to refer to size. Samson, for example, is a Gibor but not a nephil. What is involved here too is the interweaving of Jewish and classical myth (Japhet equals Iapetos; Ashkenaz equals Ascanius, and so on). The Oxford English Dictionary has not the slightest awareness that in seventeenth-century usage, "giant" did not necessarily refer to size.

For the Alexander legend, see F. P. Magoun, Jr., The Gests of Alexander of Macedon (Cambridge, Mass. 1929); A. A. Vasiliev, The Goths in Crimea (Cambridge, Mass., 1936); A. R. Anderson, Alexander's Gate, Gog and Magog, and the Inclosed Nations (Cambridge, Mass., 1932); A. H. Godbey, The Lost Tribes, A Myth (Durham, 1930).

chantium historiam retulisse." [22] In the *Talmud Yerush-almi,* *(Yer. Megillah* i. 11,71b) Magog is rendered Gothia. Higden's *Polychronicon* records the modern knowledge of Magog: "Gothia is a region of Scythia... That londe was callede Gothia of Gog, the sonne of Iapeth, the people of whom be callede rather Gothos than Gogos, whiche be mighty men and terrible." [23] Raleigh also connects Magog with the Gothic invasion: "S. Ambrose and Isidor take Gog for the Nations of the Goths: belike because they invaded Europe, and sacked Rome, and many other places and Cities thereabout." [24] The nationalistic revival in Sweden was one of the prime forces bringing to light the Magog parentage of the Goths, since the object of the Swedish nationalists was to account for their national beginnings either on the basis of the Scandza theory of Jordanes or the Biblical theory. In the *Historia de omnibus Gothorum* by Johannes Magnus (1540), Sueno is the eldest son of Magog and progenitor of the *gens Suenica,* the Swedes. [25]

We come finally to Tuisco, the god and progenitor of the Germans. There is, of course, no Tuisco in the Bible, but his mention in Tacitus *(Germania* ii) and the authority of the ethnographic Genesis 10 appeared to constitute reason enough to install Tuisco in the line of descent from Noah. The main reason probably why Tuisco was introduced into Noah's line was that his presence there accounted for the gap between the Flood and the fall of Troy. This is certainly the reason

[22] *Quaestionum hebraicarum in Genesim,* chap. x verse 2, in Migne, *Patrologia Latina,* vol. XXIII, col. 999.

[23] Volume I, p. 145; for the Alexander story see III, 69-70: "Over the hilles Caspy where kynge Alexaunder includede twyne peple, Gog and Magog, whom Antecriste schalle delyver when he commethe, and shal brynge theyme furthe."

[24] *History,* 77, left column; for Saint Ambrose, see *De fide ad Gratian,* bk. iii, ch. 16, in Migne, *Patrologia Latina,* vol. XVI, col. 612.

[25] See C. F. Barnouw, "Early Danish and Swedish Writers on Native History," *Studies in Honor of John Albrecht Walz* (Lancaster, 1941), p. 168.

for the enormous popularity in the Renaissance of the pseudo-Berosus, probably the main source of the idea that Tuisco is of the Noah posterity.

The pseudo-Berosus was compiled by Annius of Viterbo (his real name was Giovanni Nanni, or Anni) and published in 1498 under the title *Commentaria super opera diversorum auctorum de antiquitatibus loquentium,* supposedly the authentic writings of Berosus, Manetho, Metasthenes, Archilochus, Fabius Pictor, and others. This text is the "Berosus" referred to by Spenser, Milton, Raleigh, Camden, and a host of others, usually in indignation at the scope of the fraud. The pseudo-Berosus tells the story of the division of the earth among Noah's progeny, Tuyscon inheriting Germany. [26] In the English translation (1602) by Richard Lynche, under the title *An Historical Treatise of the Travels of Noah into Europe,* Tuyscon appears in the midst of Noah's family, Titans, giants, Hercules, Saturnus, Nimrod, and so on, in a manner to leave a reader gasping:

It is written that Noe begat of his wife Tytea after the floud, thirtie children, viz. Tuyscon the Giant, Prometheus, Japetus, Macrus, and the sixteen Titans which were all Giants... And over Almaign, (now called Germanie) governed the Giant Tuyscon, one of the sonnes of Noe... The names in like manner of the people of Germanie varied and differed very often and severally: For the first name that the people received were Tuyscones, of Tuyscon, one of Noe's sons. [27]

In Verstegen's interpretation, Tuisco accounts for the name "Deutsch." He places Tuisco in Noah's family and adds the amusing information that if some wonder that Noah should have had so many children, he can personally testify that a woman in Paris by the name of Yoland Baillie had "two hundred fourscore and fifteen children." Tuisco was "the

[26] Page 31 of the 1612 edition under the title *Berosus sacerdotes Chaldaici...cum commentariis Joannis Anii.*
[27] Leafs B2, B4, K4.

father and conductor of the Germans, who after his name even unto this day do in their own toung call themselves Tuytsh and there countrie of Germanie Tuytschland." 28 Among the endless repetitions of the Tuisco legend, one is selected to represent all. Drayton's *Polyolbion* (song iv, line 375) tells of "Tuisco, Gomers sonne"; Selden's notes to the *Polyolbion* comment on Tuisco and the forger Berosus:

According to the text, the Jews affirm that all the sonnes of Noah were dispersed through the earth, and every one's name left to the land which he possessed. Upon this tradition, and false Berosus testimoney, it is affirmed that Tuisco (sonne of Noah, gotten with others after the flood [Munster. Cosm. lib. 3] upon his wife Arezia) tooke his parte the coast about Rhine, and that thence came the Name of Teutschland and Teutsch, which we call Dutch, through Germany. Som make him the same with Gomer, eldest sonne of Gomer (by whom these parts of Europe were peopled) out of Notation of his name, deriving Tuiscon or Tuiston (for so Tacitus calls him) suppose him to be Gomer and take him for Aschkenaz (remembered by Moses as first sonne to Gomer) and from whom the Hebrews call the Germans Aschkenazim (whose reliques probably indeed seeme to be in Tuisco, which hath beene made of Aschen either by the Dutch prepositive article die or tie... 29

To those writers interested in the origins of fiction, there were available, therefore, three theories which would provide an Oriental setting for the peoples connected with the origins of fiction: Jordanes' Scandza theory, the Odin legend, and finally the rabbinical tradition synchronizing German, Gothic, Scythian, and Biblical history. The ubiquitous Noah-progeny have an additional interest for the Gothic tradition of democracy and constitutionalism arising out of the fact that in Lynche's translation of the forger Berosus, the name Japhet is explained as meaning liberty! 30

28 Verstegen, *Restitution*, pp. 3, 9.
29 *Polyolbion*, in *Works*, IV, 89-90.
30 Leaf A4 verso: "Japhet, which signifies libertie or freedome."

# INDEX